More praise for *Meeting at the Crossroads*

"*Meeting at the Crossroads* is a crucial exploration of the way girls lose their 'voice' and with it, their opinions and their sense of self. Nothing less than America's future leadership depends upon whether *all* of us—from the schoolroom to the White House—heed Gilligan's and Brown's analysis, and make new social policy in light of it."

—Naomi Wolf
Author of *The Beauty Myth*

"According to this challenging and provocative study, girls approaching adolescence often disavow their feelings and suppress their experience in order to preserve 'relationships'; women excuse, justify, or actively impose on girls the self-censorship that they themselves once suffered. In their honest, self-critical, and passionate book Lyn Brown and Carol Gilligan attempt to disrupt this inter-generational cycle of silencing which deadens relationships and undermines the potentialities for a resistant, politicized ethics of care."

—Sara Ruddick
Author of *Maternal Thinking*

"Lyn Brown and Carol Gilligan have given us a magnificent book. They show us how and why girls lose voice and withdraw from themselves and society. They illuminate the ways we can reverse the truncation of humanity that occurs whenever girls are pushed to the margins of the community. Like *In A Different Voice*, this book casts a lifeline."

—Mary Field Belenky
Coauthor of *Women's Way of Knowing*

Meeting at the Crossroads

WOMEN'S PSYCHOLOGY AND GIRLS' DEVELOPMENT

Lyn Mikel Brown
Carol Gilligan

Ballantine Books • New York

Library of Congress Catalog Card Number: 93-90004

ISBN: 0-345-38295-1

Cover design by Georgia Morrissey
Art by Brad Teare

Manufactured in the United States of America
First Ballantine Books Edition: September 1993
10 9 8 7 6 5 4 3 2 1

Acknowledgments

This book, itself a deeply collaborative effort, is an outgrowth of years of relationship and work with many other women, with girls, and also with boys and men. Here we are especially grateful to the girls whose voices and experiences are at the heart of this book—the girls from whom we have learned so much about women's psychology and girls' development. Year after year, they came to tell us what they knew, to speak with us of the pleasures and the pains of their intensely relational lives, to teach us, in part by living through with us, the process of changing relationships, to take us into the underground of their feelings and thoughts. Much as we would like to name each girl individually and thank her for her contribution to this work, in the interest of confidentiality we cannot do so. While we have endeavored to preserve the authenticity of the girls' voices, we have changed personal details and have disguised the girls' identities in order to preserve their privacy.

The journey we record in this book was initiated by an invitation from Leah Rhys on behalf of the Laurel School to join with them in an effort to think more deeply about women's psychological development and to improve girls' education. Leah's dedication to opening this dialogue and bringing the work of the Harvard Project to Laurel led her to seek and gain support from Hazel Prior Hostetler, a 1911 Laurel alumna, and from the Cleveland Foundation. As the work grew, the circle of support widened to include the George Gund Foundation as well. We especially thank Steven

ACKNOWLEDGMENTS

Minter, Judith Simpson, and Victor Young for their lively interest in this work in its early stages. Crucial support for this joining of women with girls and encouragement to explore further its implications for psychology and education came from Joan Lipsitz and the Lilly Endowment, from the late Lawrence Cremin and the Spencer Foundation, and from Wendy Puriefoy and the Boston Foundation. We are grateful to Joan Lipsitz, to Lawrence Cremin, Marion Faldet, and Linda Fitzgerald of the Spencer Foundation, to Wendy Puriefoy and Don Zimmerman of the Boston Foundation, and throughout to Patricia Albjerg Graham, Dean of the Harvard Graduate School of Education, for actively supporting our work with women and girls, for helping us to believe in what we were hearing and seeing, and for encouraging us to go further in developing its educational and political implications.

In this process, the company of other women and men was essential to us. Our colleagues at Harvard and our relationships with them made possible many of the discoveries of this work. Our relationship with Annie Rogers was crucial to working out the account of women's psychological development which we present in this book. We have learned immensely from our ongoing conversations about this work with Elizabeth Debold and Judith Dorney, and also with Barbara Miller, Steve Sherblom, Mark Tappan, Jill Taylor, Deborah Tolman, and Janie Ward. In addition, we thank Peggy Geraghty, Lisa Kulpinski, Susan Libby, Laura Radin, Anna Romer, Melanie Thernstrom, Tina Verba, and Gwill York, who gave freely of their time and energy and offered valuable insights into girls' and women's lives. We are especially grateful to Sarah Hanson for her thoughtful, generous, and excellent help.

We would also like to express our appreciation to the other women and men with whom we have worked over the years. Their insights into psychological growth and healing are woven into our research: Dianne Argyris, Jane Attanucci, Betty Bardige, Mary Belenky, Dana Jack, D. Kay Johnston, Sharry Langdale, Nona Lyons, Catherine Steiner-Adair, Lori Stern, Grant Wiggins, David Wilcox, and Birute Zimlicki.

At Laurel, Patricia Flanders Hall, the Dean of Students and our

ACKNOWLEDGMENTS

liaison for the final two years of the study, brought a profound understanding of girls and a keen sense of the need for change in women's lives. Jo Ann Deak, Lynne Feighan, Peter Hutton, Marlene Roskoph, Marilyn Sabatino, and Nancy Strauss made this project possible. Teachers welcomed us into their school, allowed their classrooms to be disrupted by students coming and going to interviews, spoke with us about their experiences with girls, and contributed their understanding of the changes we were hearing in girls' voices.

We were deeply affected by the women with whom we 'went on retreat in the course of this work: Denise Andre, Claudia Boatright, Renee Bruckner, Jo Ann Deak, Judy Dorney, Pat Flanders Hall, Nancy Franklin, Terri Garfinkel, Louise (Skip) Grip, Marilyn Kent, Linda McDonald, Susie McGee, Sharon Miller, and Almuth Riggs. The close relationships that developed among us have changed both our work and our lives.

Our work with Laurel School is part of a series of studies undertaken in different contexts by the Harvard Project on Women's Psychology and Girls' Development. The joining of women with girls begun in 1981 at Emma Willard School has continued with studies of 11- and 15-year-old boys and girls, first in a suburban public school and then in three ethnically diverse neighborhoods. Two studies of high-school-age girls and boys followed—one in an urban public school and one in a coed private high school. At the moment, two other studies are in process: a study of adolescents in public school considered at risk for early pregnancy or parenting, or for dropping out of school; and a prevention program with girls and boys at two schools, one private and one public.

We would like to thank Mary Belenky, Blythe Clinchy, and Dana Jack for their careful reading of earlier drafts of this book. We would also like to express our appreciation to Angela von der Lippe and Susan Wallace, our editors—Angela for envisioning what this book could become and offering a wonderful image of girls and women dancing at the crossroads; Susan for her vigilance, her good ideas, and her incredible patience.

We wish to extend our appreciation to two people: Mark Tappan

ACKNOWLEDGMENTS

has been a central member of our collaborative project and has joined us in this work by reading drafts, talking over questions, and providing care and emotional support. Bernard Kaplan has been our teacher and good friend and has given generously in ways that were at once freeing and challenging, thus encouraging our most radical impulses.

Finally, in developing our work on voice, we are profoundly indebted to the brilliant voice work of Kristin Linklater. Her teaching and writings (*Freeing the Natural Voice* and *Freeing Shakespeare's Voice*) have given us a physics for our psychology—an understanding of how disconnection happens and how it sounds. Our discussion of resonances in relationships draws centrally from the bold and luminous theater work of Normi Noel and from the subtlety of listening which she has brought to the Harvard Project—specifically to the Strengthening Healthy Resistance and Courage Project, directed by Annie Rogers. We have learned about women and girls, relationships and truth in ways that pertain directly to this book from Toni Morrison, Jorie Graham, Jamaica Kincaid, Maxine Hong Kingston, and Michelle Cliff, whose novels and poems we have taught for many years, and from Charlotte Bronte and Emily Dickinson, from Adrienne Rich, Margaret Atwood, Jeanette Winterson, Sharon Olds, and Elizabeth Socolow, and from the theater work of Tina Packer.

Most centrally, in exploring the paradox in women's psychology—the giving up of relationship for the sake of "relationships"—we find a deep affinity and joining between our work and the work of Jean Baker Miller. She has powerfully articulated this paradox ("Connections, Disconnections, and Violations") and seen it as central in the development of psychological problems. Such convergence of work is strong validation. And we find in her radically insightful writing a touchstone—a resonant insistence on the relational nature of psychological processes, the reality of conflict in women's lives, the need for courage in women's psychological growth, and the link between women's development and societal change.

LMB
CG

Contents

CONTENTS

Meeting at the Crossroads

1

A Journey of Discovery

Anna is twelve. She is tall and slender. She looks at me, her green eyes intense, her pale skin somewhat flushed. It is my first interview after lunch, and she is waiting for me at the room when I arrive. We chat about the day. She has a concert tonight and a test tomorrow, and this concerns her. We begin the interview, and she seems somewhat wary. It takes me some time to feel comfortable. She responds to some of my questions with lengthy answers, to others with terse, almost abrupt acknowledgment. By the end of the interview, we are feeling tired. After we finish, I ask her if she has any questions for me. She wants to know why we are here—What do we hope to learn? What do we get out of this?

This scene—a girl, wary and curious, and a woman, also curious, listening, taking in a girl's voice, a girl's questions, and following that voice as it mingles with her own thoughts and feelings—is at the center of this joining of women's psychology with girls' development. We begin with twelve-year-old Anna because she stands at the edge of adolescence.[1] We will mark this place as a crossroads in women's development: a meeting between girl and woman, an intersection between psychological health and cultural regeneration, a watershed in women's psychology which affects both women and men.

In speaking of early adolescence as a crossroads in women's lives, we call up old stories about crossroads—in particular, the Oedipus story. The murder at the crossroads—Oedipus' killing of his father, Laius—has come to symbolize the strife between fathers and sons within a patriarchal civilization: the fight over who holds power.

Psychologically, this murder is rooted in the abandonment of Oedipus by his parents in early childhood—the radical separation decreed by his father and enacted by his mother, Jocasta, who gives the child to the shepherds. The consequence is a relational deafness and blindness.

Our studies of women's psychological development began with listening to women's voices and hearing differences between the voices of women and men.[2] Privileged men often spoke as if they were not living in relation with others—as if they were autonomous or self-governing, free to speak and move as they pleased. Women, in contrast, tended to speak of themselves as living in connection with others and yet described a relational crisis: a giving up of voice, an abandonment of self, for the sake of becoming a good woman and having relationships. This early work left us with a profound sense of unease. In one sense the women in our studies seemed to know what they were doing—to see the folly in trying to connect with others by silencing themselves. In another sense, they seemed not to know. It was when we decided to follow women's psychological development back through girls' adolescence and then further back into girls' childhood that we came to witness a relational crisis in women's psychology—a comparable crisis to that which boys experience in early childhood—and to unravel a long-standing mystery in girls' development.[3]

For over a century the edge of adolescence has been identified as a time of heightened psychological risk for girls. Girls at this time have been observed to lose their vitality,[4] their resilience,[5] their immunity to depression,[6] their sense of themselves and their character.[7] Girls approaching adolescence are often victims of incest and other forms of sexual abuse.[8] This crisis in women's development has been variously attributed to biology or to culture, but its psychological dimensions and its link to trauma have been only recently explored.

Our journey into this hitherto uncharted territory in women's psychology—this land between childhood and adolescence—has been guided by girls' voices. Over a period of ten years, our project has taken us into private schools for girls, inner-city schools, coeducational day and boarding schools, large urban high schools, and boys' and girls' clubs in culturally diverse neighborhoods.[9] Listening to girls, we hear a naturalist's rendering of the human world—detailed accounts of what is going on in relationships. Girls watch the human world like people watch the weather. Listening in to the sounds of daily living, they pick up its psychological rhythms, its patterns. From girls, we heard a child's frame-by-frame description of what happens in the world in which they are living, a more or less articulate tracing of how life goes, psychologically.

Anna's questions are questions about relationship, and more specifically about our relationship to this work: Why are we here? What do we hope to learn? What do we hope to get out of this? These questions can be answered simply: we hope to learn about women's psychological development by joining women with girls. From girls, we hope to learn about girls' experiences, girls' feelings and thoughts. In previous work, we listened for differences between women's and men's voices and followed changes in women's voices as they moved through crisis and through time.[10] Together with Jean Baker Miller and her colleagues Judith Jordan, Irene Stiver, and Janet Surrey, we found that an inner sense of connection with others is a central organizing feature of women's development and that psychological crises in women's lives stem from disconnections.[11] In light of this work, our interviews with younger girls have proved invaluable in elucidating a fundamental paradox in woman's psychology. In coming to understand this paradox, we were struck (and validated) to discover that Jean Baker Miller described it as central in women's lives and key to the development of what has been called psychopathology. Connection and responsive relationships are essential for psychological development and underlie women's knowing, as Mary Belenky, Blythe Clinchy, Nancy Goldberger, and Jill Tarule have observed; yet women often silence themselves in relationships rather than risk open conflict or disagreement that might lead to isolation or to violence. Listening to seven- and eight-, ten- and eleven-year-old girls, we—working with our colleague Annie Rogers—have heard in girls' voices clear evidence of strength, courage, and a healthy resistance to losing voice and relationship, even in the face of difficult relational realities. Against the backdrop of adolescent and adult women's voices—the voices which have in the past defined women's psychology—the young girls' voices are striking as they speak freely of feeling angry, of fighting or open conflict in relationships, and take difference and disagreement for granted in daily life.

Our surprise in discovering the strengths in girls' voices and the revision this implies for theories of women's psychological development suggests that adolescence is a time of disconnection, sometimes of dissociation or repression in women's lives, so that women often do not remember—tend to forget or to cover over—what as girls they have experienced and known. As the phrase "I don't know" enters our interviews with girls at this developmental juncture, we observe girls struggling over speaking and not speaking, knowing and not knowing, feeling and not feeling, and we see the makings of an inner division as girls come to a place where they feel they cannot say or feel or know what they have experienced— what they have felt and known. Witnessing this active process of not knowing swirl into confusion in the back and forth of our interview conversations between girls and women, we began to listen in the moment and to trace in the transcriptions of our interview sessions how girls struggle to stay in connection with themselves and with others, to voice their feelings and thoughts and experiences in relationships—to show what Annie Rogers has called "ordinary courage," the ability "to speak one's mind by telling all one's heart."[12] And we saw this struggle affect their feelings about themselves, their relationships with others, and their ability to act in the world. The sounds of this struggle in girls' voices re-sounded similar struggles in ourselves and other women; listening to girls, we began once again to know what we had come not to know.

After taking in the voices of younger girls, we had a new way of understanding the losses and confusion we heard in adolescent and adult women—a way of documenting both what was lost and girls' resistance to these losses. Our research raises a major question about the relationship between women's psychological development and the society and culture in which women are living: Are these losses of voice and relationship necessary, and, if not, how can they be prevented? The hallmark of this loss in women's lives and also in men's is the move from authentic into idealized relationships. Recent work in psychology documenting the capacity of infants to know relational reality—to respond to breaks in human connection, to pick up when connection falters or stops[13]—grounds our observation that girls in general continue to develop this capacity up to the time of their adolescence, and then they show signs of losing their ability to know what is relationally true or real. In tracing this process, we will join the problems which have been seen as central to the psychology of women—the desire for authentic connection, the experience of disconnection, the difficulties in speaking, the feeling of not being listened to or heard or responded to empathically, the feeling of not being able to convey or even believe in one's own experience—with a relational impasse or crisis of connection which we have observed in girls' lives at the time of their adolescence.

In this book, then, we record a journey of discovery. At the heart of our narrative are the voices of nearly one hundred girls between the ages of seven and eighteen. They were students at the Laurel School for girls in Cleveland, Ohio, during the years 1986–1990. Because the Laurel School is a private day school, the girls can be seen as fortunate; they have access to many of the privileges which this society offers those who are born into favorable conditions or who are particularly talented or motivated to succeed. Although most of the girls come from middle-class or upper-middle-class families and the majority are white, it is important to emphasize that about 20 percent of the girls are from working-class families and are attending the school on scholarship, and that about 14 percent of the girls are of color. In this group of girls, color is not associated with low social class, and low social class is not associated with educational disadvantage.

Given their fortunate and privileged status in many respects, one might expect that these girls would be flourishing. And according to standard measures of psychological development and educational progress, they are doing extremely well.[14] Our study provides clear evidence that as these girls grow older they become less dependent on external authorities, less egocentric or locked in their own experience or point of view, more differentiated from others in the sense of being able to distinguish their feelings and thoughts from those of other people, more autonomous in the sense of being able to rely on or to take responsibility for themselves, more appreciative of the complex interplay of voices and perspectives in any relationship, more aware of the diversity of human experience and the differences between societal and cultural groups. Yet we found that this developmental progress goes hand in hand with evidence of a loss of voice, a struggle to authorize or take seriously their own experience—to listen to their own voices in conversation and respond to their feelings and thoughts—increased confusion, sometimes defensiveness, as well as evidence for the replacement of real with inauthentic or idealized relationships. If we consider responding to oneself, knowing one's feelings and thoughts, clarity, courage, openness, and free-flowing connections with others and the world as signs of psychological health, as we do, then these girls are in fact not developing, but are showing evidence of loss and struggle and signs of an impasse in their ability to act in the face of conflict.[15] Thus, while in one sense the girls we have studied are progressing steadily as they move from childhood through adolescence, in another sense adolescence precipitates a developmental crisis in girls' lives. In other words, the crossroads between girls and women is marked by a series of disconnections or dissociations which leave girls psychologically at risk and involved in a relational struggle—a struggle which we heard and sometimes experienced as enacted with us in our interviews with girls, a struggle which is familiar to many women.

Meeting at this crossroads creates an opportunity for women to join girls and by doing so to reclaim lost voices and lost strengths, to strengthen girls' voices and girls' courage as they enter adolescence by offering girls resonant relationships, and in this way to move with girls toward creating a psychologically healthier world and a more caring and just society. In providing this account of our meeting with a particular group of girls and describing the relation-

6

ships that developed between girls and women, we report a way into what has been a dark continent in women's development—a crisis of relationship which has been covered over by lies. The horror, psychologically speaking, which is at the center of this crisis is the realization that girls are not only enacting dissociation but also narrating the process of their disconnection—revealing its mechanism and also its intention. The girls in our study, as they approached adolescence, were finding themselves at a relational impasse; in response, they were sometimes making, sometimes resisting a series of disconnections that seem at once adaptive and psychologically wounding: between psyche and body, voice and desire, thoughts and feelings, self and relationship. The central paradox we will explore—the giving up of relationship for the sake of "Relationships"—is a paradox of which girls themselves are aware. Psychologically, girls know what they are doing and then need not to know, in part because they can see no alternative. In reporting work which in its very nature is relational and therefore open-ended or incomplete, we bring to others the evidence from our work with girls and women—voices which we believe are worth listening to, in part because of the questions they raise. From this work, we take the strong conviction that resonant relationships between girls and women are crucial for girls' development, for women's psychological health, and also for bringing women's voices fully into the world so that the social construction of reality—the construction of the human world that is institutionalized by society and carried across generations by culture—will be built by and acoustically resonant for both women and men.

The Underground

In beginning this work, however, we were not aware of these dimensions of our study. We came to Laurel School to continue our exploration of women's psychological development by including younger girls and to test the effects of our conversations with young women—their potential educational value and their usefulness as a preventive or therapeutic intervention. In our previous studies we had no way of knowing whether the changes we observed were due to the nature of our conversations with women—the way we approached girls and women, the questions we asked, the way we listened and responded to what they said and to what happened between us in the course of the interview session—or whether it was simply our presence as psychologists or psychologists from Harvard, or simply the experience of being interviewed regardless of approach or method. Following standard procedures of research design, we randomly assigned twelve- and fifteen-year-old girls (all of the members of the seventh and tenth grades) to experimental and control groups. With the experimental group, we would use our own approach: an interview composed of a series of questions which were open-ended and designed to encourage people to take us into their psychological world by exploring with us their feelings and thoughts about themselves, their relationships, and their experiences of conflict. With the control group we would use a standard psychological method, by asking girls to respond to a series of hypothetical dilemmas and standardized probe questions. We predicted that it was the relational nature of our conversations with girls that was responsible for the effects we had observed—clinical improvement, developmental progress, a strengthening of voice in relationship.

We joined our interest in exploring systematically the potential benefits of our research interview with our continuing investment in discovering where girls and women experienced conflict in their lives and how they moved in the face of relational problems. Leah Rhys, who was then head of the Laurel School, encouraged us to bring our ongoing project on women's development into the school and involve the full age range of girls at the school. Thus we also decided to interview all of the six- and nine-year-old girls (members of the first and fourth grades) and set up a longitudinal, cross-sectional design by interviewing and then following all of the girls in the first, fourth, seventh, and tenth grades. Our goal was to extend our investigation of women's development to younger girls, to continue to explore changes in adolescent girls over time, and to look for connections between our interview data and standard measures of personality development, social growth, cognitive and emotional capabilities. We planned to use academic records, teachers' evaluations, disciplinary records, and girls' own assessments of their experiences as ways of corroborating our interview data.

Yet we proceeded ambivalently with this plan. Our wish to do good psychological research led us into assumptions about control and objectivity and concerns about validity and replicability which left us with a sense of discomfort and unease. The source of our discomfort came over us like a wave as we entered the school to conduct the first set of interviews: the halls were alive with activity, with girls of all ages and from a variety of racial and ethnic backgrounds, dressed in every variation of green and white, working together, eating together, moving from class to class. Over the course of the day, we—a group of thirteen women,[16] most of us strangers to the students—became increasingly aware that we were being watched, labeled ("the tall one," "the young one," "the 60s looking one"), and compared by the girls. Not privy to our lives, our thoughts and feelings—as we soon were to theirs—we were, understandably, regarded with curiosity and suspicion.

And soon after our arrival, as is often the response to situations of inequality, we saw signs of an emerging underground. Within an hour after the first round of interviews, the word was out: there are two interviews—the personal one and the one with the "little stories." The girls responded to our research by aligning themselves against this strange intrusion. In private, we later discovered, they shared their memories of the questions with one another and their parents, reassured their soon-to-be-interviewed friends, began to prepare for their own interviews as best they could by taking in bits of information gathered here and there and rehearsing their "lines." And we could not miss the irony. We came to the school to learn from girls; our work depended on girls' willingness to speak to us from their experience; we hoped that by taking girls' voices seriously we could arrive at a better understanding of women's psychology, and yet we came with a research design that, by definition, presumed no relationship that we would call real relationship—between ourselves and the girls, among the girls, between the girls

9

and their teachers and parents. We had come to the school to understand more about girls' responses to a dominant culture that is out of tune with girls' voices and for the most part uninterested in girls' experiences, which objectifies and idealizes young women and at the same time trivializes and denigrates them, and yet unwittingly we set into motion a method of psychological inquiry appropriated from this very system. Constrained by our own design, we found ourselves losing voice and losing relationships in our own research project. "The master's tools," Audre Lorde warns us, "will never dismantle the master's house."[17]

Let us add here that this was not our first visit to the school—that by most psychologists' and educators' standards, we were very much *in* relationship. We had traveled to Laurel many times before we began interviewing the girls; we met with administrators and with the women and men on the faculty; we sat in on classes, consulted with teachers and psychologists working at the school about the phrasing of our interview questions, talked with girls about their thoughts and feelings about being involved in this project, spoke at an Upper School assembly, and answered girls' questions about the interview process, confidentiality, and the research project. Our previous successes and failures left us with a keen sense of the value of working collaboratively; we had learned the importance of involving the people with whom we were working at every level of activity, the need to provide choices and to be sensitive to and work with the particular nuances, climate, atmosphere of the school or community or clinical setting in which we were working. Our own project at Harvard was a collaborative working group of women and men, faculty and students, and we were, we thought, especially sensitive to girls' desire to know about the process, about the nature of the questions we would be asking them, about the safety of the relationship, about our reasons for being at Laurel.

Moreover, some years earlier, we had begun to confront questions of distance and disconnection in our practice as psychologists. We saw our voice-sensitive method lose its psychological resonance when we attempted to bring it into line with standard research practices and to create mutually exclusive categories of analysis.

Specifically, attempts to create either/or categorizations resulted in simplistic and ultimately untrue ways of describing both women's and men's experiences. To call women connected and men separate seemed to us profoundly misleading; to say that men wanted domination and power while women wanted love and relationship seemed to us to ignore the depths of men's desires for relationship and the anger women feel about not having power in the world. And yet we were consistently hearing differences in the ways in which women and men speak about themselves in relationship and also seeing differences in the positions of women and men in the world.

In trying to bring our work on psychological theory and women's development into line with the practices of our field—to use widely accepted methods and thus to render our work comparable to that of others—we struggled with the problems inherent in commonly used methods of psychological assessment. We wished to create a way of working that sustained other people's voices and our own—to voice the relationship that was at the heart of our psychological work. We were looking for a way to capture the layered nature of psychological experience and also the relational logic of psychological processes. We were trying to understand and respond to and also sustain in our analysis the complex associations people make as they struggle with difficult experiences of conflict in relationships or speak about difficult moments in their lives.[18] Yet although our way of working was centered on voice and listening and thus was akin to clinical and literary methods, our attempt to bring this work into line with standard practices of psychological research broke connection in a myriad subtle and not so subtle ways. Holding firmly to the same questions for each girl, for example, prevented us from following girls to the places they wished to go. We—neutral outsiders, strangers on a train—would ask the questions (provide the stimulus) to which the participants (we *had* stopped calling them "subjects," which really means, in psychology, "objects") would answer (respond). Then we, the knowing but hidden (powerful, god-like) psychologists, would interpret these responses in the hope of finding in them something true or meaningful (from our viewpoint). Although questions of truth and power and interpretation continuously occupied us, when push came to shove, we fell back on the safety and predictability of old methods—the way we were trained to do psychological work. And although we spoke about the importance of context, of the particularities of a person's life or story, we continued to justify the appropriation of that story into our terms.

Yet as we proceeded with our "experiment" at Laurel, we began to sense that by staying with our method we were in danger of losing the girls. Because we were in some relationship with the school, the girls, and ourselves, we were attuned to what was happening around us. What did it mean, given what felt to us like careful preparation and honest communication, that our presence in the school caused a kind of subterranean shock wave (subterranean for, to the untrained eye, it was barely visible and no one was speaking openly about what was going on) that rippled through the surface calm and quiet of daily activity? What did it mean that our research design, rather than encouraging girls' voices, caused them to scramble for information, to join with those they could trust to tell them what to expect and how to prepare? What did it mean that our presence caused the girls to withdraw their thoughts and feelings, clutch them tightly to themselves like some old familiar handbag full of prized belongings, the contents of which are brought forth and displayed only to the most trusted people in the most private places? Within hours of beginning our research with girls on the experience of being listened to, we had simply become a new version of something to guard against, someone to protect themselves from, to be suspicious of, to be warned against. Perhaps most insidiously we became another reason for girls to feel bad or feel judged—because they were not being open enough with us, not able to speak freely in our presence, not courageous enough or clear enough to contribute to what was generally regarded in the school, and perhaps by them as well, as important work on women's psychology and girls' development. We felt this, and then we overrode our own feelings. As women we found this easy to do.

These impressions, however vivid and pressing in the moment, however alive in our research group immediately after the first round of interviews, faded somewhat over the next year as we began what we then considered to be the more important work of data analysis—the slow, deliberate process of transcribing tapes, taking in and interpreting girls' voices. But in September of the second year, a singular event in the life of the study occurred: an event that would bring these passing impressions and questions about relationships to the very center of our work.

We had made the increasingly familiar journey to Cleveland at the beginning of the second year of the project to talk with the faculty and staff at the school about what we were learning from our interviews with the girls. We gathered in the Middle School library, the walls covered with bright paintings, mobiles floating overhead depicting scenes from the girls' favorite books. The faculty sat in rows with a long aisle running down the center of the room. Reflecting our relationship to the school at that time, we sat in front on a just slightly raised platform.

We spoke about an initial finding of the research: that many of the girls had publicly agreed to an honor code in which they did not believe. In the privacy of our interview sessions, girls spoke about their responses to honor code violations, describing the relational problems they faced.[19] Because they did not see any way to speak of these problems in the public arena, many girls had taken matters of public governance into a private world of relationships and settled them in private places. Drawing on their extensive psychological knowledge of relationships and feelings, they often arrived at complex and creative solutions to difficult relational problems. Yet these solutions, although sometimes elaborate, were unknown, and therefore unacknowledged and unappreciated, within the public world of the school.

We suggested that to educate girls who as women would be likely to participate fully as citizens of a democratic state, it seemed necessary to encourage girls to treat matters of public governance as political matters, to bring their relational knowledge into the public arena, and to speak openly of their differences and their disagreements. At this, Louise Grip, an upper school teacher, sitting in the front row, to our right, raised her hand. "How can we help girls learn to deal with disagreement in public," she asked—scanning the faces of her colleagues, women and men—"when we," meaning now women, "cannot deal with disagreement in public ourselves?" Her question electrified the room. Afterwards, outside in the hall, another teacher spoke of her eleven-year-old daughter, who said that she was angry at her mother because when her mother and father disagreed, her mother always gave in. "I was so humiliated," the teacher said; "I was so ashamed."

The initial discomfort we felt when we entered the school with our experiment came flooding back. Like the teachers and administrators in the school, we had been tracing the visible activity and movement of the girls in response to our presence, choosing to ignore the low rumblings of trouble and respond only to their compliance, to welcome their cooperation and their public courtesies. Like the honor code system in the school, we had imposed a structure that had created the need for an underground. The word "collaboration" we used so freely to describe our work now seemed to take on a darker meaning. While as researchers we could question the discrepancy between the surface reality of girls' compliance with the school's honor code and their underground knowledge from a safe, professional distance, we now recognized our unwitting contribution to this discrepancy in girls' lives. Not wanting to collaborate in silencing girls' public voices, we began to take our study, as it was designed, apart and listen to the girls who expressed frustration with the limits we imposed on relationship. We began to hear girls' anger at feeling used when we asked them to fill out standard psychological measures, we began to hear their questions and their requests to spend more time with us so that we could talk together about what we were finding, their wish for a chance to add to and disagree with our interpretations, their desire to know what we were saying about them in public settings and to say how this made them feel.

We had come to this school to study girls with clear questions and a research design to implement, with a sense of our role and authority, and we found ourselves increasingly in the throes of an ever-changing and uncertain relationship, moved along by deep feeling for the girls we were coming to know more intimately from one year to the next. Questions that were once distinctly ours were transforming as we began to take in questions posed by the girls and the women at the school. No longer steeped in a dispassionate discipline of testing and assessment, we entered into relationships which changed with each new encounter, and we began to learn from the girls and the women who were now joining us in this study.

Clearly we needed a different way of working and a method which did not interfere with our ability to listen to ourselves and to others but which enabled us to bring our knowledge as women and as psychologists into relationship with our work. And since part of what we know as women has to do with the pervasiveness of androcentric and patriarchal norms, values, and societal structures, such a practice would be both responsive to others' voices and yet resistant to the dominant voices, the cultural overlays that serve to drown out, mute, or distort the voices of those with less power or authority. We needed, it seemed, to create a practice of psychology that was something more like a practice of relationship. Acknowledging our own power to listen and name and potentially distort the words of others, we sought to create a responsive and resisting practice that was tied to a way of listening to others. Thus we created a "Listener's Guide" that had, built in, the space for a girl to speak in her own voice and thus to refuse the established story of a white, middle-class heterosexual woman's life, a story all girls in this culture—whether they are white or of color, rich or poor, heterosexual or lesbian—struggle against, albeit in different ways. Our goal was to create a collaboration and a relational method that, rather than upholding the usual lines of division, provided a way to come into relationship with another person.

We could not have made this move without the girls—without their insights, their questions, their resistance. As we moved into more genuine dialogue with one another and with the girls in the study, the girls in turn invited us to join them in deeper levels of understanding. Our work gained a clarity we had not experienced before. Out of what could be seen as a collapse in form—a letting go of our planned research design for the messiness and unpredictability and vulnerability of ongoing relationship—a way of working emerged which felt more genuine and mutual, precarious at first, disruptive, unsettling to those of us used to our authority and control in professional situations and in the conduct of psychological research.

This book reports our journey of discovery. Listening to girls and to ourselves over the five years of this study, we heard something we had not heard before. In the next chapter, we present our Listener's Guide—a voice-sensitive way of working that allowed us to follow girls' thoughts and feelings and to hear girls' struggle at adolescence. Then, following the presentation of our method, we turn to a developmental narrative, listening to girls at three different ages speak about themselves and their relationships and then following individual girls over time, listening closely to the changes in their distinct voices from one year to the next, addressing at times our successes and failures in responding to what girls feel and think and therefore know. Listening to these girls over the five years of the study, we attempt to describe the psychological parameters and the developmental or educational implications of the struggle we heard as they moved from childhood into adolescence—a struggle most visible and audible at the edge of adolescence. We interpret this struggle as a healthy resistance to losses and disconnections that are psychologically wounding.

In elucidating how a group of girls travel through childhood and adolescence and reporting on our own journey of discovery as well, we will focus on the tension between political resistance and psychological resistance. The tendency for a healthy resistance to turn political and for a political resistance to turn into a psychological resistance becomes central to our understanding of the difficulties and psychological suffering that many of these privileged or fortunate girls experience. At adolescence, we saw women's psychological development becoming inescapably political.

Although it seems at first counter-intuitive that women would learn from girls, we have been profoundly affected by the girls who took part in our research. We do not claim that these girls are representative of girls in general, but that their voices are worth listening to and taking seriously. From this particular group of girls we have learned about some of the darker places in women's development, including the processes of dissociation and disconnection which play a central role in women's psychological lives. By joining our understanding of these girls' development and its implications for the psychology of women with the creation of a psychology that is a practice of relationship, we are brought face to face with difficult questions of truthfulness and authenticity in relationships between girls and women and among women as well. Widening the conversation to include ourselves and our profession, we have found ourselves in the presence of what Adrienne Rich calls amnesia—the silence of the unconscious. More specifically, we came to remember the forgetting of our girlhood by going back through the disconnections of adolescence. Truth, Rich adds, is "not one thing, or even a system" but "an increasing complexity,"[20] and in this work we attempt to move to deeper understanding by staying with the complexity of what girls know from their experience and not abandoning what we—in part through this work—have come to know ourselves.

2

The Harmonics of Relationship

In the early spring of 1988, prior to the third year of interviews, we and our research group—Elizabeth Debold, Judy Dorney, Barb Miller, Annie Rogers, Steve Sherblom, and Mark Tappan—gathered for our weekly project meeting.[1] In retrospect this particular meeting was significant, since we began to name the tension we had been feeling about the research design of the study. Sitting around an oblong wooden table in a small windowless seminar room, those of us who had interviewed the girls began to articulate what first felt like a general feeling of concern and a vague sense of loss: the outspokenness and resilience of the younger girls seemed to be in jeopardy, and we had been unable or unwilling to express the sadness and disappointment we were feeling. Many of the questions we had asked, moreover, did not seem right; they were no longer useful, they seemed to be cutting off girls' voices, preventing them from speaking from their experiences.

In the face of this emerging awareness, we considered the costs and benefits of continuing with our research design: if we repeated the questions we had asked the previous years, we would gain a standard comparison, but at the risk of ignoring what we were seeing and feeling and turning away from our emerging questions, perhaps even at the risk of losing the girls. The answer suddenly seemed clear—we would stay in relationship with the girls and move where they seemed to be taking us, change our design and rewrite our questions so that we could explore the changes we were hearing in

18

girls' voices. We would give up the experimental and control groups and talk with all the girls in a more open-ended, flexible manner.

Giving ourselves the freedom to stay with our feelings and articulate our most pressing questions, we had to face more difficult issues: What, in fact, did the girls seem to be struggling to say? Where were their moments of silence and resistance, their moments of pleasure and ease? What questions would we ask to encourage their voices? Over the course of hours, we attempted to sort out which questions worked and also to create new questions that we felt addressed directly what girls seemed to be saying indirectly over and over. For example, we heard girls at the edge of adolescence imply that what they were experiencing seemed at odds with what others were calling reality. After a long discussion, Annie Rogers phrased the question: "Can you tell me about a time when what you were feeling and thinking was not what others were saying and doing?" Elizabeth Debold and Judy Dorney, who had been reading girls' responses to questions about their ways of knowing,[2] guided us as we developed new questions that we felt would draw out girls' experiences of knowing and not knowing—recognizing that girls became more engaged when asked to speak and tell stories about their lives. In addition to these changes in the content of the interviews, we decided to let go of the self-imposed pressure to cover every question on the interview protocol. Instead, we would use questions as openings, as pathways into relationships with girls in which they would feel free and able to speak their thoughts and their feelings. We would follow the associative logic of girls' psyches, we would move where the girls led us.

This decision to listen to ourselves and to the girls led us away from standard procedures for analyzing interview data and to the creation of a voice-centered, relational method of doing psychological research. Initially, our approach in listening to women's voices and the voices of psychological theory had been clinical and literary, and this approach led us to hear and specify differences between women's experiences of self and approaches to relational conflicts and the conceptions of self and morality that were prevalent within psychology, institutionalized within society, and part of the dominant culture.[3] Women's voices, in articulating a connected sense of self and approaches to conflict that centered on strengthening or maintaining relationship, were different voices within a male-voiced world. In an effort to bring this work into line with standard practices of psychological research, Nona Lyons created a coding system to explore further the contrasts between a connected sense of self and a separate sense of self and the relationships between different conceptions of self and the moral voices of justice and care.[4] When we engaged more deeply with the psychological struggles we were hearing and feeling in listening to girls, we returned to a more clinical and literary approach and listened for movement within the interview session, for stops and starts, for silences and struggles. And we turned our attention to developing and formulating a systematic method for interpreting these movements and listening to the complexities of voice in relationship.[5]

Voice is central to our way of working—our channel of connection, a pathway that brings the inner psychic world of feelings and thoughts out into the open air of relationship where it can be heard by oneself and by other people. The physicality of voice—its sounds, resonances, vibrations—gives our work its naturalistic grounding, and the re-sounding by girls of voices that may have been muted or covered over by women is key to the physics of relationship and the relational nature of our psychological work. Voice, because it is embodied, connects rather than separates psyche and body; because voice is in language, it also joins psyche and culture. Voice is inherently relational—one does not require a mirror to hear oneself—yet the sounds of one's voice change in resonance depending on the relational acoustics: whether one is heard or not heard, how one is responded to (by oneself and by other people).[6]

As we listened for voice (girls' voices and our own) and followed girls' moving in and out of relationship with us and our moving in and out of relationship with them, we began to hear girls enacting and describing psychological processes such as dissociation and found ourselves witnessing the onset of relational struggles that plague many women. Voice became key insofar as girls feel pressure to become selfless or without a voice in relationships, and the experience of self in the sense of having a voice became central to girls' experience of authentic relationship. Following girls' voices, we listened for girls' sense of themselves—the way they spoke of themselves, the presence and absence of an "I" in their stories of relational conflicts. Morality, or the voice that speaks of how one should or would like to act in relationships, became of interest to us at this point primarily insofar as moral language carries the force of institutionalized social norms and cultural values into relationships and psychic life. Listening to girls' voices, we heard the degree to which morality, in a male-voiced culture and a male-governed society, justifies certain psychologically debilitating moves which girls and women are encouraged to make in relationships and creates internal as well as external barriers to girls' ability to speak in relationships and move freely in the world.

Over the course of many meetings, many conversations, we came to the way of working that guides our interpretations of the interviews in this study, a method that centers on voice and that offers a guide into relationship with another person.

Centering on Voice

Four questions about voice attune one's ear to the harmonics of relationship: (1) Who is speaking? (2) In what body? (3) Telling what story about relationship—from whose perspective or from what vantage point? (4) In what societal and cultural frameworks? To ask who is speaking tunes one's ear to the voice of the person as a distinct voice, a new voice—a voice worth listening to. To ask about the body, about the relational story which is being told, and about the societal and cultural frameworks is to inquire into differences that are psychologically meaningful—one's body, one's experience of relationships and how one tells that story at a particular time, one's societal position, one's cultural groundings. These questions about voice reveal the dominant voice in the field of psychology (the voice generally taken to be not a voice but the truth) to be oracular, disembodied, seemingly objective and dispassionate. Yet, paradoxically, this "objective and disembodied" voice has presumed, at least implicitly, a male body, a story about relationship that is, at its center, a story about separation, and a society that men govern within the framework of Western civilization. By listening to women and to girls and bringing their voices into the center of psychological theory and research, we are changing the voice, the body, and also the story about relationships (including the point of view on the canonical story), shifting the societal location, and, by the work itself, attempting to change the cultural framework. In essence, we have been reframing psychology as a practice of relationship by voicing the relationships that are at the heart of psychological inquiry and growth.

To ask what relationships are good or beneficial for girls and for women—as we asked in setting out to discover whether our research interview was preventive of psychological problems or served to encourage psychological health and development—is also to ask about ourselves and our practice. As psychologists, we are in positions of some authority and power, able to (licensed to) treat people, assess people, test people, write about people in ways that affect their lives, their feelings and thoughts about themselves and about others, their economic and social opportunities. Questions about voice, authority, truth, and relationships, which may be academic within other disciplines, become, within the field of psychology, highly personal and highly political questions.

Recasting psychology as a relational practice, we attend to the relational dimensions of our listening, speaking, taking in, interpreting, and writing about the words and the silences, the stories and the narratives of other people. Our way into relationship with another is through the avenue of voice, and we have built into our method the space for a woman or girl to speak in her own voice. Since each voice is different and every relationship is, by definition, a fluid, ever-changing, and unique experience, we have created a "guide to listening"—a pathway into relationship rather than a fixed framework for interpretation.

Maintaining voice, and therefore difference, we ask not only who is speaking but who is listening, and this relational understanding of the research process shifts the nature of psychological work from a profession of truth to a practice of relationship in which truths can emerge or become clear. Instead of holding as an ideal a no-voice voice or an objective stance—a way of speaking or seeing that is disembodied, outside of relationship, in no particular time or place—we seek to ground our work empirically, in experience, and in the realities of relationship and of difference, of time and place. Our claim, therefore, in presenting this work is not that the girls we spoke with are representative of all girls or some ideal sample of girls, but rather that we learned from this group of girls and young women, and what we discovered seemed worthy of others' attention.

Our effort to find ways of speaking about human experience in a manner that re-sounds its relational nature and carries the polyphony of voice, as well as the ever-changing or moving-through-time quality of the sense of self and the experience of relationship, has led us to shift the metaphoric language psychologists traditionally have used in speaking of change and development from an atomistic, positional, architectural, and highly visual language of structures, steps, and stages to a more associative and musical language of movement and feeling that better conveys the complexity of the voices we hear and the psychological processes we wish to understand. At times we pick up and extend metaphors that girls and young women we interview use in describing their experiences, at times we draw on language used by women poets and novelists who write about girls' and women's lives, at times we draw from music a language of voices, counterpoint, and theme.[7] We make these shifts in metaphor in full awareness that androcentricity is deeply rooted in the language of psychology and that the metaphoric quality of that language is often given the status of reality or truth.

We know that voice, as a channel of psychic expression, is polyphonic and complex. Our Listener's Guide lays out both a literary and a clinical approach—a method or way of working that is responsive to the harmonics of psychic life, the nonlinear, recursive, nontransparent play, interplay, and orchestration of feelings and thoughts, the polyphonic nature of any utterance, and the symbolic nature not only of what is said but also of what is *not* said.

23

We know that women, in particular, often speak in indirect discourse, in voices deeply encoded, deliberately or unwittingly opaque. As white heterosexual women living in the context of twentieth-century North America—as women whose families in childhood were working-class and Jewish, respectively—we know from our own experience about certain strategies of resistance, both the dangers of an outspoken political resistance and the corrosive suffering of a silent psychological resistance. We also know about capitulation—about complicity and accommodation. Therefore, our Listener's Guide—as well as being a relational method, responsive to different voices—is also a feminist method, concerned particularly with the reality of men's power at this time in history and its effects on girls and women as speakers and listeners, as knowers and actors in the world.

We provide, below, a general description of our Listener's Guide and the way it enables relationship by taking in another's voice. In doing so, we attempt to clarify the literary, the clinical, and the feminist nature of our method. Then we address three questions: Why use this method? What can it offer a listener interested in exploring psychic life? How can it help someone who is invested in the process of healthy psychological development—a parent, a teacher, a therapist, a friend—to hear and follow the clarity, confusion, encouragement, and discouragement of voice and relationship? Listening to Neeti, a student at Laurel, first at twelve years of age and then at thirteen, we follow her voice and listen to the ways her voice guides us into her relationships and brings into our relationship with her a rendering of what we have come to identify as a critical moment or crossroads in women's psychological development.[8] We suggest that the moments where Neeti struggles to know what she knows and to speak her feelings and her thoughts reveal the canonical no-voice voice that girls take in to be a real voice—that is, Neeti's experiences of relational impasse make clear what is tacit, what goes unsaid because it is so much a part of the culture that it is assumed to be real and taken for granted. Embedding voice in a body and in a relational and societal context thus paradoxically allows girls' and women's voices (and those of others

24

who struggle to speak and be listened to within the current framework) to be heard and at least partially understood. The fact that Neeti is bi-cultural and of color may underscore these realities and these differences for her.

A Listener's Guide

Guided by our voice-sensitive method, we listen to a person's story at least four times. In this way, we begin to sort out different voices that run through the narrative and compose a polyphonic or orchestral rendering of its psychology and its politics. We use the term "listening" to describe our way of working because it joins our conversations with girls with our listening to audio-tapes and reading over interview transcripts. Our voice-centered approach thus transforms the act of reading into an act of listening, as the reader takes in different voices and follows their movement through the interview.

In the course of many years of interviewing or speaking with people about their lives, we have come to appreciate the power and the complexity, as well as the oddity, of this experience for both speaker and listener: two strangers, sitting together, speaking together—sometimes for the first time, sometimes for the only time—one initiating the conversation by asking questions, the other responding, separated always by the quiet murmuring of the tape whirring and running its course. There is something strange and fascinating in the way these separations can fade into intense conversation over the course of an hour or more. When a conversation has different meanings for the people engaged in it and especially when one of the two has the power to structure the meeting, it is important to ask whether there can be genuine dialogue. The interview, to be sure, is a conversation of a different sort from the conversations we are used to in everyday life: it is both private and public, informal and formal, lived in the present but preserved for the future.

Although, as we have explained, we came to Laurel with an agenda, carefully worked out and in part recorded on the pages of questions we brought to our interviews, our explicit reason for talking with the girls was to learn from them about girls' experiences. Over the years of the study, conversations that were at first somewhat stilted and formal became more relaxed, more mutual—in part because the girls came to know us and feel more comfortable, in part because we revised our questions and shifted our approach. We became more curious and less directive, more interested in following the girls' lead; they in turn became more invested in teaching us what they know, more disruptive, more outspoken, and also more playful, warmer, more genuinely in relationship. As a result, our later interviews were distinctly different from the earlier ones—more clearly in the spirit of genuine back-and-forth conversation, more dialogue than question and response. This shift affected the development of our Listener's Guide and also turned our attention to the relational dynamics of the interview process, the dramatic nature of this meeting between a girl and a woman. Embracing our participation in the interview led naturally to questions about the nature of these relationships—the importance of acknowledging our power to shape or expand the dialogue, the ways in which we came to love and care about the girls and to feel their connection with us, the ways in which our feelings and thoughts and experiences moved in response to what we were taking in and affected the ways we spoke with girls, and the ways we interpreted the interviews and heard their voices.

The four listenings suggested by our guide are ways into the complexity of voice and relationship. Working with audio-tapes and transcriptions enables us to sound and re-sound, trace and retrace voice(s) through the interview process. At the same time, we note the myriad shifts that occur in moving from the present moment of the relational drama to the audio-tape of the conversation, to the written record or transcription.[9]

Listening for the polyphony of voice, we hear the voice of the speaking self or first-person "I" and the relational voices that carry different ways of being in relationship. Individual words and phrases are meaningless in and of themselves to explain the "living utterance,"[10] because the living language, like the living person, exists in a web of relationships. A person's meaning becomes clear only if the relational context of speaking is maintained. By voicing the relational context of human living and also the dialogic nature of speaking and listening, our method offers a way of tracing and untangling the relationships that constitute psychic life, including our relationships with the people involved in our studies and our responses to their experiences and stories.

The first time through the interview, we listen to the story the person tells: the geography of this psychological landscape, the plot (in both senses of the word). Our goal is to get a sense of what is happening, to follow the unfolding of events, to listen to the drama (the who, what, when, where, and why of the narrative).[11] Like a literary critic or a psychotherapist, we attend to recurring words and images, central metaphors, emotional resonances, contradictions or inconsistencies in style, revisions and absences in the story, as well as shifts in the sound of the voice and in narrative position: the use of first-, second-, or third-person narration. In this way, we locate the speaker in the narrative she tells. In addition, this first listening requires that we reflect on ourselves as people in the privileged position of interpreting the life events of another and consider the implications of this act. An awareness of the power to name and control meaning is critical; and to avoid abuses of this power, we name and think about the meaning of our own feelings and thoughts about the narrator and about her story. In what ways do we identify with or distance ourselves from this person? In what ways are we or our experiences different or the same? Where are we confused or puzzled? Where are we certain? Are we upset or delighted by the story, amused or pleased, disturbed or angered? Writing out our responses to what we are hearing, we then consider how our thoughts and feelings may affect our understanding, our interpretation, and the way we write about that person.

The second time through the interview text, we listen for "self"— for the voice of the "I" speaking in this relationship. We find this listening for the voice of the other to be crucial. It brings us into relationship with that person, in part by ensuring that the sound of her voice enters our psyche and in part by discovering how she speaks of herself before we speak of her. Thus we include her voice in our description of her, attempt to know her on her own terms, discover the resonances in our own psyche, respond to what she is saying emotionally as well as intellectually. Like Adrienne Rich, who describes her own process of coming to know the work of Emily Dickinson, we encounter not simply a text but rather the "heart and mind" of another; we "come into close contact with an interiority—a power, a creativity, a suffering, a vision—that is *not* identical with [our] own."[12] As the other's words enter our psyche, a process of connection begins between her thoughts and feelings and our thoughts and feelings in response, so that she affects us and we begin to learn from her—about her, about ourselves, and about the world we share in common, especially the world of relationships.

Once we let the voice of another enter our psyche, we can no longer claim a detached or objective position. We are affected, changed by that voice, by words that may lead us to think or feel a variety of things—that may turn our thoughts in new directions and may cause us to feel sad, or happy, or jealous, or angry, or bored, or frustrated, or comforted, or hopeful. But by taking in the voice of another, we gain the sense of an entry, an opening, a connection with another person's psychic life. In this relational reframing of psychology, relationship or connection is key to psychological inquiry. Rather than blurring perspective or clouding judgment with feelings, relationship is the way of knowing, an opening between self and other that creates a channel for discovery, an avenue to knowledge.

These first two listenings—for the plot and for the voice of the "I" or self—bring the listener into responsive relationship with the person speaking and thus are key to what we mean by calling our approach a relational method. Moreover, in emphasizing the importance of becoming an empathic and responsive listener, we connect our way of working with empathic approaches to psychotherapy and reader-response approaches to literary analysis. But in so doing we are mindful of Patrocinio Schweickart's critique of such approaches for making no claims to feminism and thus neglecting "issues of race, class and sex," and for giving "no hint of the conflicts, sufferings, and passions that attend these realities."[13] Our *responsive* Listener's Guide, in attending to realities of race, class, and sex (who is speaking, in what body, telling what story of relationship—from whose perspective, in what societal and cultural frameworks?), is therefore also a *resisting* Listener's Guide, that is, a feminist method. As resisting listeners, like Judith Fetterley's resisting reader, we question "the very posture of the apolitical"; we give "voice to a different reality and different vision . . . [bring] a different subjectivity to bear on the old 'universality'" and thus politicize it.[14] In listening to girls' and women's voices, we listen for and against conventions of relationship within a society and culture that are rooted psychologically in the experiences of men.

In the third and fourth listenings, then, we attend to the ways people talk about relationships—how they experience themselves in the relational landscape of human life. In working with girls and women, we are particularly attentive to their struggles for relationships that are authentic or resonant, that is, relationships in which they can freely express themselves or speak their feelings and thoughts and be heard. And we are also attuned to the ways in which institutionalized restraints and cultural norms and values become moral voices that silence voices, constrain the expression of feelings and thoughts, and consequently narrow relationships, carrying implicit or explicit threats of exclusion, violation, and at the extreme, violence.[15] As resisting listeners, therefore, we make an effort to distinguish when relationships are narrowed and distorted by gender stereotypes or used as opportunities for distancing, abuse, subordination, invalidation, or other forms of psychological violation, physical violence, and oppression, and when relationships are healthy, joyous, encouraging, freeing, and empowering. Because girls come up to a chasm between what they know about relationship through experience and what is socially constructed as Relationship within a male-voiced culture, and because women struggle with this experience/"reality" split, it is particularly important to name not only the vulnerabilities inherent in relationship but also the dangers in the prevailing conventions of relationship.[16] Specifically we are referring to the encouragement of self-sacrifice or self-silencing and the holding out of purity and perfection as conditions for relationship and the mark of good women, in the case of the feminine ideal, and, in the case of the masculine ideal, the encouragement of self-aggrandizement and the desire to be in the dominant position, to be in control.

As resisting listeners, we thus are aware of, and through this awareness attempt to extricate ourselves from, the constraints of a patriarchal logic, to create a space to define or "revision" the experience of self and the nature of relationship in a way that is in tune with the voices of both women and men. We do this by listening in the interviews for signs of self-silencing or capitulation to debilitating cultural norms and values—times when a person buries her feelings and thoughts and manifests confusion, uncertainty, and dissociation, which are the marks of a psychological resistance. We also listen for signs of political resistance, times when people struggle against abusive relationships and fight for relationships in which it is possible for them to disagree openly with others, to feel and speak a full range of emotions. This process of voicing, as Kate Millett says, "a system of power [so] thoroughly in command, it has scarcely [a] need to speak itself aloud,"[17] provides, we suggest, a way to move beneath the prevailing conventions and to understand how those not heard as full human beings within such a system exist and resist, how they create and maintain their humanity both above ground and underground.

Our voice-centered method thus is an attempt to maintain the relationships which are central to the process of psychological growth and also the process of our inquiry by maintaining voice and thus articulating difference. Within the societal and cultural contexts in which we are working, our method strives, as Fetterley puts it, "to expose and question that complex of ideas and mythologies about women and men which exists in our society,"[18] and also "to see," as Rich says, "the assumptions in which we are drenched."[19] In pursuing these relational truths and realities (the need for both self and other to have a voice, the social and cultural context of speaking and listening), we have learned from our work with girls and women, from other psychologists who have stayed with women's voices,[20] and from feminist literary critics who have contributed to what Rich calls "revision"—"the act of looking back, of seeing with fresh eyes, of entering an old text from a new critical direction."[21] In Virginia Woolf's terms, we are attempting "to find new words and create new methods"[22] by bringing women's voices into psychology and thus creating a new voice for psychology—a voice more resonant with people's lives.

Voicing Resistance

To illustrate the use of our Listener's Guide, we turn to Neeti, a twelve-year-old girl of Indian descent, the daughter of a biochemist and an executive, a seventh grader at Laurel School. Using this method, what can a responsive, resisting listener say about Neeti's experience of herself and her relationships? Here we listen to Neeti speaking at age twelve, and then a year later at age thirteen.

Listening the first time, we hear Neeti tell a story of relational conflict in which she is willing to take on an intransigent camp guide, and risk getting yelled at, on behalf of her homesick cousin:

When we were at camp [two years ago], I went to camp with my sister and my cousin, and he was really young . . . He was, like, maybe seven, and he got really, really homesick. It was overnight. And he was, like, always crying at night and stuff. And we had this camp guide who was really tough, and I was kind of afraid of him . . . And he said, "Nobody's allowed to use the phone." And so my cousin really wanted to call his parents. And it was kind of up to me to go ask the guy if he could. So, either, like, I got bawled out by this guy and asked, or I didn't do anything about it. And he was my cousin, so I had to help him. So I went, so I asked the guy if he could use the phone, and he started giving me this lecture about how there shouldn't be homesickness in this camp. And I said, "Sorry, but he's only seven." And he was really young, and so he finally got to use the phone. So he used the phone, and then we had a camp meeting, and, um, the guy started saying, "Any kid here who gets homesick shouldn't be here." And he didn't say my cousin's name, but he was, like, almost in tears.

Neeti's story, it seems to us, is about her cousin's homesickness, the intransigence of a camp director, and her decision, despite her fear, to help her cousin call his parents. The conflict was, she says succinctly, "me saving myself or saving him." She decided to help her cousin because "nothing bad was going to happen to me"; the camp director might intimidate her and hurt her feelings, but he "can't beat me up or anything." Neeti realized that "it was worth, like, letting [my cousin] talk to his parents . . . My cousin was screaming, has nightmares . . . He wasn't being able to have any fun and he paid for [the camp] . . . He was like almost sick, you know. That's why I guess they call it homesick." The camp director, she thinks, "was really callous." Looking back, Neeti says that it's obvious that her decision was right, at least for her. "It might not be for you or somebody else, but it's helping out my cousin and that camp director, it's a rule, but people are more important than rules." Besides, she notes, the camp director was contradicting himself; they say, "We're here to help our kids, to make them have fun." Her cousin, she observes, "wasn't having fun, he was just contradicting the whole slogan."

Listening to this narrative of relational conflict, we note that Neeti states the problem on several levels: as a conflict between saving herself and saving her cousin, as a conflict between people and rules, and as a conflict between doing nothing and doing something in a situation where she sees the possibility of doing something to help. The relationships mentioned are Neeti's relationships with her cousin, with herself, with the camp director, and with her friends, as well as the cousin's relationship with his parents. A possible contradiction in the story is between Neeti's sense that the right thing was obvious and she did the right thing, and her experience of conflict.

As we take in Neeti's voice, we respond to Neeti's story, recording places of connection and disconnection between Neeti's experience and our own. As listeners, we ask ourselves what we know about Neeti from this story and what this might mean for our interpretation. Through this connection, we draw attention to the powerful act of one person, the listener, interpreting—"naming"—the experience of another who only speaks within a narrative about a conflict that she lived. In Neeti's case, we recall our own experiences of summer camp and how powerful the counselors were, how the rules which were enforced sometimes seemed arbitrary and unfair. As white, educationally advantaged women, we also wonder about Neeti's ethnicity and how this affects her choice or her sense of obligation to protect her young cousin, or if Neeti's privilege gives her confidence that the system will protect her—confidence we do not remember having at that age. In this way we attend to what we know and don't know about Neeti, and what she knows about herself, to raise questions about her telling and interpretation of the story.

The second time through the story we listen to the way Neeti speaks about herself. Returning to the beginning of her narrative, we now listen for Neeti as the feeling, thinking, acting "I," as the protagonist in her drama of relational conflict. Here is Neeti's story in first person:

I went to camp . . . I was kind of afraid of him . . . and I was really afraid of him . . . It was kind of up to me . . . Either, like, I got bawled out by this guy and asked or I didn't do anything about it . . . I had to help him . . . So I went, so I asked . . . I said, "Sorry, but he's only seven" . . . I said, "This guy can, he can intimidate me but he can't beat me up" . . . I'll realize . . . I have to do this . . . I mean . . . I'm sure, I was sure . . . He was my cousin, you know, and we've always been kind of close . . . Either I helped him out or, I helped my, or I didn't, like that was for him, or I couldn't go for myself because I didn't want to be like . . . I was really afraid . . . It was me saving myself or saving him . . . I mean . . . nothing bad was going to happen to me . . . So I realized . . . so I guess he did kind of realize . . . I mean I would never see that guy again . . . But I lived . . . I lived with my cousin . . . I would never see that guy again . . . It's just like my feelings being hurt and I hate being yelled at . . . I guess . . . I'm sure . . . the way I saw it . . . So I don't . . . I guess . . . I guess . . . I know . . . I was really surprised . . . I felt really good but I felt really bad . . . I did something for him . . . And it's kind of like a victory . . . I'm sure . . . I don't know what it was . . . It's obvious that was right . . . it is for me . . . I felt it . . . I could have gotten out of it easily . . . It wasn't my feeling . . . I wasn't feeling what he was feeling . . . I did have a little empathy, but, you know, not that much . . . I could have gotten out of it and said "I'm not going up to that camp director" . . . I almost felt like he did in a way, so I did, I did go up, you know, because I felt miserable having him feel miserable.

Neeti's voice carries the sound of a candid, confident, psychologically astute and shrewd twelve-year-old, concerned about her cousin and also about herself, indignant at the camp director's lack of concern, sure of her perceptions and judgments, stubborn, determined, and capable of making intriguing observations: "Either you feel it, like all the way, or you just, like, recognize it" (referring to the difference between her response to her cousin's homesickness and that of her friends).

Attending to how she speaks about herself in this drama, we hear Neeti's fear of the camp director ("I was afraid of him," she says three separate times) and also her clarity: Although the camp director says "kids are having fun," she *sees* that her cousin is not having any fun and she goes with her perceptions. Neeti's ability to do this rests in part on her certainty that, although the director, who is "a big bully and he can have anything the way he wants it," might yell at her, he cannot physically hurt her. Knowing this, Neeti speaks from her experience, saying what she sees and hears: She *sees* her cousin's obvious distress; she *hears* his crying and screaming at night. And, taking in the evidence of her senses, she trusts her experiences to guide her understanding: "He was like almost sick, you know. That's why I guess they call it homesick." At the risk of being yelled at, and in the face of the camp director's admonishments, which are supported by the camp rules, Neeti finally determines that "I have to do this." This sense of imperative comes in part from Neeti's experience of relational reality, especially her sense of herself in relationship with her cousin.

Listening a third time, we hear Neeti speak about a relationship with her cousin that seems genuine to her. Neeti describes her understanding of this relationship and her response to her cousin who is in great emotional distress:

He was really young. He was like maybe seven, and he got really, really homesick. It was overnight. And he was, like, always crying at night and stuff . . . And so my cousin really wanted to call his parents . . . And he was my cousin, so I had to help him . . . And I said, "Sorry, but he's only seven" . . . He was, like, almost in tears . . . The right thing was to go because it was for my cousin's good, you know. And he wasn't going to die or anything but, you know, he's like afraid to go to camp now, because he's like nine now. And he's like, he doesn't want to go back . . . This guy can, he can intimidate me, but he can't beat me up or anything . . . I'll realize that that's just the way he is, but I have to do this . . . just help [my cousin] out . . . The conflict was that, like, it was like, he was my cousin, you know, and we've always been kind of close . . . It was me saving myself or saving him . . . Nothing bad was going to happen to me . . . He felt a lot better . . . My cousin was screaming, has nightmares, and it was really bad, he was with all his friends . . . My cousin lives seven minutes away from us, so I lived with my cousin, but I would never see that [camp director] again . . . [What was at stake was] kind of like the ego, you know, it's like nothing physically and nothing that anybody else would see. It's just like my feelings being hurt and I hate being yelled at . . . But my cousin, he was like feeling really, really low . . . really bad. He was like almost sick . . . It's like, either you feel it, like all the way, or you just, like, recognize it, you know? . . . It's helping out my cousin and that camp director, you know, it's a rule, but people are more important than rules . . . He was just a little kid . . . My cousin wasn't having fun . . . He was, like, really close, but I wasn't feeling what he was feeling, so like I did have a little empathy but, you know, not that much . . . He was, like, very miserable and I almost felt like he did in a way, so I did, I did go up, you know, because I felt miserable having him feel miserable.

Listening in this way, we hear Neeti speak of her relationship with her cousin—"we've always been kind of close"—and her feelings in response to his pain—"I did have a little empathy but, you know, not that much . . . I almost felt like he did in a way." Neeti's attunement to the feelings of her cousin and her response to his feelings are tied in with her own feelings because her cousin's unhappiness affects her. His feelings are not the same as her feelings, as she states clearly; he is not she. Implicitly resisting conventional notions of selflessness and self-sacrifice associated with feminine ideals of love and caring, Neeti's voice draws the listener's attention, instead, to her knowledge of human relationships and psychological processes, knowledge that suggests close and careful observations. And when the camp director does not acknowledge her cousin's distress, when he responds by giving her a lecture "about how there shouldn't be homesickness in this camp," we hear Neeti's resistance to his view when she points to the visible signs of her cousin's distress and replies, "Sorry, but he's only seven."

Listening, finally, for what Neeti identifies as false relationships, as relationships in which people cannot speak or are not heard, we hear Neeti focus on the camp director and express her feelings about his power over her and her cousin:

We had this camp guide who was really tough and I was kind of afraid of him . . . and I was really afraid of him. And he said, "Nobody's allowed to use the phone." And so my cousin really wanted to call his parents . . . So either, like, I got bawled out by this guy and asked, or I didn't do anything about it. And he was my cousin, so I had to help him . . . So I went, so I asked . . . and he started giving me this lecture about how there shouldn't be homesickness in this camp. And I said, "Sorry, but he's only seven" . . . We had a camp meeting . . . and, um, the guy started saying, "Any kid here who gets homesick shouldn't be here" . . . And the right thing was to go because it was for my cousin's good, you know . . . Like, I said, "This guy can, he can intimidate me, but he can't beat me up or anything." And I, I'll realize that that's just the way he is, but I have to do this . . . I hate being yelled at . . . He wasn't being able to have any fun and he paid for it, so he had to do something . . . The way I saw it at that time was this guy is, like, a big bully and he can have anything the way he wants it. So . . . I guess it was kind of big, letting, giving in for him . . . He goes on . . . his, like, his reputation, you know, see that was a rule and he couldn't break it, but he said, "Yes, *but*," and then he started giving us the lecture . . . But I did something for him, my cousin, and it's kind of like a victory, you know, it's like you won over this guy, so be happy . . . The camp director had another point of view. He was probably like, "kids always get homesick and what difference does it make, he's not going to die," you know, but he wasn't that kid . . . And so he had a totally different point of view from my cousin and I . . . He was really callous . . . It's a rule, but people are more important than rules . . . They were saying, "Well, we're here to help our kids, to make them have fun," but my cousin wasn't having fun, he was just contradicting the whole slogan.

Neeti reasons empirically from her own experience as she notes the absurdity of a situation in which the camp directors say, "We're here to help our kids, to make them have fun," and she sees that her cousin "wasn't being able to have any fun and he paid for it." She watches a camp director place his concern with reputation over the misery of a seven-year-old, and take advantage of the fact that the seven-year-old is under his direction while he "can have anything the way he wants it." Neeti presents a complicated understanding of rules as structures that maintain order in relationships. She sees that the camp director's pride or sense of his reputation was contingent on "a rule and he couldn't break it"; thus, again, she makes, albeit inadvertently, a psychologically astute comment about the internalization of rules and standards. She also alludes to her faith in the protective power of a system of justice, when she says that the camp director could intimidate her and hurt her feelings but he "can't beat me up or anything." And we hear Neeti's resistance to oppressive authority in the form of the "callous" camp director who plays by the rules without exception: "People," Neeti says firmly, "are more important than rules."

As listeners, we are struck by Neeti's courage and ability to stay with what she knows about relationships in the face of pressure not to know and not to see and hear. We are also impressed by her clarity about her own thoughts and feelings and her intricate knowing of the psychological and social world. Speaking of her decision to act on behalf of her cousin, she says: "It wasn't my feeling, my cousin's, but he was, like, really close, but I wasn't feeling what he was feeling, but I did have a little empathy, but not that much . . . But he was, like, very miserable and I almost felt like he did in a way, so I did, I did go up because I felt miserable having him feel miserable." Here Neeti makes a distinction that reveals the full extent of her relational capacities. She contrasts empathy—that is, feeling another's feelings—with responsive relationships—responding to another person's feelings with feelings of her own. This distinction is rarely made in the psychological literature.

Listening to Neeti's age-thirteen interview narrative, we hear her tell a very different story of relational conflict. This year Neeti tells a story about feeling trapped in a scene that is not of her own making, which is not what she wants. We listen as she describes the conflict in her own terms: "One friend I have and she is supposedly my best friend, you know, and I don't talk to her, because like everybody hates her in class . . . I mean I don't even like her." The dilemma, Neeti says, is "that I don't like this girl at all, that I absolutely hate her, but I don't know how to act because I have to be nice."

Surprised already by the change we hear in Neeti's voice, we listen a second time to her story, attending to the way she speaks about herself in this relational drama. We now hear Neeti's ambivalence: "I can't say anything to her, because she'll be hurt, so I have no idea what to do." We hear her speak and then retract what she has said: "this is me, not really." We listen to a sharp increase in her use of the phrase "I don't know" as she knows and then does not know what she feels and thinks, what she can know and speak about.

Listening to Neeti speak about her understanding of relationships in this situation, we now hear her describe what sounds like a series of fraudulent relationships based on her desire not to hurt or upset anyone—her "friend," her friend's mother and sisters who, she says, are friends with Neeti's mother and sisters. Unable to speak what she feels and thinks, Neeti describes a false and "suffocating" closeness that feels like "being married" to someone she does not love. Unspoken, unvoiced, and thus taken out of relationship, her thoughts and feelings have come to seem out of proportion and out of perspective—too large or too small, too monumental or too trivial. Unable to gauge her friendship with this girl (is she her best friend or someone she hates?) or know what she wants, it feels impossible for Neeti to be in this relationship. What she wants to say now is to her unspeakable: "I hate you. Please leave me alone." What she wishes for openly is an end to conflict.

Unlike at age twelve when she spoke her thoughts and feelings in relationship, when she drew from her experience and thus clearly distinguished between what she knew to be true from experience and what authorities said was the case, now Neeti seems to have taken in a conventional, authoritative voice and is modeling herself on the image of the perfectly nice and caring girl. Giving over the evidence of her own experience—that she and her "friend" are both suffering in this idealized form of relationship—Neeti struggles to authorize, to give voice to, to name, even to know her thoughts and feelings. This shift in Neeti's voice over time is, in fact, exemplary of a loss of voice, a struggle with self-authorization, and a move from real to idealized relationships characteristic of girls we have listened to using this voice-centered approach, as they move from childhood to adolescence.[23]

With our Listener's Guide we draw attention not only to the powerful act of one person interpreting—"naming"—the experience of another but to the implications of such an act for those who tell psychologists stories about their lives. A relational practice of psychology moves beyond a revisionary interpretation of voices or texts. Such interpretation, in fact, ought to mark only the beginning of a dialogue, the initial move by the listener toward the forming of questions, and ultimately toward a relationship in which both people speak and listen to one another. Rather than focusing on objects to be studied or people to be treated, judged, tested, or assessed, we speak about authentic or resonant relationships, that is, relationships in which both people can voice their thoughts and feelings, relationships that are as open and mutual as possible, in which partially formed thoughts and strong feelings can be spoken and heard. In creating a method that allows for (and encourages) a polyphony of voices, we cannot, in a relational practice of psychology, cut off or appropriate the voice of the person speaking, especially if her voice is discordant with our own. A shift from encouraging (enforcing) consensus or agreement to engaging diversity creates the possibility for real rather than fraudulent relationships with those with whom we engage in our work.

We spoke with Neeti over the course of five years in formal interview settings. And during that time we listened and interpreted and wrote about the changes we heard in her voice as she spoke about herself and her relationships. Since then we have been in dialogue with Neeti about our interpretations and our writing. Our relationship with her has moved forward and changed; we have learned from her and she has learned from us. In the course of a day-long retreat we met with Neeti and other members of her eleventh-grade class to discuss this research. After talking with us about her response to a paper we wrote, Neeti wrote us a letter: "At first I was overcome with a helpless feeling of self-exposure," she said. "I was struck, for it never occurred to me that what I had been saying for the past five years of interviews was of any importance . . . It was an odd feeling to see my voice in quotes."

Neeti then conversed with us about our interpretation of the changes in her life. She told us of her dismay when at fifteen she was asked to write an essay called "Who Am I?" and she realized she did not know. Unhappy with her "fascination with the perfect girl" and her "fraudulent view" of herself (phrases from our writing that resonated with her feelings about herself), Neeti spoke of a "voice inside" her that "has been muffled": "The voice that stands up for what I believe in has been buried deep inside of me."

Neeti, whose relational world seemed to us to have darkened over time, continues to surprise us with her resilience, her determination to be heard clearly, her perceptiveness, and her ongoing struggle with conventional feminine ideals. "I do not want the image of a 'perfect girl' to hinder myself from being a truly effective human being," she writes, "yet, I still want to be nice, and I never want to cause any problems." Neeti is caught in a paradox between wanting relationship and feeling that in order to have relationships she must muffle or bury her voice. Although she sees the impasse clearly, she cannot see a way out.

A relational psychology informed by literary theory, by the insights of feminist literary critics, and by clinical insights about psychodynamic processes—that is, a voiced, resonant, resistant psychology—offers an opening, a way of voicing the relational nature of human life. As psychologists working with people rather than literary critics interpreting texts, we have to ask why, as Neeti moves from age twelve to age thirteen, does speaking about what she feels and thinks in her relationships, once so simple and genuine for her, become so fraught with difficulty and danger? As we saw, Neeti struggles to hold on to her experience—to know what she knows and to speak in her own voice, to bring her knowledge into the world in which she lives—in the face of authorities, conventions, and relational conflicts that would otherwise lead her to muffle her voice and bury what she most fervently wants and believes in: the possibility of authentic or genuine relationship. As psychologists who are women, who were once girls, we struggle to hold on to what we know about relationships and feelings, about psyches and bodies, about political and social realities, and about the ways in which women's voices have been trivialized, dismissed, and devalued. In so doing we use our authority and power to make it easier for girls' and women's voices to be heard and engaged openly in relationship—to encourage the open trouble of political resistance, the insistence on knowing what one knows and the willingness to be outspoken, rather than to collude in the silencing and avoidance of conflict that fosters the corrosive suffering of psychological resistance: the reluctance to know what one knows and the fear that one's experience, if spoken, will endanger relationships and threaten survival.

3

Whistle-Blowers in the Relational World: Three Guides through Childhood

Anita, eight years old, is wearing a green and blue plaid jumper with a crisp white blouse. She has just returned from recess, thrown her coat in her locker, and is ready now to begin her interview. The two of us sit in a corner outside her classroom; the murmur of girls' voices edge into consciousness whenever we pause. She is shy but interested. We remember each other from last year when I visited her class to describe the study, and she thinks she remembers something about the stories in the interview. Some of the questions are hard for her, nevertheless, and there are starts and stops, pauses and silences now and again. As we near the end of our time, she begins to fidget in her seat, her eyes wander to the pencil she holds in her hand, her ears to the sounds behind the door. She asks if she can hear her voice on the tape. Better yet, can she have the tape? After we finish, we listen to our voices for a few minutes. It's funny and a little embarrassing. It doesn't sound like us.

This memory of Anita captures our impressions of the seven- and eight-year-old girls we listened to. Before talking to each girl in the second grade class, we observed these girls for a short time, watched them work together and ready themselves for recess and dance class. Their brightly painted pictures and projects lined the halls, claiming this space in the building as their own. Bringing these small bodies to rest even for a short period of time seemed almost unnatural, so used were we to seeing them in constant motion, both at work and at play.

Anita and her classmates speak of their thoughts and feelings about relationships in direct ways, describing their willingness to speak out to those with whom they are in relationship about bad or hurt feelings, anger, resentment, or frustration, as well as feelings of love, fondness, and loyalty. These seven- and eight-year-old girls say matter-of-factly that people are different, that they may disagree, and, as a result, sometimes people get hurt. While they speak about the importance of being nice, they openly acknowledge that sometimes they do not feel like being nice; they know that they can hurt others, and they speak about being hurt by others. In this sense, their relationships seem genuine or authentic.

These young girls tell stories of times when they refuse to take no for an answer. If they think someone is not listening, they will try again; and if that doesn't work, they can find creative, though perhaps disruptive, ways to be heard. Tuning our ears to the voices of eight-year-old girls in this study and to the stories they tell about relational conflicts, we begin with Diana, who says that she feels bad because her brother and sister keep stealing her mother's attention at dinner, interrupting her when she tries to speak. One night Diana's response to this problem was to bring a whistle to the dinner table. When she was interrupted, she blew the whistle. Mother, brother, and sister, she says, abruptly stopped talking and turned to her, at which point she said "in a normal voice, 'That's much nicer.'"

Diana's classmate, Karin, tells of a time when she was so upset with her teacher for not calling on her that she walked out of the classroom. She explains:

She picked someone else, and the same thing happened yesterday, so I walked out . . . I just lost my temper, I guess . . . I don't do it very often.
Was there anything you were thinking about?
When people walk in [to class] and see me and think that I got in trouble and that's why I was outside [the room]. And I wasn't

in trouble. I just couldn't take it. So, I guess I just left . . . because I didn't want people to make fun of me. I wanted to answer something, because she always chooses someone else and for once I wanted her to have chosen me for a problem that was really hard.

So your decision was to walk out of the room. And do you think that was the right thing to do?

[Yeah]. Because I just don't think that—if I want to do something, I should be able to do it, and I just lost my temper. So I guess that's why I left . . . I think I should have my chance to do . . . a hard problem.

Does [the teacher] know why you left the room?

She wouldn't listen to me, but I told her, so I guess she knows.

Karin, like someone explaining simple laws of physics, says that because she said what she was thinking and feeling her teacher knows it—though she may have chosen not to listen. These girls carry with them a strong belief that they know what is going on in the relational world and are willing to act on their knowledge. To ignore her feelings and ideas is a mistake, Melissa warns, "Because maybe you have something important to say . . . and if they don't listen to you, then they may miss out on something."

These seven- and eight-year-old girls blow the whistle on relational violations, such as interrupting, ignoring, hurting people's feelings, by dramatizing their experiences. Diana's whistle recreates in others what she feels when she is interrupted. By leaving the room, Karin suggests she might as well not be in class when her repeated efforts to answer a question are not attended to. These girls interrupt the surface calm and quiet of daily life with their insistence on saying what is happening between people. Tracy, who understands her parents' inattention and at times is even willing to make excuses for it, draws the line at a certain point. "I understand they're busy, but . . . if it was really important, I would have to say, grab them . . . even if they wouldn't listen to me then, I would be really mad . . . if it was really important." If "my mom . . . doesn't answer," Lidia explains, "I have to yell. Then she gets to hear me. I mean, I want her attention . . . I wouldn't have yelled . . . if she had listened." The capacity for these eight-year-olds to be openly angry—to be "really mad"—to be disruptive and resistant, gives them an air of unedited authority and authenticity, and reveals their simple straightforward relational desire to speak and to be listened to.

Yet these young girls are already intensely aware of the reactions of others to their voices and actions. Though she walked out of class, Karin is painfully aware of what her classmates will think and say about her: She fears "that someone will make fun" of her, "whisper about" her, "laugh at" her; they will "think that I got in trouble and that's why I'm outside." And so while Karin and her classmates speak directly to each other and frequently act on their strong feelings, they are quick to point out the risks of speaking up or acting on impulse. They know that in order to be accepted or liked or included by others, they must also be "nice girls" who heed the advice of their teachers and parents and friends to "wait their turn," "be polite," or "be patient." Nice girls "make more friends," Tina confides to her interviewer. "It's better to be nice than not nice—you get more friends . . . and relationships."

Anticipating the reactions of adults, these seven- and eight-year-olds begin to monitor each other and report on "nice behavior." Word of some misdeed or "rude" remark travels fast among the girls, at times revealing the dark underside of their relationships. Indeed, the demand for nice and kind can be oppressive, a means of controlling and being controlled. "Whispering," "telling secrets," "making fun of," and "laughing at" others are ways to prevent girls from risking too much or acting in ways that are too threatening, too different. And so, in the face of pressure to not know or not speak, these young girls sometimes retract their initial strong feelings rather than face the painful consequences. Stories with "happy endings" then emerge, revealing the power of "nice and polite" to cover over strong feelings and mask conflict. Lauren, for example, begins to tell her interviewer about a time when she was treated unfairly at school. "I had [the computer] first," she says, "and I'd just left to put my spelling book away and stuff. And when I came back *she* was there." "Another girl?" her interviewer asks?

Yeah, that's in my class, and she said, "Well, I got here first," and I'd say, "No I did." And so our teacher . . . said we couldn't do it unless we both do it or we agree on doing it together or just not do it for like the rest of the day, so we decided to do it together, and that meant a lot to me, so I said, "Thank you for letting me play with you," and I felt very happy when it was time to leave and stuff.

What is, at first, a story of unfairness and Lauren's direct confrontation with the girl who took her place at the computer is muffled, in part by the teacher's influence, and turned into a story of happy cooperation. Lauren soon reveals, however, that much of what she has told the interviewer about her own actions and the actions of the teacher in this account actually took place in her thoughts. Her decision to cooperate, she tells the woman who sits with her, was in response to an inner dialogue that includes both her awareness that speaking politely will reflect well on her, and her appreciation of the wishes and the power of her teacher:

I said to myself, "Well, why don't I just ask her if I can?" I'd say, "May I please have the computer?" and she'd say, "No." And so the teacher would come and tell us that—those things—and that's why I decided to do it together, and she decided to do it together . . . cause I wouldn't want to get in trouble and have the teacher yell at me.
Was the other girl happy with the solution, do you think?
Sort of . . . but after, when I said, "Okay. You can do it by yourself," she was very happy, and she said, "Thank you."

Not wanting "to get in trouble and have the teacher yell at me," Lauren capitulates to the anticipated wishes of the teacher, giving up her desire to work on the computer alone. Thus what we are led to believe is a polite and happy ending turns out to mean that the other girl is happy because she finally has the computer all to herself and Lauren doesn't actually say how she is feeling. Lauren, it seems, lost her chance to work on the computer alone, and thereby gave up her feeling that she could or should have the computer. The teacher, in this case, makes it impossible for Lauren and her classmate to work out their conflict in a way that responds to Lauren's perceptions and feelings. It is as if what Lauren saw never happened, as if her feelings were unacceptable feelings.

Such stories reveal the second grade girls' clear recognition of pressure not to want what they want if it brings them into conflict with others. Yet underneath talk of cooperation, or perhaps in spite of such talk, Lauren clearly says what happened: "I said, 'Okay. You can do it by yourself.' She was very happy, and she said, 'Thank you.'" The teacher who involves herself in assuring happy cooperation and sharing between the girls presumably does not protest or even interfere with Lauren's decision to give up the computer, and give over her strong feelings.

Other girls, like Lauren, talk about giving over their strong feelings—feelings of frustration, anger, fears of abandonment—to "happy endings." They offer and retract their desires, reconsider or dismiss or reframe their feelings and thoughts in ways that cover over their initial reactions. Sandra tells of her feelings when her sister was born. "I felt like I was left out of the family . . . 'cause I didn't get any attention . . . when my sister was born . . . She's three." When Sandra told her parents how she felt, she says they said to her, "Well, you're older . . . and you don't need as much attention . . . because you have more privileges." Sandra then concludes, "Well, that's right . . . to look on the bright side." Sandra's conclusion suggests there is no place in such a reformulation for her initial feelings, her thoughts, her observations that she was sometimes left out of the family. The distinction between her feelings of exclusion and the glib solution "to look on the bright side" suggests she may hear in her parents' response a message about her feelings—that they are negative, unacceptable, or ineffective and may, in fact, lead her to be left out of the family, her worst fear. The "happy endings" heard from other girls seem more like wishful thinking on their part, something heard in a fairy tale, a pleasing and acceptable cover for experiences of feeling left out and fears of being abandoned.

These young girls are certainly conscious of the power of adults to affect their lives—to control them or support them or punish them, to love them or abandon them—and often express strong anger in response to what they perceive to be abuses of power. Dana was furious when her ballet teacher told her to sit down for talking in class. Her dark eyes flashing, she exclaims, "Well, I think she should have listened to me. It's not fair . . . I think she should have listened to me, 'cause it isn't fair that she listened to the girl that . . . was talking in class, but she wouldn't listen to me . . . She does the thing where she doesn't listen to your half of the story, she does that to everybody. She just doesn't let you tell your half of the story." "What would happen if she heard your side of the story?" the interviewer wants to know. "Well, I think that she might have understood more," Dana replies, "and she might not have—I might not have had to sit out and stuff." Frustrated by her teacher's unwillingness to listen to her or take her explanation seriously, Dana is rendered ineffective by "the thing"—unable to speak on her own behalf. Dana and her classmates are angered at what seems to them to be the adult "thing"—cutting off relationship or rendering girls helpless and powerless in relationships by not listening, and thereby making it impossible for them to speak. These girls repeatedly reiterate their wish for honest conversation and dialogue, conversation that would not always be pleasant or "nice" but full of genuine disagreement and feelings.

These seven- and eight-year-old girls speak clearly and at times passionately about their feelings of friendship. Strong feelings of loyalty and love for friends are matched only by the anger and pain of fighting and disagreeing with them. Experiencing face-to-face conflict with friends makes these girls feel "sad" more often than any other experience they describe, an emotion that seems appropriate to the feelings of loss they talk about. While these girls have little recourse for action, except perhaps to cry "unfair!" when adults treat them badly, when their friends do so they react by expressing strong feelings, by asking questions, or actively protesting. And yet, though they tell of hurt feelings or exclusion, anger, and frustration, they tell us they are less likely to react with physical violence than verbal outbursts. Words seem, in some ways, more powerful to them.

When these second-graders do complain of violent acts or bullying behavior, they almost always speak of boys, most often their brothers. Telling about her relationship with her sister, Carrie compares her fight with her sister to her brother's fight with her sister: "And once when my brother was in a fight with my sister, and he was hurting her real bad, I got real mad and I didn't know what to do . . . I felt pretty mad at my brother for hitting her. Then I decided I would go tell mom, because he was hurting her more than our fight, the fight that she and I had." "How could you tell?" the interviewer asks her. "Because she was crying and stuff," Carrie responds, "I was glad I did that to get my brother off of her." Carrie's decision to tell her mother is based on the evidence of her senses; what she sees and hears leads her to judge that her sister's distress has gone beyond the usual. Other girls talk about the importance of paying close attention, of observing carefully, in determining the existence or extent of another person's pain. Part of knowing how much another hurts depends on remembering their own painful experiences as well as the knowledge of the other person gained over time and in relationship.

Tessa tells her interviewer about how a group of boys, friends from her neighborhood, taunt her and her girlfriend as they walk home from school. "They all went in a group," she says, "and me and my friend [were walking home] from school. They were being really mean . . . and they just ganged up on us . . . We didn't do anything to them." Her wish is that "we could all play together and play a game of tag or something," but in order for that to happen the group of boys would have to say "we're sorry." The boys don't comply, and Tessa tries to understand their behavior, even excuse it—"Maybe," she says, "they were jealous that they didn't have another friend"— though she remains both indignant and uncomfortable. The only other recourse she can imagine is a private conversation: "We could talk to one of the kids by himself and ask him to say 'I'm sorry.'" But, perhaps after measuring her discomfort and the unlikely possibility of such a dialogue, Tessa and her friend leave the scene. "We just ignored them . . . We went inside and played our game," she explains, since she suspects that to stay around would invite more verbal abuse—"Maybe they'd get a little madder, and they'd start calling us names again."

Tessa, willing to give the boys every opportunity to explain their behavior, first imagines that a private face-to-face dialogue has the best chance of being effective, offering her an opportunity to reason with one of the boys. But after surveying the situation and deciding that conflict would seem only to create more conflict, Tessa and her friend move their game inside. Choosing to ignore—to not know—what the boys are doing, Tessa and her friend allow themselves to be displaced. And yet, at eight years old, they are clear about what has happened and why, and how they feel about the situation.[1]

These seven- and eight-year-old girls are aware that another person's emotional hurt is not always visible at first glance, and their response may change as stories of hurt or meanness emerge and become known. They understand that people are different and that difference can be the basis for real disagreement, but they also experience difference as a part of the life of relationships. The willingness of these girls to change in a relationship, to grow to like someone, to create common ground in relationships for the sake of staying together seems to reflect what psychologists and sociologists have documented in girls' play—their willingness to change the rules of the game rather than to argue over differences.[2] And yet, this is not to say these girls will back away from open disagreement, only that they judge which disagreements are worth having. Consider Marianne's story:

> There was someone that was a new girl and moved into someone else's house . . . and I didn't really like her that much, but my friend did, but then I learned to like her.
> *How did you learn to like her?*
> Oh, I just played with her a lot. It was because she always was like the boss, but then I told her, "Hey, I don't like you being the boss," and so, "And I know another friend who played with you before, and she doesn't like you being the boss." And then she stopped being the boss and I liked her.

Marianne, who has clear reasons for not liking the new girl, says that she expresses her feelings directly and openly to her. By explaining what it was that she did not like, she was able to initiate

In summary, the seven- and eight-year-old girls we listened to only partially reflect more common descriptions of children their age: while they can be egoistic and concrete in their thinking—the most common view put forth by psychologists in this culture—they also reveal psychological capabilities we have not seen explored fully.[3] These young girls know how they feel and what they want; they also know what others want them to do and be and so they anticipate others' reactions to their voices. They have a capacity for careful attention and concern for others, as well as strong voices and a clear sense of both the pleasures and the pains of relationships.

Having listened to this chorus of lively, outspoken, psychologically astute seven- and eight-year-olds, we turn to three girls—Jessie, Sonia, and Lauren—to be our guides through childhood. We choose these three girls because they represent three very different pathways, three separate journeys through childhood, and yet even in their distinctiveness we can follow the broad outlines of similarity. Jessie is European-American; at eight she is both somewhat shy and boldly expressive; she is direct about her strong feelings. Sonia is African-American; as she talks to a white woman about what is happening in her relationships, she is wary, quiet, but clear as she narrates the difference between what she feels and what others, including her interviewer, seem to expect. Lauren is European-American; she is lively and outspoken, a performer whose physical and emotional energy are difficult to contain, even as she herself anticipates how others will react and tries hard to control herself. As we follow these three girls from one year to the next, we wonder what they will come to know about themselves and their relationships over time, and how what they experience might inform our understanding of girls' and women's development.

Jessie: The Tyranny of Nice and Kind

Jessie, a slender eight-year-old with wavy brown hair and white skin, exemplifies with particular clarity the characteristics of the other eight-year-old girls in this study by offering a poignant description of girls' willingness to voice difficult and painful feelings.[4] Jessie talks with her interviewer about her feelings when "sometimes my friends have friends over when I'm playing with them and I feel left out." Such exclusive treatment is unfair, she says, "because you should like all your friends together. If you had a friend over, you shouldn't just play with one and leave the other one out . . . and feeling down and out of the game." What could she do to make things different? the interviewer wants to know:

> I would just go over to them, and go in the other friend's ear, I would kind of take them over somewhere else where the other of her friends couldn't hear, and I would say, "This is really making me feel bad, for leaving me out. Can you please play with me too?" That "I will go home if you don't, cause this isn't any fun for me, just sitting here."
> *Have you tried that?*
> Yeah, but one friend just said, "Just go home."

Jessie does go home, but she does not let the issue rest. "It takes me a couple of weeks to understand it," she says, but in time she devises an elaborate plan to teach her friend a relational lesson by treating her friend the way she was treated, to make them, as she says, "even." In the end, she explains, "I would have a friend over and also have her over . . . I would show her how I felt." For Jessie, being "even" meant her friend would know the bad feelings of being left out. "If we're even," Jessie says—meaning the friend knows what she knows about exclusion and abandonment—"then we could start being friends again."

As we have heard, Jessie and her classmates describe a human world in which feelings are spoken directly. These eight-year-olds voice a full range of human feelings and thoughts. What can we learn if we begin here with Jessie, in her directness and with her strong feelings and with a sense of her own authority, and follow her as she moves from one year to the next in order to see what she comes to know about herself and how her relationships change over time?

Jessie, like the other eight-year-olds in this study, is aware that people are different, that they may disagree, and, as a result, sometimes people get hurt. Jessie's appreciation of differences is apparent when she responds to a common relational problem initially posed by D. Kay Johnston in the form of an Aesop's Fable[5]—a story about a large and stubborn porcupine who has been invited to spend the winter by a family of well-intentioned moles, who then discover that living with a porcupine is essentially unbearable.

> It was growing cold, and a porcupine was looking for a home. He found a most desirable cave, but saw it was occupied by a family of moles. "Would you mind if I shared your home for the winter?" the porcupine asked the moles. The generous moles consented, and the porcupine moved in. But the cave was small, and every time the moles moved around they were scratched by the porcupine's sharp quills. The moles endured this discomfort as long as they could. Then at last they gathered courage to approach their visitor. "Pray leave," they said, "and let us have our cave to ourselves once again." "Oh no!" said the porcupine. "This place suits me very well."

Jessie says, "The mole is asking him to leave, but the porcupine doesn't want to, because the porcupine is comfortable; but [the mole] keeps on forcing him and [the porcupine] keeps on saying no." "Porcupines and moles," Jessie decides, "shouldn't be together because they make a really bad combination." And so it would be best, she says, to make the cave larger and to "make bigger paths" for the animals to walk. While Jessie's solution would make the animals happy and the forest "settled," it also takes the differences between the animals, and the ways they are hurting one another, seriously: "They could make their own tracks," she concludes, "they could make their own paths."

A full year later, at nine, Jessie returns to the story of the porcupine and the moles. We begin to hear her speak about what she thinks and feels in different voices, voices that co-exist but do not at this time speak directly to each other: In one voice Jessie says she would have the moles say to the porcupine, "I'm sorry, but please get out. This is my house. I'm not going to let you in anymore, so leave." And then, in another quite different voice, she ponders the situation: "It's the only shelter they have. If it's snowy they would be so cold and they would freeze . . . and they can have a hole to be warm in . . . it's like having a baby in your house."

Jessie's world is one of complicated feelings, a prism of feelings, from anger and feeling wretched to love and warmth—"like having a baby in the house"—a world of emotions that has a sense of edge and color and distinction. She holds all these feelings, moving from one to the next, speaking in one voice then another. Along with these voices we hear what sound like disembodied lines from parents and teachers that drop into Jessie's ears and into her world about what to know and what not to know, what to say and what not to say: "Cooperating is better than fighting," Jessie says, referring to the porcupine and the moles, and with this blanket statement the complexity of what she has felt and thought about their differences seems to dissolve. In the end, she summarizes, "You should be nice to your friends and communicate with them and not . . . do what you want." And her wish for the porcupine and the moles is that they "are happy and they don't have to fight anymore. They could just be friends and they could stay like that forever."

But despite this idealized vision, which covers over strong feelings and earlier distinctions, conflict and disagreement are commonplace in Jessie's relationships, part and parcel of the ordinary. As Jessie says of herself and her best friend in third grade, "We usually get in fights, because she wants to do one thing and we don't know what to do and we get all bored. And then finally she goes, 'Are we friends?' So we are and we try to find something to do."

Jessie has changed in subtle ways between second and third grade. As one might guess, she is more articulate, she describes her thoughts and feelings more vividly. Yet, there is an emerging awareness of the knowledge and the danger in authentic encounters. Having taken in the message "cooperating is better than fighting," Jessie begins to equate fighting with trouble from authorities, with anger, meanness, and noise, and cooperating with praise, niceness, calmness, and quiet. She is, it seems to us, undergoing a bit of ear-and voice-training. Though she claims that people "can keep their different ideas and . . . still be friends," she struggles with disagreement, recognizing early the dangers in speaking directly or expressing anger. Jessie is now sometimes willing to be nice to make the relationship "calm" and her friends happy so they will play with her, rather than because she feels like being nice. "Cooperating" in this way is better, she says, because "you don't get into fights and it's just calm and so it is not noisy and you can play." The interviewer asks her to explain:

> *Why don't you feel good about [getting into fights]?*
> That you are losing a friend and that you are both unhappy.
> *If you said, "no" to her, "I don't want to do that," would you risk losing her?*
> Yah.
> *How do you know that she might go away?*
> Because she always, well, I am not going to lose her for a long time, because always the next day at school we hug and say we are ready and say hi, because we both forget about it. I think I would lose her because she's very easy to lose, you know. If I say no and I walked out the door, she would come and drag me in again and she would start screaming at me. And she would start crying and I don't want that to happen.

The irony of this story, it seems to us, is that Jessie has not described a friend who is "easy to lose" at all. In fact, if Jessie *were* to say no, her friend would not let her go; "she would come and drag" Jessie in the room again and "start screaming" at her. Jessie, it seems to us, has presented the most authentic and gripping scene of relationship yet, and has almost in the same breath ruled it out as an example of relationship at all. Yet, at the same time, we can understand her fear. The risk is real and substantial to her. Losing a friend is "horrible," Jessie says, "because you wouldn't have a best friend to play with all the time . . . and I don't think you could find a friend just like that person."

Indeed, in her third-year interview, Jessie is consumed with what is and is not a relationship. Her strong feelings, spoken directly and with passion, can be dangerous since they are disruptive. Signs of disruption—anger and noise, getting riled up and anxious—are cause for being "ignored," left out, abandoned. Repeatedly Jessie speaks about her discomfort with anger, with noise, with yelling, and about the value of "talking quietly," of being "calm," and of dealing with disagreements in private. This is a good way to handle disagreements, she says, "because it doesn't get anybody mad . . . everybody doesn't get all riled up . . . so that you are mad for the rest of the day and your mom starts yelling at you because you are so mad and you get anxious and do things you are not supposed to do." From such situations, Jessie says, "I learn to agree with people . . . and don't get nervous and all riled up because it will just start more trouble." And so what once were the signs of authentic relationship for Jessie, the possibility of feeling another's pain as well as their joy, and the potential for difference and disagreement, are now withdrawn as too dangerous and risky.

Jessie, now eleven and in the fifth grade, responds to the porcu-pine and moles fable. Whereas, at eight, Jessie considered that perhaps the moles and porcupine were "a bad combination," at eleven, Jessie wishes to make the hole bigger because "it would be nice to have a neighbor in the house." It would be possible, she says, for the moles to say to the porcupine, "'I really don't want you here . . . ' and tell him to get out," but that would not be "a nice way to do it . . . because the porcupine would feel left out." What sounded like advice from adults at nine—"cooperating is better than fighting"—is replaced by a stronger message with a similar ring: "Always be nice to a friend." Unlike her self at eight and nine, Jessie at eleven no longer mentions the moles' discomfort as they are stuck by the porcupine's sharp quills, but speaks only about the porcupine's loneliness and hurt feelings. The moles no longer say no to hurt or inattentiveness; they do not confront the porcupine directly or with any sense of anger or indignation. Differences and potential conflict between these animals who once "made their own tracks" is now covered over by a sole concern for niceness and neighborliness as prerequisites for friendship.

Speaking up about her feelings, no problem at all for Jessie at eight, and of some concern for her at nine, is now, at eleven, the basis for real trepidation. If a girl doesn't like another girl, Jessie says, she "should pretend that [she] likes her." The source of this new fear is the "perfect girl." In white middle-class America she is the girl who has no bad thoughts or feelings, the kind of person everyone wants to be with, the girl who, in her perfection, is worthy of praise and attention, worthy of inclusion and love. Jessie describes her as the girl who is "so good in math."[6] Other girls describe her as the girl who draws perfectly. The girl who speaks quietly, calmly, who is always nice and kind, never mean or bossy. The girl, Jessie implies, she wished she could say she hates. And sometimes, Jessie says, "your attitude just goes bonkers because you are really jealous of [her]."

In the presence of the perfect girl, Jessie, who has strong feelings, who says, "Sometimes I have to just get my anger out of me," cannot speak, since strong feelings, spoken or acted on, carry severe consequences. Saying the wrong thing or saying something in the wrong way, Jessie says, is "terrifying." Asked to tell about a time when she wanted to say something but didn't, Jessie explains:

When you are really mad at somebody and you want to say something really bad, but you can't, you just can't. It's like it comes out of your mouth and you forget what you are going to say . . . or I don't say something because . . . somebody says a real good idea and everybody agrees and mine is like the exact opposite and you don't want everybody to leave you out and say, "Oh, that's horrible! Why, we don't want to do that." Because you sort of feel bad when that happens.

Can you say more about that?

Sometimes when you have friends and they are being real nice to you and you are trying to be nice to them and usually when you are nice to them, they are nice to you and sometimes when other people say something that everybody likes, and they say, "Oh, that's a good idea," and you have the exact opposite, you feel like "Oh oh, they really won't want me to do this, or they won't want me in the club since I don't have good ideas," and you sort of get afraid to say it. And sometimes you get afraid to say things like "I hate you" when you're mad at somebody.

Why are you afraid to say that?

Because a lot of times they get really mad and it really terrifies you because you feel like they are going to tell somebody and they are going to get almost the whole class on her side and it would

be one against, I don't know, ten.
In those situations, how do you feel?
I don't feel very good. I feel like I'm making this whole fight, that
it is really turning out to be a mess.

Jessie's choice to speak will upset the precarious "nice and polite"
scene with her friends—will, in fact, reveal it as a false scene since
people will not be nice to her if she is not nice to them, that is, if
she says what she thinks. This gives her "a weird feeling," makes
her "confused sort of," and "really terrifies" her. Jessie, who at eight
would tell her friend "this is making me feel bad, I'm going home,"
is now at eleven "afraid to say" what she thinks, "terrified" of what
might happen if she says what she feels.

Thus, what seemed matter-of-fact, ordinary life to Jessie at
eight—people play and people get angry, they have strong feelings,
people wish to speak and expect to be heard—has become momen-
tous to Jessie at eleven. Faced with the potential to "upset the whole
class" and afraid of being ignored, embarrassed, ridiculed, Jessie
carefully chooses when to speak. Talking about a time when "a
whole group of friends are mad at one of my really good friends,"
Jessie illustrates the conflict other girls describe between speaking
up or choosing to remain silent. If she chooses to stay out of the
disagreement, Jessie risks herself and her feelings. She says, "I usually
just stay away and I know how I act when that happens, I can tell
. . . I am not really me. I can tell when it's not really [me]." On the
other hand, if she stays with herself and her feelings and gets
involved in public confrontation, she risks the "terrifying" feelings
of starting fights she cannot stop.

When can Jessie afford to stay with herself and speak? When
should she distance herself and "stay out of it," "forget it," choose
to "agree" for the sake of relationships with others? Like her other
classmates, Jessie shows an emerging propensity to separate what
she knows and loves from what she believes she ought to do in
order to be seen as cooperative, kind, and good—the kind of girl
others, she thinks, want to be with. If she stays with what she wants
and says what she thinks, she fears she may be the cause of social

chaos, abandoned by others in her undesirable feelings, her messiness. If she "pretends" and "agrees" and is nice when she does not feel nice, she abandons herself, her thoughts and feelings, and becomes, as Jessie says, "not really me."

Jessie, like the other girls her age in this study, seems caught between speaking what she knows from experience about relationships and increased pressure to negate this knowledge for an idealized and fraudulent view of herself and her relationships—the view rendered credible by the possibility of being a perfect girl. In a world of cliques and in-groups, the image of the perfect girl is powerful—being her can assure Jessie of inclusion, love, attention. The terrifying or terrorizing nature of this image lies in its power to encourage Jessie to give over the reality of her astute observations of herself and the human world around her—or at least to modulate her voice and not speak about what she sees and hears, feels and thinks, and therefore knows. Voice-training by adults, especially adult "good women," undermines these girls' experiences and reinforces images of female perfection by implying that "nice girls" are always calm, controlled, quiet, that they never cause a ruckus, are never noisy, bossy, or aggressive, are not anxious and do not cause trouble, and also by implying that such girls exist and are desirable. And so Jessie becomes preoccupied with what is and is not a relationship, consumed with the difference between what she knows from experience and what is taken increasingly by other girls and by the adults around her to be reality.

This impending division that arises for Jessie, between what she feels and thinks, and therefore knows, and what is said to be reality, leads her to pay close attention and to describe the relational world like a naturalist, carefully portraying the changes caused by her every move, revealing with remarkable clarity the motives and intentions and perspectives of others, and also listening to the way this world is named and described. Yet the model of the perfect girl threatens to keep Jessie from seeing what she is looking at and listening to what she is hearing.

And so we mark losses and gains for Jessie over time. While she is more subtle, cognitively more sophisticated in her understanding of herself and the social world, Jessie is also more willing to forget what really happened or to say that what she knows through experience probably didn't happen, than to feel out of touch with what others say is reality. Jessie, at eleven, is still able to name the spectrum of feelings and hear the range of voices. But she is able to integrate these voices and these feelings and thus to blur their distinctiveness. At eleven she is more cautious, more aware of what it means to know what she knows, perhaps more likely to stay in relationships in which she is hurt, more willing to silence herself rather than to risk loss of relationships by public disagreement.

Sonia: Genuine Relationship, Real Conversation

Wiggling about in her chair, swinging her legs back and forth, eight-year-old Sonia first looks at her hands, then glances around the classroom, and finally focuses her large dark eyes on the woman asking her questions. "Can you tell me about a time when you didn't know what to do?" her interviewer asks her. "I don't get that," Sonia replies. "Any times when you didn't know what was the right thing to do?" the woman asks again. A pause, and then Sonia begins, "When I pick someone, like to do something, I don't know who to pick . . . Sometimes I just pick . . . I don't know . . . sometimes I just pick people that I don't like so I don't have to like decide who I'm going to pick." "Now why would you do that?" the woman wants to know. "I don't know," Sonia responds. Her interviewer asks whether other girls also find it hard to pick between friends. "I don't know," Sonia again replies. "I never watch them."

In this way Sonia, one of two African-American girls in her second grade class of twenty-seven, begins her interview. The woman who sits with her, like all the teachers and administrators in the school, is white, and Sonia, tiny in comparison with her classmates, reveals in a rather shy and quiet way a modicum of wariness and resistance to the questions she is being asked. "I don't get that," Sonia responds to the first question, and as the interview proceeds she sprinkles phrases like "I don't know . . . I don't know" or "I don't get the question" throughout the interview, creating in her soft-spoken but determined manner a sense of space, of distance, between herself and the woman who interviews her.

Yet as we listen we find that Sonia does know, though she seems uncertain about whether or how much she wants to tell this woman. She goes on to explain the tortuous nature of her dilemma: who to pick when there is no choice that will keep her from being left out or talked about by the other girls in her class. "They tell secrets, like mean things about me, so that's why I just don't pick any of them," she says. "And if I don't pick any of them, they tell secrets too." "And these are your close friends? What do you think about that?" her interviewer wonders, trying to understand the nature of such friendships but also, perhaps, shying away from the logical next questions: "Why do they treat you this way? Why are they mean and what are they saying about you?"—questions that might raise painful feelings and bring to the surface what Sonia experiences and knows about being a black child in this mostly white school. "Well," Sonia responds—offering, in kind, only the slightest hint of what might be going on with these so-called friends or perhaps pointing to her means of self-protection—"they're not really, really, really close."

As Sonia's interviewer reads to her the porcupine and moles fable—a story about differences and, for some who hear it, a story about the painful feelings of being hurt or excluded—Sonia continues to move about in her chair, listening and yet visibly unsettled. "What do you think the problem is here?" the interviewer asks, referring to the conflict between the animals. Identifying with the moles and speaking in a direct, straightforward way that echoes other eight-year-old girls in her class, Sonia says, "I would just tell [the porcupine] the truth, that your pines are scratching me, and we don't like that." "And . . . if the porcupine says, 'No, I'm not going to leave?'" the interviewer wonders. "I would just say, 'If you don't, we'll push you out.'"

In the safety of this imagined fable Sonia speaks directly and frankly, perhaps having the animals say what she wishes to say but feels she cannot to the girls in her class who whisper and tell secrets about her: "I would just tell [them] the truth, that your [words] are [hurting] me, and [I] don't like that." For Sonia, playing the role of the uncomfortable moles living in a closed space with an abrasive porcupine, there is a limit to the pain she will endure. If necessary she would push the intruder out of the cave and admonish him for his short-sightedness—"You should have found a home in the springtime that you could've stayed in the wintertime." Perhaps recalling her own experiences of exclusion, Sonia would, however, treat the porcupine with a measure of "kindness": "I'd give him a blanket and some food." But then Sonia pauses, and in a voice that does not seem to reflect what she has said about her feelings and her experience—that sounds to us like the voice-over-her-voice Jessie, too, has taken in, a voice that speaks of nice and selfless behavior—Sonia says to her interviewer, "because if you're not kind to other people, you won't have any other friends."

Real life for Sonia is similar to the life she imagines in the fable. Sometimes people are kind and listen, sometimes they hurt others and are unfair. "Sometimes," Sonia confides—perhaps wondering if this woman who sits with her will listen to her astute observations of the relational world—"sometimes I get in fights with other people, and the teacher blames me when other kids start it." Again her interviewer does not invite Sonia to speak the unspoken—to say how this feels or why she thinks the teacher responds this way. Instead of staying with Sonia's experience, the woman—who is a good woman and a good researcher—dutifully recites the next question as it is written on the paper in front of her: "Can you tell me about a time when that happened?" Sonia, perhaps sensing that this experience may not be very much different from the experience she had with her teacher—that here, also, her feelings may not be heard or responded to—replies simply, "I can't remember."

Instead Sonia shifts the focus of her complaint from her teacher to her classmates and, in a move both creative and astute, introduces the word she knows has the greatest power to please the women in this private girls school: "nice." When other girls are mean to her, or when they start fights, Sonia says, "I don't keep on fighting." Instead, she says "nicely": "I don't like to be in fights, so can we please stop fighting." If people continue to be "mean" or to fight, Sonia—who earlier said she would push the defiant porcupine out of the cave rather than endure discomfort—now says, "I would just ignore them and just walk to another place." Outwardly aligning herself with the powers that be—with her interviewer, her teachers, the unwritten code of favorable behavior in her classroom—Sonia gains the approval of adults, in this case, the white women who wield power in her life. Adept at reading subtle relational cues, Sonia learns that if she is to give these women no good reason to be dissatisfied with her, she will need to remain silent when her teacher blames her for things she did not do and she will have to ignore—that is, come not to know, or at least not to speak about—what is really happening around her and what she is really feeling and thinking.

A year later, we listen as the patina of niceness that settled over Sonia's second grade interview seems to permeate her third grade responses. Now nine years old, Sonia, her black curly hair pulled back with purple barrettes, again speaks with a white woman, and still she struggles to express her feelings of exclusion. This year Sonia is a member of a triangle; she and two girls in her class negotiate their friendship on a daily basis. "Well last week we were on the bus and Julie wanted to sit with me and then Melissa wanted to sit with me," Sonia explains, "and I didn't know who to sit with." Melissa "didn't want to sit with all three of us," Sonia adds. "So . . . I decided to, I don't know, I sat with both of them . . . I said why don't we all sit together?" "And what did they say?" the interviewer asks. "Well one said 'no' and one said 'okay' and I said, 'I can sit in the middle and then you can sit on both of my sides, so if you don't want to sit together you don't have to see the other person or talk to them.'" Putting herself in the middle, becoming both the nucleus of this relationship and a barrier to sight and sound, Sonia tries her best not to have anyone "sit alone" or hurt anybody's feelings, since "you could lose a friend and it could make them feel bad," or worst of all "they could tell everyone what you did . . . It would be a rumor," Sonia replies. "Then it would hurt my feelings . . . Because she said she would start a rumor."

Sonia is still terrorized by the whispering and secret-telling of the year before, afraid that someone—presumably one of these two friends—will "start a rumor" and "tell everyone" how Sonia hurt them if she fails to make them happy. And so when Sonia says, "I felt weird . . . I didn't know what to do," her feelings of confusion seem a realistic response to a truly perplexing relational scene, a scene in which things are not what they are called: friends are not really friends since they will spread rumors; relationships are not really relationships since one false move will jeopardize them. Unable to walk confidently on such a slippery surface, Sonia, echoing Jessie, says, "I could go bonkers." Exasperated with the whole scene, Sonia figuratively throws her hands up in frustration and exclaims: "I will sit with anyone! Anyone can sit with me . . . I don't want them fighting against me."

Sonia, who the year before seemed to speak her strong feelings clearly and directly through the porcupine and moles, now brings her response to the fable in line with what she has been saying about her relationships. The porcupine, she explains, "should try and look for another place of his own, because then that wouldn't bother anyone." "Is that important?" her interviewer wonders. "Yes," says Sonia, "because then no one will get mad at you, they won't be complaining about you. And you can have your nice little home." Not wanting to be a bother herself, to be complained about, to have people mad at her, Sonia seems willing, at least in the presence of the woman who interviews her, to be a living representative of the nice and kind.

But Sonia also seems to feel the pressure of her own difference in this school. The porcupine, she suggests, could "go with other porcupines, so then they couldn't be scratching each other, because they all have quills, so it wouldn't matter." Hinting at what she knows about the dangers of being too different, Sonia tells her interviewer how important it is that the animals "agree on one thing" so "they don't have to fight over it," since if the porcupine got "real mad" he could overpower the moles. Ignoring their own discomfort and agreeing in this way—perhaps like Sonia agrees to let anyone sit with her—allows the moles to "have peace."

Difference, for Sonia, is a relational issue with real consequences in her life. Like the porcupine and moles, people disagree about how they feel about different things and different people, but, Sonia states firmly to the woman who interviews her, no one should judge another person by "just how she looks." "It doesn't matter how you look, it just matters how nice you are," Sonia says. The undercurrent of race, hidden well beneath the sugary glaze of nice and kind, now ripples to the surface. But the opportunity for real conversation comes and passes quickly. The woman interviewer does not ask what would seem, in hindsight, so obvious: If it doesn't matter "how you look," but "just . . . how nice you are," why must Sonia, who is always so nice and kind, worry about rumors and whispers? If she is so nice and looks don't matter, why are the other girls mean to her? Why does she "feel weird" or "go bonkers" in her relationships with her so-called "friends"? Is it possible that nice and kind aren't enough, or worse, that they cover over disruptive feelings and dangerous thoughts? In the context of this interview—a conversation in which there are differences in power on a number of levels—nine-year-old Sonia is willing to profess her faith in perfectly nice behavior. Even if someone is mad, Sonia goes on to say to her interviewer, she should "try to make up still and try to get her to like her"; even if someone thinks another person is "not nice, she should still be nice to her."

But covering over real feelings and thoughts can be extremely trying, as Sonia can attest. Revealing a wry sense of humor, Sonia describes another classmate, Wendy, who "tells me everyday a story about a half-hour long, and I try, I am listening to her, I half-listen, because she tells me these stories that I don't know what she is talking about, so I listen, but if I ask her what is happening, she will tell the whole story over again." Wendy not only goes on and on but, even worse, Sonia says, she "mumbles" and Sonia feels held hostage by these incomprehensible harangues. It's hard because "I can't hear what [Wendy] is saying," Sonia explains, "I try to listen . . . because if I [ignore her] and she is talking to me, then she might get mad at me for not listening and she might say I'll never listen to you or something . . . or she might act nice to listen." Trapped daily in the confines of a car-pool driven by Wendy's mother, Sonia is truly held hostage to Wendy's stories. Not only would Wendy get mad if Sonia said, "I can't hear you, you are mumbling"—"I have said it before to her and she got mad"—but Wendy's mom would hear and she might get mad too because, as Sonia points out, "she doesn't like anyone telling [Wendy] what to do." And so, Sonia, who knows about nice appearances and doesn't want to appear not nice, suffers through her friend's stories "pretend[ing] that I am listening."

Thus Sonia at eight and nine, speaking to white women interviewers of the virtues of nice and kind, also points to the difficulty of being nice to her friends and still knowing what she knows, speaking what she feels and thinks, addressing what is happening around her. In a mostly white school, Sonia hints at her feelings about difference, but it is her commitment to the nice-girl image that her interviewer, her teachers, and her friends seem to respond to. But being always nice seems exhausting for Sonia, who feels the craziness of "friends" who say mean things, who threaten to spread rumors, or who fight against her when she says what she feels and thinks. Not wanting to bother anyone or to have anyone mad at her, Sonia walks a delicate line in which she can only hint at what she knows about differences in power and the consequences of disagreement.

Two years later, now in the fifth grade, Sonia sits in a chair across from her interviewer, fiddling with the silver bracelets she wears on her wrist. This year Sonia is interviewed by an African-American woman, and her voice carries the sound of a self-assured, clear-headed, and confident eleven-year-old. While her earlier interviews were peppered with such phrases as "I don't know" or "I don't care" or "I don't remember," Sonia no longer hesitates or resists—such phrases are all but absent in her responses this year.

Speaking about the porcupine and moles fable, for example, Sonia would now have the moles say directly to the pushy porcupine, "Beat it! Because he won't listen you've got to do something about it." If the porcupine still refuses to listen, Sonia adds, then the moles in "the middle of the night . . . could have shoved the porcupine out . . . so then he can't come back again." Unlike the previous interviewers, the woman who talks with Sonia this year does not shy away from this response, does not imply that the moles' solution, carried out in the safety of darkness, is unspeakable or unknowable: "So in the middle of the night, just deal with it?" she asks Sonia. "Yes," Sonia replies.

This year, talking about relationships between friends who disagree, Sonia and her interviewer engage in a dialogue that has all the signs of a real conversation, a conversation in which two people seem genuinely interested in each other. When Sonia explains that people "have different feelings" because they have different "personalities," her interviewer asks, "How do you know this?" "Because everyone has feelings," Sonia says, bringing what she knows firmly into the interview. And later, when Sonia barely responds to the question, "Who is right when two people disagree?" her interviewer wonders aloud: "Is that even a good question to ask?" "Yes," Sonia replies, explaining her silence and perhaps assuring the woman of her interest, "because it makes you think."

This year Sonia is ready to talk about differences and what happens when people disagree, and she is willing to bring herself, her thoughts and feelings, into this relationship. "Not everyone in this school is going to like one person," she says with a kind of self-assurance absent in the previous two years, "different people like different people." "When people disagree about who they like, can they come to an agreement?" her interviewer asks. "Some people," Sonia explains, "that's why they have wars." "Tell me more about that?" the woman presses. "Why did you say that?" "Because," Sonia says, "people, one side, they don't agree with the other side."

Sonia, an African-American girl coming of age in a white society, casts disagreement in the light of war, making it a life-and-death issue, an issue of violence and control. And Sonia speaks openly about disagreement and hurt when she tells about unfairness in her life. It's unfair, Sonia says, now speaking what before she only hinted at, "when someone treats other people better than they treat you and they are your friends." Speaking about a time when "both my friends . . . were playing together and they weren't including me" and "I wanted to play, too," Sonia now tells of her refusal to retreat in the face of such unfairness. "I started playing with them," she says, figuring if "I play[ed] with them . . . then they [would] start to play with me." Her plan worked, but Sonia, reflecting on the scene, is aware that there was another way to solve the problem. "Somebody could have said, if somebody was left out, 'You are not playing with me at all.'" "Somebody like who?" her interviewer asks, again pressing Sonia to say what she knows about the benefits of power and privilege. "Somebody," Sonia says again, "somebody could say, 'you are not playing with me at all.'" Perhaps Sonia, who has had the experience of speaking and not being listened to, of saying what she feels and still being left out, takes a different route because she senses she is not one of the somebodies.

This story of unfairness and exclusion, the interviewer says—speaking into the tape recorder after Sonia has left the room—has really moved her. And it seems that Sonia, too, has felt the sense of an opening, of familiarity with this woman, since immediately after she finishes this story of exclusion she offers, in quick succession, two more. Now seemingly encouraged by an attentive listener, Sonia tells the story she began but did not finish the year before—a story about being blamed for something she did not do: "One time [I was] standing next to these people who always fool around . . . and [my teacher] thought it was me, and I didn't say anything." Afraid that this teacher, who, she says, "is real mean," would "yell at me for talking out in class" rather than listen to her side of the story, Sonia says she decided to say nothing. "What would you have said if you had spoken up?" her interviewer asks. "I would have said, 'That wasn't me who did it,' and that she shouldn't blame me until she knows who it is." Though Sonia is silenced by what sounds like the same old dilemma—"If I had said something, then she would yell at the other people and not me" and her friends would end up mad at her—for the first time we hear her say what she wants and what she would have said if she thought someone would listen.

Sonia then tells her interviewer the third story in her trilogy, a story that finally, openly, clarifies the struggle she has experienced in various forms since she was eight: how to stay connected with herself—what she feels and thinks and what she knows from experience—and also stay in relationship with others. "The teacher," Sonia begins, "told me I couldn't read this one book . . . because she only likes [books that have won awards]." Sounding very much like eight-year-old Karin who feels she should be able to choose to answer a hard problem, Sonia adds, "I didn't want her to choose my books, I wanted to choose something." In conflict with her teacher, Sonia wonders, "should I tell my mom about this book that I want to read and [about] the teacher [or] should I not tell my mom." "It wasn't right for her to choose my books," Sonia says, but "I shouldn't have to go through getting a note and all that." "I understand," her interviewer responds. "How did you feel about it at the time?" "I was sort of mad at the teacher," Sonia explains, "because she chose my book . . . Because we should all have to read our own book, read a book and decide, and not have to read it like with the whole class . . . And I think it's important to know which books you want to read because I think it's important that you should choose which books you want to read because maybe you don't like one."

Though Sonia does not tell her interviewer what book she did not want to read or why, her resistance seems healthy, even admirable given that awards and prizes in this culture are more often handed out by those to those who would reflect and sustain the privileged status quo.[7] Sonia's struggle, however, focuses less on her choice of books and more on whether or not to tell her mother about the conflict with her teacher: On the one hand, she says, "I wanted to choose something . . . and I shouldn't have to suffer with that book"; on the other, "I didn't want my mother to know . . . because she might get mad at the teacher and I didn't want her to get that mad."

For Sonia to speak what she knows and be heard—for her to stay in relationship with herself—she would have to bring her mother into this relational drama. But her mother, Sonia tells her interviewer, "has gotten mad at the teacher before," and to bring her mother into the conflict will put Sonia in a very difficult situation:

"My mom doesn't get real mad, but she would call the teacher and then I'll get embarrassed because the teacher likes to say stuff, she would say something about it."

Afraid that the teacher would say something out loud in class, Sonia struggles not only with potential embarrassment but with the possibility of more rumors and whispers among her friends. And upsetting the teacher might mean "bad grades" and risking what she and her mother most want, for Sonia eventually to go to "the best college in the United States," where she can get "the best education." If Sonia's mother does not get involved, Sonia's voice may be drowned out; but if her mother responds and expresses her feelings, Sonia will be out of sync with her teacher and her class-mates, left all alone to deal with her teacher's anger and her classmates' whispers when her mother leaves.

"I told my mother," Sonia confesses finally, "and she wrote a note to the teacher saying that it was a fine book . . . and I got to read another book that I liked." Doubling her voice and vision, Sonia tells her interviewer that she learned two lessons from this experi-ence: One about the public world of school—in this teacher's class, she says, "I always have to choose award-winning books"—and one about herself, with the support of her mother—"I shouldn't let the teacher choose what I want."

Though Sonia begins her interview at eight years old less out-spoken and bold than Jessie and most of the other girls in her class who are white, she is nonetheless determined and resistant. Through her silence and hesitancy Sonia effectively creates a space between her and the woman who interviews her. This woman, perhaps because of her own discomfort with Sonia or with what this young girl calls attention to and says is happening, does not ask Sonia what she is feeling when she is whispered about or excluded, does not seem to notice when Sonia chooses to ignore cruel behav-ior and silence herself in the face of conflict, does not comment when Sonia, in the name of nice and kind, decides not to speak her thoughts and feelings.

As Sonia at nine becomes less likely to speak publicly about what is really happening in relationships, words like friendship and relationship begin to lose their meaning. Like the porcupine and moles, if she wants "peace" she will ignore what is happening and agree, she will be nice to people who are not nice to her, pretend to listen to long, boring stories mumbled to her, she will not start fights or fight back. But Sonia knows if she does these things, if she pretends not to know what she knows to be true from her experience, she could go bonkers.

It is not fully clear whether Sonia has simply become outspoken at eleven, whether the change from white women interviewers to a black woman interviewer has affected Sonia as much as it seems, or whether both things have happened. In any case, eleven-year-old Sonia sounds confident and clear. Speaking with an African-American woman who, like her mother, will listen to her—will respond more to her than to standard questions written on a page—Sonia says both what she wants and what she knows to be true from her experience. Though Sonia and her interviewer do not talk explicitly about race, about what it feels like to be left out or drowned out because of skin color, there is, it seems to us, a palpable communication, a shared knowledge. Sonia and her interviewer are moved by each other, by familiar language and experience, and when her interviewer breaks from the structure of the interview to respond to Sonia's feelings and thoughts, when she invites real conversation and genuine relationship, Sonia tells a story of courage and resistance in bold, straightforward terms.

Lauren: Play and Courage

When we meet Lauren she is kneeling on her wooden chair, her ankles and feet sticking out between the slats in the back, her body draped rather lazily over the table-top, one long red braid coiled on the table as her head rests on her outstretched arm. Within this group of second-graders, Lauren claims a rather substantial space for herself. She plays with a pencil through most of this preliminary group interview—she rolls it, drops it, taps it, first close to herself and then, impishly, closer and closer to the microphone placed carefully in the middle of the table. Grinning and rolling her eyes, moving about and poking those near her, Lauren is a handful.[8]

Later eight-year-old Lauren reveals her lively, creative mind as she speaks out in a clear, if not abruptly direct, voice to the woman interviewer who sits with her. Talking about her relationship with her mother, Lauren tells of a steady inner dialogue in which she tries to anticipate how her mother might respond to her direct questions: "I decide before I ask," Lauren explains. "I say to myself, 'yes' and 'no,' because I think maybe she'll say something . . . so . . . if I said like 'no' or something to myself, then I'd go and ask my mom, and after that, if she said, 'maybe' then I expect it would be 'no.'"

Lauren, we discover, has been encouraged by her mother to consult with herself in this way, to anticipate others' reactions to her voice, to think before she speaks or acts. Lauren describes how this works when she is in charge of "bossing my sister around." "Sometimes my grandmother and my mom and dad are gone," Lauren explains, "and [my sister] like goes in places that she's not supposed to, and I say, 'No, you're not allowed,' and then I say to myself first, 'Well, I don't know, I'll have to think about it.'" But Lauren does more than "think" before she acts; she tells her interviewer about a book she refers to, a concrete reservoir for her continually evolving observations and impressions of right and wrong, good and bad: "Well, see, I write like a book for myself, when I have something to do and my parents go out, and my grandmother . . . and then what I do is I just read the book and stuff and I just talk to myself a while and then if my sister's going to do something . . . I find the right page and go and do what I wrote there, 'cause my mother helped me write that book."

In relationship with her mother, Lauren writes a book "of like what I should do while my parents are gone," a book in which she writes: "Decide first what you're going to do before you tell someone what you think or should do or something." Lauren's inner dialogue, which she makes so apparent to her interviewer, reveals how surely she has taken in her mother's voice and her mother's advice to think (of what her mother says to do) before she acts.[9]

But Lauren also remains very much her own person—lively, funny, dramatic. Swinging her legs back and forth in rhythm with the conversation, she tells of running "as fast as I could" after her sister: "I'd say 'Stop!' and she'd freeze like a statue." Later she creates a vivid impression of herself, her sister, and her grandmother together in a thunderstorm, "outside with our umbrella . . . we'd sit under the patio, and it would be so fun, we'd play games and all sorts of stuff." Lauren's pleasure in herself and other people is both physical and deeply relational. But her voice, firmly grounded in her experience and her senses, may be too bold, too uninhibited to go unchecked by those around her, and we begin to wonder whether Lauren's "book" is meant to guide her into herself, to help her hold onto her thoughts and feelings, or whether it is meant to keep Lauren in connection with what her mother wants her to do, a way to contain her lively and impulsive expression. Will it be possible, we wonder, for Lauren to stay in connection with herself—with her thoughts and feelings—while she is taught by her mother and other women how to read and anticipate the relational world she is entering?

Lauren's pleasure in her own voice and vision, her insistence on naming the relational world as she experiences it, and also the response her sometimes irreverent playfulness evokes in others, are apparent when she and the woman who interviews her talk about the porcupine and moles fable. The porcupine, like the "pencil-holder" Lauren has at home, has sharp quills and is prickly and, Lauren explains, is "stabbing" the moles, "hurting them with his things." It is striking to us that Lauren, like Sonia and Jessie, speaks clearly about the fact that someone is being physically hurt in this story. The mole and porcupine fable depicts a scene of domestic conflict—potentially a scene of violence. And eight-year-old Lauren, like many other girls her age in this study, names the physical hurt the moles experience—that they are being stuck by the porcupine's quills.

The "uncomfortable" moles, Lauren tells her interviewer, "could have moved out" in response to the constant "stabbing." "But," she adds, "since they had baby moles . . . they couldn't." Her interviewer, rather than respond to Lauren's depiction of the intolerable situation the moles and their babies face, echoes Lauren's mother by reminding Lauren of what she should know—in this case, the details of the story she has been told: "How do you know they have babies? . . . I don't think it says [that]," she says to Lauren. But Lauren holds to her position: "Because they have little ones!" she exclaims, and continues: "If I had babies, I would want them not to be pinched . . . so I'd just move out."

Lauren, who imagines the mother, father, and baby moles, and who is interested in playing with different solutions, also envisions that, like her pencil-holder's quills, which are, of course, pencils, the porcupine's quills are removable. "The porcupine, when he goes to sleep, could stick his pines in the dirt," she suggests. "Oh," her interviewer responds, seemingly caught off guard by such an unorthodox idea. "Stick his pines in the dirt!" Lauren squeals louder, delighted in this possibility and undaunted by the interviewer's hesitant reaction. In fact, Lauren's exuberance seems to increase as her interviewer hesitates, and when her interviewer asks for the one best solution to the problem, Lauren resists: "I'd say 'yes' and 'no' to [his leaving]," she replies. "'No' would mean that he should go out and 'yes' means that it would be very unkind, because it's very cold in the winter."

Although concerned with not being unkind, Lauren is not preoccupied with being nice and polite or, for that matter, with delivering a docile performance in her interview. People can disagree because, she exclaims, "it's a free world!" Confiding in her interviewer that she had overheard part of the porcupine and moles fable that very day in the toilet, "while I was changing," we hear in Lauren's voice a mix of candor and playfulness. Delivering her thoughts and feelings with gusto and also impishly playing to the edges of appropriate behavior, Lauren appears to enjoy being interviewed—or perhaps just being herself and speaking her thoughts and feelings—immensely.

But so far as we can see up to this point, the women Lauren encounters, except perhaps her grandmother, do not seem willing to play with Lauren, to enter into a conversation that bends the rules or into a relationship that plays to the imagination. Unlike her grandmother, who plays games outside with Lauren and her sister in a storm, her mother and the interviewer choose to play by the rules rather than with Lauren. While her mother helps Lauren write a book of what she should know and her interviewer checks her voice and calls her back to the story, eight-year-old Lauren, who is, it seems, a little wild and a little hard to contain, reacts, maybe at times even overreacts, to this effort to control her.

Given Lauren's joyfulness and candor and also the response it calls forth, the story we described earlier, about her teacher and the computer, seems key to understanding the changes we see in Lauren, especially Lauren's realization that, while women are made uncomfortable by her outspokenness, they—her teacher and also her mother—will look away from Lauren's choice to give up what she wants. As Lauren learns to anticipate what her mother will say—to say to herself, in her head, her mother's response—she also has learned how her teacher responds to her if she says what she feels in the moment. Knowing from experience that speaking up will surely mean that she will "get in trouble and have the teacher yell at me," Lauren, in effect, silences herself—"decides before [she] asks" and, instead of asking, has the argument with the teacher in her head. This girl who was so open now talks about hiding her thoughts and feelings. And the teacher, like her mother and her interviewer, rewards Lauren's silence, calls it good behavior—"compromise"—and seems not to notice what Lauren gives up by playing according to these rules.

A full year later Lauren, now nine and in the third grade, continues to be aware of how her actions interplay with the reactions of others; and though still very creative and lively, she seems increasingly concerned about how others, especially adults, will respond to her. Telling her interviewer what seems, on the surface, like a simple story of procrastination, when "I didn't have something done on time," Lauren points to a deeper struggle to find a way to say what she thinks and feels when she anticipates how others will respond to her.

> I had this project and I didn't turn it in on time. And I was in trouble because it was on a Sunday and it was due the next day and it was time for my bedtime and . . . I told my sister and she told my mom and that got me in trouble that my mom wanted to yell and scream at me. So I started to work on it but . . . I couldn't really, I just didn't want to do it right at that moment, because I was really tired and it was really hard for me to tell her why I didn't do it over the weekend.

Lauren, who finds it "really hard" to explain to her mother why she put off her homework, makes a lot of excuses to her interviewer as well: Her mother, she says, "made me read all weekend . . . because she likes me to read biographies." Also, Lauren quickly adds, "I forgot all about it." Moreover, she complains, "when I start it . . . it always turns out bad, whatever I think of." Yet following this string of excuses, Lauren suddenly shifts and explains her procrastination in a direct voice that sounds more genuine, more simple, and, perhaps for these reasons, more persuasive: "It's like, I really didn't want to do it right at that minute . . . I just really didn't want to do it at that point and it was like really dumb to me to do it and I really didn't like to."

In this moment, Lauren's resistance to what she sees as a "really dumb" assignment is clear, and she contemplates speaking her feelings straightforwardly to her mother and even telling her teacher what she wants to tell her: "I have so many lessons a week that I want to tell my teacher that I might turn in something late. But," Lauren adds, anticipating her teacher's response as she did her mother's, "I know she would come to me and say, 'You will just have to turn it in on time,' so I don't say it and I try to get things in on time." From past experience Lauren concludes that it is useless to say what she feels and thinks and does not speak. And she also knows that doing the assignment on time, in spite of her feelings and thoughts, means she won't "get a bad grade" and "my parents

78

will be proud of me," and "I can go somewhere of my own choice . . . like to Burger King or Wendy's." In the plethora of good grades and burgers, no one seems to notice that Lauren doesn't say what she wants; no one seems to know what she has not said—eventually, we might assume, not even Lauren. Burying her feelings about the "dumb" assignment and also her growing "rage" at her sister for telling her mother, Lauren describes a reality in which, once again, like with the computer, selflessness pays—at least as far as she can tell from adults' responses to her selfless behavior.

But Lauren's capitulation or self-silencing seems only surface deep. Unable to speak directly and openly, since holding her own becomes truly difficult right now and costly, Lauren stays with her feelings and thoughts and finds other, less direct ways to speak, such as procrastinating. Initially "really shook up" about her sister's indiscretion and unable to speak her feelings directly, Lauren irritates her father and mother by doing what's she's asked very slowly, and later, in private, "shakes" and "pinches" her sister. Though she covers her actions and voice to give the appearance and sound of happy cooperation, Lauren's real feelings show through.

As the interview progresses, it is perhaps not surprising that Lauren characterizes herself in the way she might imagine others characterize her when she insists on speaking her thoughts and feelings: as a troublemaker. Talking about the porcupine and moles fable now, at age nine, she decides that the porcupine "was causing so much trouble with the moles." When Lauren personalizes the story, saying, "I would listen to the moles and help them move [out] if they wanted to," her interviewer becomes curious. "Who are you?" she asks. "The porcupine," Lauren responds. "And the moles would be uncomfortable and they would want to move, just to get away because they already know that I have sharp quills and I would scratch them and they would do anything [not] to lay near or to sit or be next to him."

Identifying herself with the porcupine—"because," as she says, "usually sometimes I am really obnoxious, like a porcupine is"— Lauren seems to see herself as an irritant, a troublemaker, literally, as the one doing the poking. She also refers to the porcupine, surprisingly, as "him." She does not think of having the porcupine remove his quills or move out—now the troublemaker stays rather than leaves. Yet Lauren still struggles with what it means to stay with her thoughts and feelings in the midst of relational conflict. "If the moles were unhappy, I would be 'Fine,'" she begins. But as she has learned to do, Lauren then stops herself, perhaps in anticipation of the interviewer's response, and recites what sounds like a sentence from the book her mother helped her write: "I would just think of it for a minute and say to myself, 'Why don't I just stop being obnoxious and treat that person like they would treat me?'"

By being herself and staying in genuine relationship, by not leaving in the face of conflict but saying what she feels and thinks, Lauren has reason to believe others will find her abrasive, obnoxious, insensitive to their needs. And people do seem happier when Lauren does not say what she feels—the girl who took her place at the computer, her teacher, her parents, even her interviewer. But Lauren finds it difficult to give over her thoughts and feelings. In the face of such pressure, switching back and forth between being herself and being the porcupine, Lauren pleads the "obnoxious" porcupine's case: "I could have moved out but I would be in cold weather, like sitting there in the snow and I'd be cold and I would die because I think that porcupines are cold-blooded . . . I'd freeze and maybe I would die." Staying in the cave, in the midst of this relational conflict, is now, it seems, a matter of life and death for the porcupine and for Lauren. And yet to stay Lauren risks being called, and calling herself, "obnoxious" and a "troublemaker" and "him."

Still the pressure to be less trouble seems so great. "I was just thinking," Lauren adds, bringing in moral language like a protective shield to cover over the conflict she had just so vividly described— "I was just thinking of a way for both of us to be happy and to live like we should during the winter." In the wake of this sudden shift to nice and kind, we wonder if the porcupine has learned what

Lauren knows, and what Jessie and Sonia also suspect by age nine: that it is better not to speak, to pretend things are fine when they are not, to act as if nothing has happened—especially maybe if you are a girl.

Two years later, eleven-year-old Lauren, her thick red hair pulled back in a pony-tail, her socks bunched around her ankles, sits with a different woman interviewer. Playing with a plastic flower—taking it apart and putting it back together—she begins her interview talking straightforwardly about the porcupine and moles. The moles "need their space" to "eat and walk," she now explains to her interviewer, so they "could either throw [the porcupine] out" to "live by itself," or "they could say 'get out of my house.'" Sure, Lauren says, it would be "bad" if the moles "just kicked him out . . . in the open to freeze half to death," but, she adds—creating space in the conversation for her own voice—"I wouldn't care." "You wouldn't care?" the interviewer asks. "Well, see," Lauren explains, "I'm not an animal . . . and I don't even see porcupines because they're not even near where I live . . . I don't even know what one looks like."

Lauren who, at eight, compared the porcupine with her pencil-holder and, a year later, identified herself with this troublesome animal, who, just a moment before, described these animals as "very prickly" and "fat" with "spikes sticking out," now claims not to "know what one looks like." Lauren's answer signals a break in the interview, a moment of resistance, a firm step outside this structured performance. But rather than respond to Lauren, her interviewer asks the next question—"Can you think of another way to solve the problem?"—and again Lauren interrupts the flow of the interview. "Not now," she responds, setting limits on what she is willing to offer and when—"Maybe in an hour or so."

As her interviewer dutifully stays within the rules of this pseudo-conversation, Lauren continues to resist. Asked if she can "think of a rule that would solve this problem for everybody," Lauren questions whether a relationship is ever possible between these different animals—"I don't even know how the porcupine can live with the moles, because they are enemies. I read [that] in a book"—and then challenges the very idea that animals can think and talk and remember—"No [a rule wouldn't work], because they can't remember it; they have brains the size of an acorn."

But Lauren knows all about rules and their justification, as she explains to the woman: "Like here we have rules, like no running in the halls. They're to prevent us from falling." "Rules"—like the book Lauren used to keep—"help you control your life, you know. They might bore you," she adds—perhaps as this interview, so far played strictly by the rules, is beginning to bore her—"I don't know. If they had a rule that everything would go smoothly, they wouldn't have any fights or stuff like that." Staying within the rules of this structured interview, Lauren implies, nobody would "fall," there wouldn't be "any fights," things would remain "controlled," run "smoothly," but things would also be "boring," there would be no lively exchanges, no movement, no space for genuine relationship. So what if someone wanted to break the rules, the interviewer suddenly asks—perhaps sensing she is about to lose the lively, straightforward girl who spoke in the first few minutes of the interview—"Would that be okay?" "Well if they didn't tell anybody," Lauren responds, hinting at the underground and the possibility of a real conversation. "But," she adds—perhaps uncertain about this woman and what she is willing to know—"but . . . there's always a way that somebody is going to find out."

As the conversation turns to friendship and disagreement, Lauren seems ready to push the boundaries of this exchange further, if given the chance. "Everybody has their own opinion on everybody," she says, explaining how people go back and forth between liking and hating. "What would two friends who disagree say to each other?" her interviewer wonders. "Well, it would probably go something like . . . I should say it?" Lauren asks, almost incredulous that this woman will now drop the questions and follow her lead. "Yah," her interviewer responds, "If I get lost in it, I'll just ask you." With this opening before them, Lauren eagerly breaks into a three-way conversation, acting the parts of two friends sorting out their feelings about another girl. Her face alive, Lauren changes expression and switches position in her chair as she enacts the dialogue back and forth between the two friends:

> Okay. Let's see. Um, first girl: "Well, I thought she was really nice and I thought maybe she could come over again." Second girl: "Well, I didn't like her that much, so don't invite her over again." First girl: "Let's talk about this for a while." Second girl: "Okay." First girl: "What did you see in her that you hated?" Second girl: "Well, she was bossing me around."

Suddenly the third girl appears on the scene. The second girl, the one who hates her, addresses her:

> Girl two: "What's your family like?" Girl three: "Well, I'm an only child, my mom's 22, my dad's 58, and I'm 12. I have one pet. It's a bird and its name is Duster." Girl two: "Well, I have a pet and I have a bird too, and his name is . . . Sky." Girl three: "Bring yours over to my house sometime." Girl two: "Is yours a male or a female?" And then girl one interrupts: "Wait a minute, I have a bird too." Girl two: "How about we bring ours all over in twenty minutes, okay?" Girl one: "That's a great idea." So, narrator: They start talking about the birds and the girl who hated her before likes her now.

Lauren has succeeded in drawing her interviewer into this drama, and the woman, now genuinely curious, begins to ask real questions. If "girl one" and "girl two" can disagree with each other openly, what happens when girl three enters the scene? Why would the girls talk about the birds rather than the real issue, which was that "girl two" felt "girl three" was bossy? "Why didn't she just tell her that?" the woman wonders. "I don't know," Lauren responds, "maybe she'd feel sort of mean saying that . . . At the beginning you don't really know what that person is like. But after a while, and you get to know that person, you might change your feelings about her."

Lauren knows that "it hurts people's feelings" to make faces or laugh at them or even to say "mean" things, and, as we have seen, she tries not to make trouble—especially when she concludes that she cannot or will not be heard. But in the presence of someone who listens, the eight-year-old Lauren—impish and playful, and also direct and open—seems to reappear in the body of this eleven-year-old. Invited to speak what she really feels and thinks, Lauren tells about a time in school when she tried to offer her ideas on a group project and no one would listen, "because they want to do their own thing." Annoyed, Lauren says "I walk[ed] off . . . I was off just sitting reading a book . . . I just sat back and started reading my book. And I finished it." Lauren who struggled at nine to speak her thoughts and feelings directly, who became silent in anticipation of what others might say or do, now tells her interviewer, perhaps because her interviewer will now listen and play, that she refuses to give over her ideas for the sake of false relationship, refuses to pretend it is okay that no one listens. "It's like why would I help somebody if I didn't have time to say my idea?" she asks. "I don't want to help you if you don't even listen to me."

Perhaps wanting to tell her interviewer about what, for her, is a genuine relationship—a pleasurable, mutual relationship—Lauren then describes her "best friend," Nina. Nina is expressive and kooky, "and if she heard something funny, she'd like make a weird face . . . when something smelled she'd [make faces]." The friendship between Lauren and Nina formed when they started riding the bus together and "every week we'd get in a fight." Now fighting and making up daily, Nina and Lauren find it safe to say what they think and feel and need from each other, and Lauren trusts, ironically perhaps, that because she can say what she thinks and feels Nina will not abandon her. In turn, Lauren feels a deep loyalty to Nina. "I promised not to tell," Lauren says of a secret Nina told her, "and I will never tell anybody."

So when the "cool" girls, the ones who "brag a lot," dismiss Nina, Lauren gets angry and supports Nina publicly:

> We were in a group with Ellen [a cool girl] and after all the ideas were given, Nina says, you haven't heard [my] argument and Ellen goes, well, who cares, let's do this anyway . . . I go, "Excuse me, you forgot somebody, and she has a good idea."

When Ellen dismissed Nina, Lauren felt "sort of sad" for her friend and "worried that she might start crying." "I['d] comfort her if she were to start to cry," Lauren explains. "I'd help her and I'd get her through her misery." Lauren speaks up in Nina's defense, believing she, Lauren, has a certain degree of power in her class: "Sometimes I can get people's attention because I'm popular here," Lauren explains. "Like I'm smart in math and I'm good in school and I guess they think of me as a smart person and they really, like, listen to me." Though Lauren is aware that if she says what she thinks out loud "I might lose a friend," her genuine, trustworthy relationship with Nina gives her the courage to speak directly to the other girls in her class—"I say, 'Excuse me.' I don't say, 'Shut up,' but I say like excuse me, you forgot someone . . . to bring people's attention, people that are careless, [that] just forget about other people."

But Lauren, who says she stands up to the "cool girls," still struggles to speak what she feels and thinks around adults, especially her mother. She still sometimes hides when she does things wrong, pretends "that I didn't know that I did that." Following what "they say," Lauren plays by the rules, at least on the surface, since "parents have this instinct of finding out things." "My mom always gets things out of me. The truth or not, she gets it out. She knows when I'm telling a lie." Guarding herself against such omniscience and also tempted by the rewards of appearing good, Lauren moves her thoughts and feelings underground, at times publicly mouthing the right response to protect her private knowledge, but also waiting for someone who is interested in the lively, creative Lauren who lingers, waiting for someone to play with, someone who will really listen.

In the computer story, eight-year-old Lauren tells of taking herself, her thoughts and feelings, out of relationship to make others happy. But in the presence of a woman interviewer who listens, eleven-year-old Lauren, like eleven-year-old Sonia, directly and clearly refuses what she has, up to this point, accepted—to be in relationships that are not genuine relationships. "I don't want to help you if you don't even listen to me," Lauren now says, and by voicing a refusal to stay in relationships in which she cannot speak, Lauren points to a touchstone of women's psychological health. In the presence of a woman who chooses Lauren over the rules, Lauren embodies what Annie Rogers calls the most natural, ordinary kind of courage.[10]

"We do not, cannot, know the meanings of all these words, for we are nine and ten years old. So we watch their faces, their hands, their feet, and listen for truth in timbre."[11] Like Claudia and Frieda in Toni Morrison's *The Bluest Eye*, Jessie, Sonia, and Lauren learn to anticipate what the adults in their lives—including the women who interview them—want to hear, want to see. Ready at eight years old to blow the whistle on relational violations, to dramatize their strong feelings, to disrupt the polite silences with their observations about what is happening in the relational world, these three young girls narrate the process by which, over time, they begin to replace their voices with the foreign voice-overs of adults, their feelings and desires with others' wants and expectations.

Eleven-year-old Jessie tells the woman interviewing her about being terrified as she experiences the relational world of her childhood disappear, the world where girls said go home and they meant go home and where it was possible to voice the full range of human feelings—anger, hurt, sadness, and jealousy as well as comfort, joy, pleasure, and love. Jessie fears that if she voices her thoughts and feelings—acts on her desire, thus bringing herself into relationship with others, she will disrupt, perhaps irreparably, the human world she lives in. And yet to pretend to agree when she disagrees and be nice when she does not feel like being nice is to abandon herself, to take herself out of relationship with others and to be "not really me."

Sonia begins her eight-year-old interview in quiet wariness, uncertain if it is safe to say aloud to her interviewer what she knows is happening and yet subtly voicing over and over again the difference between what she feels and thinks and what is said to be happening in relationships. Anticipating the power of the nice and kind in the world of her private girls' school, she is willing, at least for the sake of this interview, to "pretend" to be nice, to "ignore" mean behavior, to remain silent when she is blamed for things she did not do. Yet she arrives at age eleven in full voice, outspoken and straightforward, revealing, it seems, the power of a real conversation with a woman who is genuinely interested in what she feels and thinks, a woman whose own experiences resonate with the stories of unfairness and exclusion and, finally, of loyalty that Sonia tells.

Lauren at eight portrays the lively, impish resister. Although she reveals in remarkable detail how she takes in the adult voices around her and learns well to anticipate what others want, she also revels in her own creativity and loves to play. We listen as her voice comes up against the framework of her interviewer's questions and also the wall of conventional female behavior, where it is considered both good and the right thing for Lauren to give up her strong feelings and give over the things she wants. Like Sonia, Lauren at eleven reveals the power of a relationship with a woman in which she can say what she feels and thinks, an experience that recalls the pleasure and the danger of playing outside in a thunderstorm with her grandmother and her sister.

At eight and nine, Jessie, Sonia, and Lauren speak in a variety of voices, a polyphony of voices that complement and contradict one another. Lauren feels no pressure to integrate her solution to the fable—that the answer to whether the porcupine should leave would be "yes" and "no" makes perfect sense to her. Sonia is willing, with some frustration but without great difficulty, to double her voice and vision as she goes about her relationships half-listening and pretending to be nice. And Jessie simply appreciates the differences between the porcupine and moles, giving the animals two clear but opposing views of the relational conflict. But over time, as these three girls become more subtle in their thoughts and feelings, as they gain a capacity and a desire to integrate the different voices they are taking in with their own thoughts and feelings, they begin to feel their voices in tension with others, to comprehend the relational consequences of speaking out, to appreciate how others will greet their relational truths. Sonia and Lauren, who begin to cover their thoughts and feelings, seem to emerge as resisters at eleven, in a responsive relationship with a woman who resonates with their liveliness and outspokenness and is willing to play with them within the interview session. But Jessie in speaking with her interviewer seems to move further out of relationship with herself, with what she sees and hears, feels and thinks. At eleven, Jessie no longer calls attention to the moles' discomfort or pain, no longer blows the whistle on the porcupine's intransigence and cruelty. We cannot help but connect this change over time—from Jessie's willingness to speak about the moles' feelings and the porcupine's abuse to her silence about both in the name of "cooperation" or nice relationship—with the tendency of some women to stay in emotionally or physically abusive situations. What Jessie is learning at ten and eleven, it seems to us, is a justification for staying in such relationships, a lesson she may carry with her into adulthood.

All three girls voice their psychologically astute understanding of relationships and point to the places where a world they know seems in danger of disappearing; all three learn to anticipate what others will say or think if they express their strong feelings; all three know the tyranny of nice and kind, the power of the perfect (white, middle-class) girl. Jessie, Sonia, and Lauren take in the relational world around them—messages about holding in their feelings and thoughts in order to be seen as good girls, as well as pleasurable experiences of being with women who really want to know them, who enjoy being with them, and who stay with them even when they are disruptive. The pressure to integrate their rich emotional lives with narrowing visions of nice and kind women leaves these girls struggling with the difference between true and false relationships. As we listen to these girls at eleven, and recall their eight-year-old voices and the voices of their classmates at that time, we begin to wonder what is happening at the edge of adolescence to call forth such resistance, and what will sustain it.

4

Approaching the Wall: Three Guides into Adolescence

Susan is eleven and in the fifth grade. I go to her classroom to tell her I am ready because my previous interview ran a bit over the scheduled time. As we move down the hall I notice she is walking on the backs of her top-siders, crunching them into something like slippers. I ask her how she's doing and how she likes school, and she responds softly in a word or two. Though she was interviewed last year, this is the first time we have met. I soon learn that much is different for her this year. As a fifth grader, she has entered the Middle School world of changing classes, tougher subjects, higher expectations. School has become more serious. But, she tells me, she and her classmates have weathered these changes; relationships have survived.

Guided to fifth grade by Jessie, Sonia, and Lauren, we now meet Susan and her classmates who, according to their teachers, are an unusually bright and sensitive, close-knit group. It is easy to understand this portrayal as we watch them engage in lively discussions, hover over science projects, read stories they have written aloud to each other, laugh heartily or glance knowingly at their best friends across the room.

In our interviews, it becomes clear to us how much these ten- and eleven-year-old girls know about people and relationships and how deeply they feel relational conflicts. Their curiosity about the human world they live in is palpable; they seem always to be listening in or keeping track of what is happening between people. Open to relationships, they talk unabashedly about vulnerability—

their pleasure in the intimacy and fun of human connection, and also the potential in relationships of being wounded. Experiencing the changing weather of relationships, they speak about the subtle nuances of relational conflict and the politics of relational experiences—highlighting especially the painful consequences of the formation of cliques, the social order so common among girls of this age. Noura, for example, ponders the consequences of speaking up to her friends about their treatment of other people:

> I'm afraid that sometimes the friends that were talking about people—sometimes they might just go on talking, and then later they'd talk about me . . . and spread it around and then no one would like me, or the other person that was being talked about would not like me, or sometimes they'd think, "Well, you did the right thing, but I don't like you," like, "I like you," but they're not going to be my best friend or something, and so I don't know what to do . . . 'cause then the other friends wouldn't like me as much or something.

From this situation, in which she could do the "right thing" and not be liked, Noura learns "how I would feel . . . I learned that it's not nice [to talk about people] and I learned what it feels like to be—to be the person that everyone doesn't like." "How did you learn that?" the interviewer wonders. "Well," Noura explains, "you learn that by just your feeling, what you feel was right or wrong . . . and your reactions to everyone talking about them or something, and you learn because you know that you wouldn't like that to be happening to you. So you know, then you kind of learn how to solve things and work things out with people."

Noura, who knows what she feels, who "learns from" her feelings, nonetheless struggles to say what she knows. She knows through her own experience that speaking up will not necessarily change her friends' behavior. In fact, it may make things worse—"the friends," who aren't really friends, "might just go on talking, and then later talk about me." Even the girl she defends may not like her if she says what she feels. And yet by staying with her feelings and paying attention to her own "reactions" Noura also knows how it would feel to be ostracized—"to be the person that everyone doesn't like." Knowing all this, she anticipates, like Lauren, the consequences of her actions. Feelings and knowing, intimately entwined, lead Noura to an awareness of the complexity of the relational world. But by not saying what she feels, Noura risks losing touch with what she knows from experience.

These ten- and eleven-year-old girls, who experience the depth of feelings and the complexity of relationships, actively resist a growing pressure not to speak what they know from experience and struggle to hold onto what the evidence of their senses tells them is happening. Yet as they respond to subtle and overt pressures to cover strong feelings with "calm" and "quiet" behavior, words like "friend" and "love" and "relationship" become slippery and begin to lose their meaning. When it is wrong to know what is happening or to express strong feelings, and when, conversely, everyone is called a friend and everyone is said to care, girls struggle to stay in touch with what they are experiencing so that they can tell the difference between genuine and false or idealized relationships.

Common prohibitions against girls' speaking what they feel and think—especially given the acuity of their perceptions—renders the relational world complex and difficult to read. Moral language can add another layer of confusion over their actions as these girls learn to separate what they know from what good girls should know, what they do from what girls should do, what they feel and think from what nice girls should feel and think. As girls attempt to connect to the world of adult shoulds, they join in reinterpreting their actions; their experiences take on double meanings, they begin to see double. Gail, for example, reflects on her life over the past year with satisfaction, as a time when "I think I've gotten along better with people . . . I don't disagree as much . . . and I don't get into fights as much. Like arguments with my friends." "How come you think that has happened?" her interviewer asks. "Maybe because I can understand how they think now and accept them . . . accept what they think, instead of being just one-way minded," Gail replies. "So I can think, I can understand how they think, as well as what I think." In the past, Gail continues, "I had more fights or arguments. Then I realized that I went along with that and I realized I was experienced I guess, because I realized that I *should* understand what they think also" (emphasis added). In this way, Gail says, she came to understand "that I'm not always right, they could have been just as right and they have their thoughts too."

The changes in herself that Gail describes would seem like clear evidence of her maturing capacity to embrace the fact of difference and to listen to other people. To insist on her thoughts and disagree a lot with her friends, as she did in the past, Gail says, was "one-way minded" and led to unnecessary fights. Now that she understands her friends and accepts them, she is open-minded because she can "understand how they think as well as what I think." This move to accept and understand frees her mind to "do something constructive" and reduces the amount of "worthless" arguing. But to make this move Gail has to suspend what she really feels, something she is now more capable of doing as an eleven-year-old but which, in effect, removes her from genuine relationship. "Do you think fighting or arguing is worthless?" her interviewer asks. In a confusing statement which seems to lead one way, but then turns another, Gail says essentially yes—that fighting is worthless and since she's stopped fighting she doesn't "have to think":

It is [worthless] . . . if it's over something that's of no importance, like little things, like something . . . that [a friend] did that you didn't think was right. If she lost something and you got really mad at her for doing that, that's sort of worthless . . . because you can just get on with it and that won't matter in what you do.
And you said since [you stopped arguing] you have a lot less on your mind?
Yah, because you don't have to think, you don't have to try to avoid that person, and you don't have to think more about, if you regret what you did, then you don't have to think about it that much.
Did you find that before, you were regretting?
Yah, because . . . you could lose a friendship if you did that.

Gail's response to her interviewer's questions about arguing exemplifies the intricate and subtle relationship between Gail's developing capacity to understand and appreciate and take in viewpoints different from her own and the fear that by continuing to speak in the presence of difference she will lose her relationship with her friends. Gail's preoccupation with what is a worthy and what is a "worthless" argument is overridden by the associations she makes between arguing and feeling "regret"—feelings which then interfere with her ability to do other, more "constructive" things. Linking arguing with losing relationships, Gail joins "thinking" and "understanding" with "accepting" what others say, suggesting that, as Gail becomes more discerning of others' ways of seeing and thinking she also becomes less able to say what she thinks and feels. Clear evidence of developmental gains go hand-in-hand with a sense of genuine loss. In this reformulation of thinking and this willing suspension of feelings, Gail "accepts" others' views and doesn't "have to think" or deal with the difficult feelings arguing may create—the wish to avoid people, the sense of having to think more about things, the lingering specter of regret. Agreement is easier and neater, but it comes at the expense of genuine relationship—that is, relationships in which Gail can say what she thinks is right, in which conflict and disagreement and strong feelings can occur. Thus, by associating arguing with disconnection and regret, and relationship with "getting along better with people," Gail reveals the fine line between genuine relationship in which she speaks and also listens to others and learns from them and false relationships in which she silences herself because she is afraid of what will happen, and also how she will feel, if she expresses what she really thinks.

As we listen to these ten- and eleven-year-old girls' struggle to know what they know and say what they feel, we begin to trace their puzzlement at the discrepancy between what they see and hear, what they know about relationships and feelings through experience, and how the relational world and the world of feelings is supposed to be known and seen. As these girls become more psychologically astute, this discrepancy between their experiences and what they hear adults saying, see adults doing, captures their attention, fascinates and frustrates them. They begin to watch and listen intently, paying close attention to how others—particularly the adult women in their lives, the people they have most closely relied on for help and guidance in navigating the relational world—feel and think, how they express their feelings and thoughts, how they name relationships, and why they act like they do. And with stunning perceptiveness, these ten- and eleven-year-olds describe what they see and hear.

Allison describes her frustration with her great-aunt who babysits for her and her sister when her mother is out of town. This aunt "writes down things and tells my mom everything that happens" and "sometimes she explains things differently," Allison explains. "Sometimes in her head it's different than it really happened. I mean, it happened the way she's telling it, but not in her thinking, it processes different than in our thinking . . . she doesn't think like we do." The problem for Allison is that her mother listens to her aunt's side, rather than to "both sides." "It might not help [if she would listen to both sides]," reflects Allison, "but at least she would understand . . . We don't want her to not listen to our great-aunt, but to listen to us too."

Allison is clear that the story her aunt tells her mother is different from what she and her sister experience, from how they "process" what happened. Though Allison knows there are two sides to the story, at least two different interpretations or ways of thinking, like Noura, she stays with what she knows from experience—what is, to her, reality. Allison wants to solve the problem not by covering over or ignoring her aunt's version of the story but by including her own. This way her mother can "get a better feel of what happened." Yet Allison and her sister don't explain this to their mother because their mother doesn't listen, she already "sort of knows":

Well . . . she doesn't really care. She cares what we do, but she doesn't really get angry or upset . . . as long as she doesn't get angry at us, it doesn't really matter if she doesn't listen to our

side. We get upset, but it doesn't really matter. But if she gets
upset . . . It doesn't matter as long as she—she sort of knows—in
her—she doesn't listen to us because she knows what's in her head
. . . in her head, she's thinking that she knows what we would
think, because she knows us, so she doesn't have to listen to what
we say 'cause she sort of has a feeling.

Her mother, Allison explains, thinks she knows what her daughters would think, has "a feeling." Yet, Allison observes, her mother
does not listen and though this means she doesn't get angry, it also
means that her "feeling" for the situation is "in her head" and does
not reflect Allison's reality. And so Allison has two experiences—
she is upset because she is not listened to, and yet "it doesn't really
matter" that she gets upset or that her mother "doesn't listen to our
side" as long as her mother does not get upset or angry. Watching
this strange interplay between love (the mother cares but "doesn't
really care") and authority (she knows though "she doesn't listen"),
Allison openly wonders what her mother is up to. What Allison
describes echoes other girls' astute observations of what is really
happening in relationships, and also their propensity, at least on the
surface, to give up or give over their version of reality to those who
have the power to name or reconfigure their experience.

Like Noura, Allison struggles with discrepancies between what
she feels and thinks, what she knows from experience, and what
she observes others—in this case her mother—doing and valuing.
For Allison, a mother who knows by "feeling" but yet knows "in
her head" without listening is confusing and leaves her speechless,
feeling ineffective. "I don't say, 'It's unfair,'" Allison explains when
her mother takes her sister's side in arguments, "because then my
mother always says . . . 'Life is unfair' . . . I can't help it if my
parents think what they really think, and even if it's not right, you
can't really do anything about it, but tell them, and if they don't
agree with you, there's no sense arguing."

Gail describes a similar feeling of helplessness at not being heard
or listened to when her older sister is allowed to go off on her own
at the mall and she is not. When Gail protests her sister's privilege,

her mother, too, says, "Life is always unfair." "What did you think of that?" her interviewer wonders. "It's probably true that life is not always fair," Gail responds:

[My mother's] probably right and I probably suggested it because she was doing it. I probably wanted to do it. I was probably jealous or something, so that's why. At that time I probably thought that's unfair and then I realized that it wasn't really unfair because she didn't want me to get lost and I didn't really want to get lost anyway.
Do you wish you had spoken up or are you glad you didn't?
Well, I'm glad I didn't, because it might have caused a ruckus over something and I probably would have another chance.

Gail's repeated use of the word "probably" suggests that her agreement with her mother is not as complete as she implies. What she initially called unfair she now describes as her problem—"I was probably jealous." Gail lets go of her feelings about the situation as she takes her mother's concern into herself—"I didn't really want to get lost anyway." Speaking up, she reflects, "might have caused a ruckus," and, like Allison, Gail feels the powerful edge of adults' disapproval and admonishments and concludes that her anger and strong feelings are not only ineffective but upsetting and un-welcomed.

While Allison, in frustration, decides "there's no sense arguing" with her parents since "you can't really do anything about it," and Gail, rather than "cause a ruckus," takes in her mother's view, Edie describes the impasse between her feelings of anger at what she experiences as unfairness and her mother's goodness. What Edie first describes as an unfair use of power, she recasts as an example of her mother's care, her selfless love.

Can you tell me about a time when something happened to you that was unfair?
Unfair? Okay, this is like, I think it's unfair, maybe it isn't. It's unfair, sort of, it's unfair to me.
If you thought it was unfair to you, that's what I want to know about.
Well, sometimes when I want to go to a party, a sleep-over, maybe, and my mom would say no, because she maybe doesn't trust the

people or something. And then I think it's unfair. But then I know that she's caring and, you know, she's like loving and she's caring about me and she's making it so I don't get hurt or anything, she's doing it for my own good, then I know that after, but then at the time I got mad, but just for a while. Especially when everybody else is going.

What would have been the fair thing to do?

I don't know, maybe like she said, well, I think it was sort of fair now that I think about it, you know, that she was right in doing that, she did the right thing.

Edie gets mad, she says, "but just for a while." In quick succession what she calls "unfair to me" becomes "sort of fair" and then "the right thing," as Edie comes to "know" that what felt unfair to her was really her mother's love and care, her mother "making it so I don't get hurt . . . doing it for my own good." Edie's struggle to name unfairness and to stay with her feelings and thoughts about being overruled by her mother is overshadowed by her mother's seemingly selfless love and concern. In the end, this reconfiguration leaves both Edie and her mother voiceless and out of relationship.

Allison, Gail, and Edie reveal girls' intricate knowledge of relationships, their awareness of what is happening between people, and also their thinly veiled attempts to cover over their thoughts and feelings as they portray others', in this case their mothers', reactions to what they really feel and think and want. Desiring connection with the world around them—with the world of their mothers—they speak of taking their feelings and thoughts out of relationship for the sake of what is being called relationship. Over and over in their interviews we hear these girls struggle as their strong feelings come up against a relational impasse that shuts out their experience or shuts down their loud voices, a wall of shoulds in which approval is associated with their silence, love with selflessness, relationship with lack of conflict. Here their anger and strong feelings are associated with danger and disruption. Our interviews suggest girls are conscious and aware of this relational impasse, this move toward false or idealized relationships—at least at age ten and eleven.

Desiring connection and approval, girls thus begin to idealize their actions and their relationships with other girls by denying what they know through experience about conflict, about meanness or unkindness, since to know about such behavior implicates them, especially perhaps in the eyes of the women who interview them. Suzanna, for example, proudly announces that there is no meanness at all in her class. When her interviewer, surprised at this remark, having listened to other girls' stories, asks her to elaborate, Suzanna responds, "Well, we all do things together and nobody's left out." Suzanna's statement flies in the face of overwhelming evidence to the contrary, since so many other girls in her class describe in rich detail those times when others have whispered about them, excluded them, said mean things about them, or left them out. Suzanna, it seems, is either out of relationship with what is happening around her or she simply chooses not to speak what she knows is happening to the woman interviewing her, chooses not to speak what is quickly becoming for her and her classmates unspeakable.

Other girls cover their experiences of being left out or talked about with such a thin whitewash of nice and kind that the grain of their real thoughts and feelings shows through. When Madeline, for example, tells of her experience with the cliques and "clubs" that exist in her class, she dilutes her feelings with the almost unbelievable power of polite behavior to cover over, to bury, the meanest remarks:

Last year people didn't think I was, like they didn't like me very much, and they would make clubs against me, they would say, "Let's make up this club against her, because we don't like her," or something, but then I found out about it, so they would say, "I'm sorry," and so it turned out okay.
Was that at this school that they did that?
Yah, but only the first month maybe and then everybody got to be good friends and everything, so it turned out very well.
How did it work itself out?
I don't know, like I would find out about it somehow and I'd ask the person why they did that, like I'd say very nicely, not "Why

did you do that?" I would just say, "Why were you making up a club yesterday?" and they'd tell me why and say, "I'm sorry," and then everything would get back together.

The key to "getting everything back together," Madeline reveals, is polite but indirect confrontation. Though she says she would speak up to the people who have made a club against her, she knows that *how* she does so is important. Thus Madeline qualifies her question—"Like, I'd say very nicely, not 'Why did you do that?' I would just say, 'Why were you making up a club yesterday?'" Her question, asked "nicely," apparently passes the scrutiny of those in the club and "so it turned out well." Yet this happy ending hardly covers Madeline's hurt feelings when she hears about the club made against her, and it does not seem adequate to explain how such ardent dislike and exclusion on the part of the other girls could change so easily into genuine friendship. And we wonder why, if things ended so well, this experience of exclusion stays with Madeline so vividly a year later.

Like Madeline, other girls speak as though "I'm sorry" or other simple expressions of apology have the power to cover cruel or mean behavior or resolve ardent disagreements. Stories in which an apology is given have almost fairy-tale-like happy endings, so that strong feelings of pain or indignation end abruptly with this final act of attrition. Since these girls are talking to adult women, we wonder whether they believe what they say or whether they are saying what they believe the women who sit with them want to hear or will approve of. Perhaps ending their stories so "nicely" allows the girls to speak also of the cruelty and anger and sadness they've experienced, to speak what otherwise might cause women to turn away.

Like Jessie who says she "pretends" to be nice, and Sonia who knows people can "act nice to listen," these ten- and eleven-year-olds recognize, even talk about, whitewashing the relational world. Able to hold on to their own experiences and also to act in ways they have come to see others will approve of and respond to, they know the benefits of being the perfect, happy girl, at least on the surface. But what is, at first, a thin disguise can become all too real. While some girls wonder how a perfect girl could be possible, much less desirable, and how adults and other girls could fall for what they see as clearly fraudulent, other girls seem transfixed by the idea of her. Poised at the edge and suspecting that people prefer the "perfect" girl to the real one, these girls experiment with her image and the protection and security and happiness she promises.

As the perfectly nice girl seems to gain popularity with adults, and also with other girls, and as many girls strive to become her, jealousies and rivalries break out. The cliques and clubs so prevalent at this age thus seem to be a response to this struggle—a way for those girls who accept and best approximate perfection to group with one another or around a girl who seems perfect, and also a way for girls who are clearly not perfect to support each other emotionally. "I think friendship is very important," writes Victoria, a less than perfect girl, in English class:

> Some girls that were unpopular like me made a club. Ever since then I know that when I'm sad or depressed I can count on those three girls. Before that I didn't know what was going to happen . . . Though we are Leftovers in the Laurel School Cafeteria, I know I'm liked. That feels *great.*
> Sincerely,
> A Leftover.

Watching a treacherous relational scene, garnering evidence of the hazards of being too different or of not fitting in, leads Madeline to vehemently protest her distinctiveness: "I was kind of mad because they thought I was a different person, but I'm really not!"

But trying too hard to fit in can also backfire. Noura explains that her friends talk about other girls in her class who "just follow them around . . . Sometimes they just push it too hard and they just follow you around and try to do everything with you and then you never have a chance to be with your other friends. A lot of people are just like that, they just follow people around." Such girls don't know how to create the right impression, can't read the unspoken social codes about what not to say and do; they just say what they want and feel; as Noura says, they just "spill their guts."

A sense of relational treachery is everywhere at this age. Divisions and cliques are visible reminders of the potential hazard of being too different, not pretty enough, not nice enough, subtle enough, smart enough. The most "popular" girls in the class move about boldly, however, comfortable with the authority invested in them and the image they portray. Often the most outspoken among the girls—though not necessarily with adults—they have the power to gather some girls around them and to exclude others. As we might guess, then, such girls become the focus of much attention and much criticism and jealousy. Madeline explains:

> OK. There is a girl here . . . and she has this group, and she thinks, "I am so pretty, everybody should like me, and I am really popular and I am going to make everyone like me." So she has this group of all the people that she thinks are pretty and nice and very smart, and she takes them into her group and teaches them not to like certain people, and then she uses other people to get information out of some people, but the—that's what some people think, that is what we think she does, that is what some people think that don't like her—and so, she's just mean, she thinks, "I'm so pretty and she's ugly, why should I like her?" So that's what she says. She just doesn't like to be around other people. But she can be nice, but she's just like, "I'm so pretty," and she just sits like fluffing her hair back and everything.

Understandably, popular girls are outwardly doted on at the same time that they are privately envied or despised. Sometimes there are attempts to police these girls, to bring them back into the group; as Edie notes, "Sometimes people get mad at people that are too popular and stuff, and then we get in fights and stuff." Other girls watch the popular girl closely since she has the potential to "use" or hurt people and also to elevate them in the eyes of adults. Girls wonder who she is aligning with and why—is she showing off, looking for the approval of adults, or is she in relationship with other girls, a collaborator behind the scenes?

Knowing very well that people can think one thing and say another—since this is something they describe themselves doing—these ten- and eleven-year-old girls observe others closely; they wonder who is genuine, whose motives are honest. They distinguish between "real, real good" friends, those they can trust will not whisper or talk about them behind their backs, and "just" friends. They point out chameleon-like people who engage in fraudulent relationships and people who really care, who are really nice—they know the difference between people who fake it and people who mean it.

Although friendships can be a place for girls to experiment with strong feelings and disagreements, a place to feel painful feelings and to test truth and falsity without too great a personal risk, these girls describe how adult women—mothers and teachers—appear at times of relational conflict to mediate girls' disagreements, to protect girls' feelings. Sounding a lot like Sonia, Margaret tells her interviewer about the difficulty of choosing a partner in gym class. "If I pick the wrong girl, then the other one wouldn't necessarily get mad at me, but would sort of be upset," Margaret explains, "and if I did it the other way, the other girl may be upset."

As Margaret tells it, before she can deal with this dilemma she is rescued by her teacher. After noting that "all year . . . everybody was picking their best friends and they weren't going with other friends" and that "it was happening to a lot of people, it wasn't happening with just me," her teacher, she says, decided "who would go where." Though Margaret is "in a way . . . glad that the teacher decided" for her, she tells her interviewer that, given the chance to work things out for herself, she would have been more deliberate in her choice—not "ending up" with a group the teacher randomly chose but choosing "another group that hadn't asked me or they weren't asking, like the other groups had been." Though "it's hard for a person to decide," Margaret explains, next time "if a person doesn't have a partner, I will probably go to them."

According to Margaret, her teacher uses her authority to put a halt to what has been an ongoing occurrence—exclusive cliques that have hurt and upset people in the class. Although Margaret is rescued from her discomfort, she is unable to end her own story in the way she imagines—enacting a solution that is not only thoughtful but psychologically astute. If it were up to her, knowing "it is hard" and risky, Margaret would nonetheless face into the difficulty and choose.

Like Margaret, Allison also finds herself in a difficult situation when her "class took to two groups," and "some people went with their friends on one side and the other group went with their friends on the other side." Telling her story, Allison points to the considerable apprehension she felt about really being "a part" of the conflict: "I forget what the issue was," she explains, "but [one person] had a lot of friends, and another person had a lot of friends, and another girl was sort of—she kind of went from group to group, and so she would go to one group and listen and then go to the other group and tell." "And tell?" her interviewer asks.

> Yes . . . and see, I didn't want to be a part of anything, because then you lose a lot of friends, and gain them, but if you just have them all, and don't take a side, then you keep all your friends.
> *So what did you do?*
> Well, I just sort of stayed out of it—some people asked me, but I just said, "I'd rather stay out of it."
> *Do you think your decision was the right thing to do?*
> Yes . . . Just to stay out of it . . . If you get into it, then other people have hurt feelings, and then they could get angry with you, and then you would . . . then, if they thought, they wouldn't be your real good friend anymore . . . because you would get in an argument, and you would lose your friends, so it's better just to keep all your friends and not have them angry with you . . . But, on the other hand, it's better to stay out of it, because if you get yourself trapped between them, and when it's over, you don't know if some people will still dislike you.

The cause of the fight long forgotten, Allison remembers the relational drama in detail. She decided, she says, to remain "neutral"; in her cost-benefit analysis of losing and gaining friends, it does not seem worth it to get involved. But Allison, revealing the intricacies of eleven-year-old girls' relational knowledge, fears something worse. If she were to get involved and choose sides, she could end up "trapped between" friends, unsure when the fight is over who is a "real friend" and who isn't. And yet choosing sides, unprofitable and dangerous as it might be, would at least be authentic. The girls who took sides at least escape fraudulence, unlike the disingenuous chameleon who "would go to one group and listen and then go to the other group and tell."

As Allison continues her story, again we hear how girls portray adult women in their lives at such moments—as coming in to protect girls from feeling painful feelings by removing them from conflict:

> After a while, the teachers made us walk in a straight line, and they would walk with us, so there were no hurt feelings . . . so no one would hurt another person's feelings, and then it stopped . . .
> *I don't understand.*
> See, by walking a straight line, the teachers would walk you to different classes, it would eliminate like any talking and hurting of feelings of other people, 'cause if you were in a straight line, you couldn't like group together with people.

What made this conflict hard, Allison says, was that "I like both of the friends on both sides, 'cause I like everybody in the class":

> And my mother always told me not to have a best friend, because it gets you into problems with other people. So, other people had a best friend, so they wanted just to . . . even if they didn't think what their friend thought, they wanted to stick together, and they told themselves that they thought that . . . and it was hard because you liked everybody, and if you went on one side, the other side would get angry; if you went on the other side, the other side would get angry, so it was difficult.

Allison portrays her teachers and her mother as intervening in ways that encourage Allison not to choose groups. The teachers, obviously witnessing the troublesome division of the class, attempt to eliminate the talking and physical grouping that sustain such divisions. They require the girls to walk everywhere in a straight line, accompanied by a teacher—a visible reminder of their unacceptable behavior. The teachers, in this way, justify Allison's decision to remain uninvolved—for now each girl must walk alone and no girl is jeopardized or hurt by being left out. In addition, Allison recalls her mother's advice "not to have a best friend, because it gets you into problems with other people."

But Allison has a problem whether she has a best friend or not; she is a part of this conflict whether she chooses sides or not. The teachers, while effectively preventing the girls from public fighting, may have simply moved the conflict underground. And while her mother's solution may allow Allison to avoid some problems, it seems to create others. Allison knows that by choosing to stay out of things, she risks being called disloyal, dishonest, or, worse, a spy. Allison's friends—who want her to choose, and choose them—do warn her of these risks: "Some people thought that I should just join—go with a group—because otherwise I might be like just pretending I didn't want to go in a group and really be in the group and just know what other people are saying."

Allison's resistance seems courageous in a relational climate where people tell themselves they think what their friends think, where words can cause psychological violation and pain, and cliques or groups or "sides" threaten to silence girls' voices. But solutions designed to protect girls' feelings by ending public conflict simply push strong feelings underground and leave the simmering residue of disagreement, anger, and sadness unspoken and out of relationship. What remains visible, then, are the nice feelings, the polite conversations. As a result, girls find it more and more difficult to tell the difference between genuine pleasure and love in relationship and the pretense of pleasure and love.

More mature than the eight-year-old whistle-blowers, involved in more complex friendships and able to take different viewpoints, Margaret, Allison, and their classmates describe the difference between what they know from experience and what others say is or should be happening. Their strong desire to remain connected to those around them leads them, at times, to cover over, to whitewash their own experiences in order to be accepted, to be seen as acceptable. We hear them narrate their disconnection from themselves as they suspend their strong feelings so they might stay in relationship with other people.

And yet while some girls pick their disagreements carefully and thoughtfully, determining when it is okay to "cause a ruckus," others speak openly, revealing the complexity and depth of their concerns in a genuine attempt to name relationships honestly, to work through the surface layers and get to what is really happening between people. These girls seem caught, then, between speaking about what they know about relationships—a sophisticated knowledge of thoughts and feelings—and pressures to negate or abandon their knowledge for an idealized view of themselves and their relationships. When women enter girls' stories as protectors—escorting them from the potential dangers of open conflict—or as idealized models of selfless love and perfect kindness, girls voice their growing suspicion that if they speak openly or have bad feelings, women will not want to be with them.

This time in girls' lives when the real and ideal divide seems critical. The move to the ideal leaves girls in danger of losing their relational reality, a reality that is crucial for them to hold onto, since once girls lose their ability to name relational violations they become, in new ways, vulnerable to abuse—both psychological and physical. Listening to these girls name what feels to them like a relational impasse, listening to them narrate their disconnection from their feelings—taking themselves out of relationship for the sake of relationship—we begin to wonder if we are witnessing the beginning of psychological splits and relational struggles well documented in the psychology of women.

Having listened to the variety of voices that populate the fifth grade, we now attend more closely and intently to the stories of three girls, three informants, who will be our guides through the late years of childhood, through the changes of puberty, and into early adolescence. Noura, Judy, and Victoria each describe a struggle to stay connected with themselves, with their thoughts and feelings, in the face of a relational impasse. Noura, who is Syrian and middle-class, brings her strong feelings and loud voice into the world of her relationships. Childhood has been an awakening of new thoughts and feelings, and she has learned from her family that she can express herself, that she can make the space and take the time to work through difficult relational problems. But as Noura comes up against the wall of good girls and perfect grades, she overrides what she has learned through experiencing the difficulties and the pleasures of her relationships and moves into an exhaustive cycle of good feeling and perfect relationships. Even as she describes the hypocrisy of double standards, where others can speak and she cannot, and voices her longing for genuine relationships, Noura becomes so frightened of what she might feel and think and say in relationships that she dissociates from her feelings and cannot speak clearly.

Judy is European-American and middle-class. Over the years of the study she narrates the gradual split she experiences between what she feels deeply in her body, what she feels with her mind, and what is being shoved into her brain. Sensing the dangers that befall girls who remain embodied, who express their strong feelings, Judy nevertheless struggles to stay with herself and her feelings. Her parents' divorce brings Judy into a different kind of relational crisis where conflict and difference are laced with the reality of loss and the threat of further separation. Unable to say what she is really feeling, Judy protects herself and shelters others from her feelings in the name of relationship. Theorizing how people lose their minds, by which she means their bodily knowing, Judy poignantly describes the losses she herself feels so deeply.

Victoria, also European-American and middle-class, describes the painful feelings of growing up in an angry and violent household, where her protests "fall on deaf ears." For a time she struggles openly to express her feelings of anger and sadness, to name and to condemn what is happening to her and around her. But Victoria cannot seem to hold on or hold out in a world of unreliable and untrustworthy relationships, and so, in an attempt to stay with her own voice, she moves out of relationship with others. Claiming her radical independence from everyone, Victoria wavers between feeling "crazy" in the intensity of her anger and disconnecting from her feelings to find solace in the ideals of romance.

Three guides, three different stories of girls' struggle for voice in the face of pressure to not know and not speak.

Noura: Knowing and Not Knowing

Nine-year-old Noura leans over the white construction paper and points to each figure in the family picture she has drawn; her straight, shoulder-length black hair falls forward and brushes the paper as she looks intently at the people and animals she has painted in primary colors: "That's my brother, and he likes animals," she begins. "A cat and a dog and a bird and a fish?" her interviewer observes. "Yeah," Noura responds, "and my dad's a doctor, and my mom and I like to paint a lot. My mom used to be an art teacher, and so I guess she still likes doing it. And, I don't know, I guess I take after her because I like art too. And that's a picture of my sister in her prom dress . . . she looked pretty in it." "Could you tell me a story about the people in your drawing?" her interviewer asks. "Just any story?" Noura replies. "Yeah, just any story," her interviewer says. Noura tells the following:

> One day my brother went out on a field trip, and they were going in the woods, and he saw a dog, and he was injured kind of, and some other animals too. So he didn't follow the rest of his group, and he just went off to go and help them. And then after he found something to bandage them up with, he forgot about the field trip, and everyone started noticing he was gone. And then he just started walking and trying to find a way out, and then he found a way to get out and there was a restaurant there, and it just happened to be the one, McDonald's, that they were going to eat at . . . But he arrived a little bit earlier, and so he waited and decided to order some food because he was hungry, and then they met there again, and the rest of the day was normal.

Noura says that this story is "a fake one." But the image of her brother, two years her senior, making his way in the world, stopping to help injured animals, becoming separated from the crowd, finding his own "way out," feeling his hunger, ordering food, and then meeting up with the others and returning to a "normal" day evokes themes that will resonate throughout this time in girls' lives—themes of separation and relationship, injury and aid, hunger and satiation and concerns about what is normal and not normal. "You told a story about your brother. What is important to you about your brother?" her interviewer asks. "Well," Noura says, "we usually fight a lot, but he can be nice sometimes . . . We just like to tease each other." "A lot?" her interviewer asks. "Yeah," Noura says.

For nine-year-old Noura, relational life is filled with playing and fighting and teasing and niceness, and, as we might expect of life with an older brother and sister, filled with voices saying how to hold it all in check. "Since me and my brother fight a lot, people always tell us to be fair," she explains to her interviewer. Rules, she adds, "keep things equal," while strong feelings—like being "mad" or "upset" as well as being excited and happy—give Noura's life passion and meaning.

Noura is Syrian; her dark skin and black eyes set her apart from the sea of fair complexions in her fourth grade class. Yet according to Noura, "Everyone is different." "There are opinions and there are opinions," she says knowingly, and some people just "think differently." Fascinated by differences, Noura is also undaunted by disagreement; "I don't get along with some people," she says, which seems perfectly understandable to her since whether people get along "depends on what they think and how they like people to be." Noura, like other girls her age in this study, paints her relational life in the same primary colors she paints her pictures, in bold colors that emphasize borders and contrasts.

But like other nine-year-old girls, Noura also hears adult women encouraging her to be more measured in her response to differences, to consider more than what she sees and hears, feels and thinks. They are, Noura says, "always saying you should try and give someone a chance . . . And if you don't like them, fine, but try at least to get along with them."

Noura seems to have taken in this advice. A year later, the primary colors that so vividly represented her knowledge of herself and her relationships appear less distinct, more subtle. Talking about what has stood out for her this past year, ten-year-old Noura says with some pride, "I stopped fighting with my brother as much." "And how did that happen?" her interviewer wonders. "I don't know," Noura replies, "I guess because, just . . . we're becoming older and we don't always fight over the stupid little things and stuff." Now when her brother teases her, instead of teasing him back, Noura explains, "I try to ignore it, 'cause sometimes it just, I don't even think about it."

This change in Noura's relationship with her brother over the past year—from the lively exchanges, the mutual bantering and teasing, to her attempts "to ignore," to not know and not "think about" her brother's behavior—is accompanied by a shift in Noura's language. At ten, Noura sounds more tentative than she did at nine, less certain about what she feels and thinks, as she becomes more aware of how she is perceived by others. No longer wanting to "fight over the stupid little things" because her brother's teasing now "embarrasses" her, she is concerned with what should and "shouldn't be said." As moral language creeps into her interviewer's questions and into Noura's speech, so does Noura's uncertainty about the value and importance of what she has to say: When her interviewer asks her to describe a time when she didn't know what she should do, Noura responds, "I don't know, it doesn't really matter . . . I guess we could talk about . . . I don't know, not like anything big or anything . . . I don't know . . . Well, I don't know, see 'cause sometimes, I don't know, 'cause I just can't really . . ." As her interviewer, like other women in Noura's life, asks her to reflect on how she should behave rather than to describe what she thinks and feels, Noura begins the difficult process of deciphering what she can or should know from what she knows; Noura is beginning, it seems, to disconnect from her feelings and knowledge in an attempt to connect to what others want.

Noura's increased sensitivity to social cues, to what should and shouldn't be known or said, works to her advantage in her relationships with the girls in her class. Noura watches and listens as her friends tease and talk about the girls who want too much to be liked, who "just push it too hard and they just follow you around and try to do everything with you," even though she herself is irritated by these popular friends who are "really smart, or they're really good athletes" but who "act like they're the best," who "brag" or who "just laugh at other people's throws or their hits for tennis." Quietly resistant but also keenly aware of what it feels like to be teased and embarrassed, Noura struggles with what to do when these friends who talk about people tell her "not to like this person and stuff":

> Well sometimes I just say [to them], "Yeah, but it doesn't really matter 'cause they didn't do anything wrong or anything," so sometimes I just say, "Yeah, and there's nothing wrong with somebody." And then sometimes I have to decide what to say . . . like if someone has a party that not everyone's invited to and they'll say like, "Well, somebody's so dumb, and she doesn't know anything and she never studies for her tests and she talks weird and she's ugly," and stuff like that . . . Sometimes I sort of go along with them, but sometimes I say, "I don't know," just to cover it up, 'cause I don't know what to say . . . but I usually think, "Well, it's not their fault if they can't do things good and stuff."
>
> *Is your problem deciding whether to speak up in front of your friends about this girl?*
>
> Yeah. And sometimes also, if you like the person, and you really think that that's not true, well, sometimes, I would say, "Well, that's not always true," but I wouldn't really just disagree with them totally—I would tell them, "Well, sometimes it's true, but not always" and if you look at the good side, you can see a lot of things that they don't do that other people do that bugs you and stuff.
>
> *What makes it a hard decision for you?*
>
> I don't know . . . I don't know . . . I guess just that—well, I like both of—I like my friends and well, they're all my friends, but I like also the other person that's being talked about, and sometimes you don't know. Like if you say, "Well, that's not true," then those friends might say, "Yes, it is, don't you know anything?" And then if someone else says, "Do you know what? I heard [that girl] talking about you," and then that person would get mad . . . and so sometimes I just don't know what to say, and it's hard to say something.

If Noura says what she feels and disagrees with her friends, she risks being ridiculed, talked about, and rejected; if she holds back what she feels and thinks, she colludes in behavior she knows from experience will hurt people and is unreal or false. In the deepest sense this is a struggle about relationship and about knowing—what can Noura know and say and still be in connection with other people? What should she ignore or not know for the sake of "relationships"? When we listen again to the above exchange, paying closer attention to Noura's language, we hear this struggle more clearly:

> Well, somebody's so dumb, and *she doesn't know anything* . . .
> Sometimes I sort of go along with them, but *sometimes I say,* "I
> *don't know,*" just to cover it up, 'cause *I don't know what to say* . . .
> *I don't know* . . . *I don't know* . . . and sometimes *you don't know*
> . . . those friends might say, "Yes, it is, *don't you know anything?*"
> And then if someone else says, "*Do you know what? I heard* [that
> girl] talking about you" . . . *I just don't know what to say.*

The two worst things Noura's friends can accuse her of, it seems, are either not knowing and saying the wrong things or knowing and saying the wrong things. If Noura speaks up on behalf of the girls being talked about, she reveals knowledge others want her to keep hidden, and she fears her friends will dislike or chastise her: "Sometimes I feel that my friends won't like me or something, or they'll say, 'What's the big deal?'" Moreover, Noura fears these "friends that were talking about people" might then "talk about me." Noura avoids these risks by speaking in measured tones, sometimes qualifying her thoughts and feelings—"not disagreeing with them totally"—and sometimes hiding what she feels and thinks under the guise of not knowing—"Sometimes I say, 'I don't know,' just to cover it up." In this way, Noura finds she can protect herself by thinking one thing and saying another, by doubling her voice, being, in a sense, two people—one private and honest, one public and acceptable. But while Noura finally comes to a precarious compromise that allows her to stay with herself privately without jeopardizing herself in the eyes of her friends—"I would tell them," she says, "sometimes it's true, but not always"—"going along with" those friends brings Noura dangerously close to disconnecting from herself and what she really feels and thinks.

But what is so striking to us is how clearly ten-year-old Noura articulates this compromise, how aware she is of her feelings and the risks she takes in speaking them aloud, and how consciously she protects herself by covering over her thoughts with the phrase, "I don't know." Remembering her own feelings when she is teased or whispered about, Noura learns how other people feel in similar situations: "I learn by just . . . feeling what you feel . . . and your reactions to everyone talking about them." And though she is compelled to qualify or cover over what she feels and thinks, Noura still wonders aloud in the privacy of her interview why people don't just "go to that person [who brags] and hurts people and . . . say, 'Why do you always do that?'" rather than talk about them behind their backs. "If I were that person," Noura adds, "I . . . wouldn't want people talking about me. I would want them to say, 'Stop bragging,' or 'Why do you brag?'"

And so, although Noura feels what she feels and knows what she thinks, she also capitulates to the pressure from her friends not to know and not to speak. Wanting to "do the right thing," to "not hurt" anyone, to "always help anyone who needs it," Noura gives us the impression she is walking on eggshells as she gingerly makes her way among these girls who "are all my friends" but who police her thoughts and feelings by threatening to talk about her if she says what she feels, who ask her to separate "what I think" from what "I say," to remove herself from relationship for the sake of relationship. Knowing how it feels "to be the person that everyone doesn't like" keeps Noura from talking about people, but also from saying what she thinks and feels to her "friends" who do. Like with her brother, Noura finds it easier to pretend not to know what she knows when she is with her friends; certainly it is less dangerous, as Noura says, "just to keep things to yourself."

Now eleven and in the sixth grade, Noura sounds, literally, more self-possessed. As though to protect herself from her friend's judgments and expectations, this year Noura fortifies her opinions with the knowledge that "everyone can have their own feelings and you can't change that, what they are feeling, you can't say, 'Yes, you do, I know it,' because you don't really know what they are thinking." Doggedly staying with what she knows to be true from her experience, her relationships have changed. When her brother teases her to the point of exasperation, for example, Noura now exclaims, "Shut up! I don't care!" And when she gets in trouble, not only for what she says to him but for her loud voice, she complains bitterly to her mother, armed with her new-found defense—that she sees things differently, that her feelings aren't her brother's. Knowing that "there are always two whole different things that happened," and that any fair resolution to relational conflict depends on hearing "both sides of the story," Noura seems free to express her strong feelings and opinions. And so when she is asked to talk about a situation in which she had to make a decision and she was not sure what she should do, Noura launches, without pause or qualification, into a long and complicated story of relational conflict.

Well, I think it was last weekend when [my friend, China] was over to my house, we were talking to [Mia on the phone] . . . and then we heard that [Heather] was like on her three-way phone, and she was just listening. And they didn't tell us that she was on, and we got into this huge fight . . . And then like, first China started crying and then, I don't know why she started crying, but I guess I just felt like I had to, so I started crying and then we kept hanging up the phone on each other and calling them back . . . and China wanted to spill her guts to them, but I wouldn't let her . . . I didn't want her to yet, because I knew that they would hang up and never talk . . . First I was asking them all these questions because I wanted to know why they were doing it, that . . . and then in the end I said, "I've got an idea, why don't we just go around and start with Heather and she can say what bothers her the most about what China and I do," and then we went to Mia and then China and then me. And we just did that . . . and we decided that we would always be friends even if we got really mad.

114

NOURA: KNOWING AND NOT KNOWING

When China discovers Heather is on the line, she cries, perhaps because she has been caught talking about Heather behind her back. Noura then speaks on China's behalf:

> And I was like [saying to Mia and Heather], "China is crying very hard . . . and she wants to talk to you." And they were like, "We are not going to feel sorry for her if that is what you want us to do." And I am like, I said, "I don't want you to feel sorry for her, I just want you to know that she is feeling bad." And then I guess we got disconnected again and I was like screaming on the phone even when they were off. I was like, "I don't care," you know. And then we were, like, laughing a little, too, and then we got upset again.

Noura and her three friends go through the gamut of emotions—yelling and screaming, crying and laughing, feeling bad, not feeling sorry or caring. But in the midst of all these feelings, as Noura describes it, "we really kept talking about like why we were mad." Calling and hanging up, but ultimately staying with the fight, the four girls gradually work their way through their relational conflict.

As we listen to eleven-year-old Noura describe her role in this drama, we are struck by her thoughtfulness, her carefulness, her presence of mind, her ability to stay with her friends and her feelings in this emotionally charged situation. Noura, it seems, wants to cut through the performances—the secrets, the hanging up, the crying that might be "for attention"—and get down to the business of knowing what people really feel and think: "I decided," she explains, "that I wasn't going to get really mad about this. I was just going to talk . . . I just want to know . . . I just want to know, because out of curiosity, I just need to know and so, I don't know." Taking her cue from the way her parents organize family meetings and solve relational conflicts, Noura suggests that the girls say to each other "what really bothers us" and "what we didn't like about each other," so that everyone would "know how everyone else is feeling. So we just, no one would interrupt while they were talking."

The results of their conversation underscore what Noura suspects: that, indeed, "there are two sides to the story." Heather and Mia,

Noura says, violated both her trust and her privacy by listening in: "It's like they don't trust me, and I didn't want them to always think I was going to be talking and then just get petrified and say, 'Oh well, then I have to listen,' or 'Tell me.' And also sometimes I just don't want anyone else to know unless they say, 'You can tell Heather, I don't care,' or something. So sort of like an invasion of privacy sort of." But Noura also recognizes and understands Heather's intense need to know, to listen in. Heather feels on the outside, Noura explains, and so she "is always afraid that we are going to talk about her," and she's "always just thinking, 'I'm afraid that she is going to talk about me, so let me hear on the phone.'" But Noura also discovers, to her surprise, that Mia had a motive for colluding with Heather. As boys have entered Noura's life, Mia has felt "ignored" and jealous: "Mia was saying that I was liking [one boy] more than her, and I was like, 'How could I like him more than you, I have known you since we were in third grade?' . . . I guess she was feeling left out."

In hindsight, Noura says, revealing her keen knowledge of relationships, this fight had been building. "I mean now that I look back on it, I think that it was something we needed to get out a while ago, because we were always having these little arguments." And it was important, she adds, that they worked their feelings out apart from adults who would only want to control their emotions and quiet them down. "We were home. No one else was there," Noura explains. "I'm glad . . . because that way I felt like we could make as much noise as we wanted and I could take a long time." If they hadn't had the time and space to work their problems out, Noura explains, "nothing would work out and somehow the whole class would end up knowing and our teacher would get into it and say well, how can we solve this and everything and . . . I just wanted it to be sort of between us."

Noura faces into this relational conflict with a clarity and a courage that are breathtaking, proposing a process that allows each of the girls, including herself, to voice her deepest feelings about the others and about the situation—to make as much noise as they wanted and to take the time they needed to work things through.

Although Noura says, "I just wanted to stay calm . . . because that is what my mom is always saying, 'Don't make a big deal out of it . . . Everyone talks a lot [about people] even though they don't really mean it,'" this is not what she did. This relational problem with her friends really frightened and upset her—this fight "was big," she says; a lot was at stake. So much could have been pre-vented if she and her friends would just say what they really think and feel to each other directly, Noura explains as she resolves that "the next time," long before things build to this level, "I'm just going to say it."

Two years later, now thirteen and in the eighth grade, Noura's voice has changed dramatically. What strikes us most is how she has shifted from the intense, lively world of relationships and the astute understanding she revealed at eleven to a preoccupation with her own perfection that seems to engulf and exhaust her. "I always feel like I'm overworked," Noura now complains to her interviewer. "It's more like just little unimportant things that are piling up . . . it kind of makes me scared, but then I think, I've just got to learn to pace myself . . . I just wish I could get more sleep." The Noura who made loud noises with her friends, who took the time she needed for herself to work out conflicts with her friends, is no longer in evidence—at least on the surface.

This year Noura is trying to understand how to deal with the increasing pressure she feels to do everything well. "I'm so pres-sured," she explains, "and I am getting good grades and stuff and if I want to keep that up, I have to keep doing as much work as I've been doing." But, she adds, "I'm realizing that I can't do everything . . . because I am really tired all the time." As Noura details the hours she spends studying to her interviewer, the late nights and early mornings, a small voice inside her wonders if maybe "it's okay to sometimes fall behind and not be perfect about everything." As though even this possibility might be giving away too much, Noura quickly overrules this voice with another: "Just . . . as long as you catch up and stuff."

Indeed, this year Noura seems to overrule or override most of her feelings and thoughts, dutifully reining herself in, trapped in a vicious circle of expectations. If she could only try a little harder, just "get more organized—I mean it's hard because I'm as organized as I can be—or try to just limit myself," perhaps she could meet all the demands of school and sports and friends.

Yet, while Noura measures herself by "doing good in school" and by "being good at anything," she knows if she doesn't escape her compulsion to do everything well, "I'm going to kill myself. I'm not getting enough sleep." Still, she worries a lot, and when her brother notices and tells her she's paranoid, this year, rather than tell him to shut up, she says, "I agree with him":

> I'm really, a lot of times I'm just so worried and nervous about anything in general and people are just like, "Why don't you just do it? Who cares?" . . . They're like, "Why are you so worried about that?" And then I feel like well . . . I can't go against what I'm thinking because that's not what I think, but then I don't want to sound like I'm some worried person . . . someone who's got to always be all perfect, they don't think that, but I just don't want it to sound, I don't know, in that situation I feel like they probably think I'm weird, I am almost too paranoid.

What Noura feels and thinks, what others think of her, and how she sounds begin to swirl together until it is no longer clear whose thoughts are whose and what Noura really wants. All the pressure for perfection, the feelings of paranoia, the worry and sleeplessness and exhaustion pile up for Noura. Though she feels trapped in her compulsion to meet the heavy expectations placed on her, Noura can't let herself express her fear of not being good enough or show her exhaustion. She does not want to "sound" worried and nervous or be seen as weird and paranoid or be judged as "all perfect." Although Noura strives for perfection, she does not want the emotional residues and relational consequences of being the perfect girl. While, before, Noura wanted her parents out of the house so she and her friends could make as much noise as they wanted, now she seems to have lost the capacity to imagine, let alone to create, this kind of space for herself and her friends.

As Noura talks about her exhaustion and unhappiness she begins to notice how out of relationship she really feels to this world of perfect grades, perfect relationships, and perfect people. "I think now I'm starting to learn more from experience," Noura says to her interviewer, "something might keep happening over and over again and you finally realize, well, there must be something wrong." Listening to herself, Noura again wonders if the pressure is too great and if the fight is worth it. Relationships can be either "perfect" or "depressing," she says. In perfect relationships people "never have any fights . . . and they are always together . . . too perfect . . . like never arguing, like, 'Oh, yeah, I totally agree with you.'" In depressing relationships someone is "really jealous and starts being really mean . . . where two really good friends break up." Somewhere between the extremes of perfection and depression, Noura imagines a place she once lived but no longer inhabits, a place where people give other people "a chance and that's all they can do"; where people struggle in the best way they know how to find a way that "sort of seems happy because . . . it's just sort of mutual I guess."

At thirteen, as Noura begins to question what goes on beneath the facade of perfection and invulnerability, she looks around for signs that others feel the way she feels and know what she knows— that others are also vulnerable, also want to be in genuine relationships, also conceal mistakes underneath the impenetrable veneer they show. Looking for signs of life, attuned to her own experience, Noura sees and hears hypocrisy everywhere: in the adults who "expect you to do everything, like be all polite and stuff" but who are not "polite to you"; and in her teacher who expects her to be a model student when "he does things that make people really mad too." When this teacher kicks her out of class for making a laughing noise, Noura describes her indignation and anger: "I was just really, really mad . . . I was like, this is so stupid . . . It's not like he's perfect . . . He just is so hypocritical . . . because he does things that make people really mad too." Observing cracks in the glossy exteriors people present gives Noura an opening to express her own vulnerability.

But Noura is having a difficult time staying with what she sees and hears, saying what she feels and thinks, tempted again and again to judge herself and other people against standards of perfection—to call people and relationships either "perfect" or "horrible" and "depressing." Though she is really mad at her teacher for what he has done, she struggles to stay with her feelings as she anticipates the repercussions of her anger:

> I never have the guts to [say what I feel] because it'll probably just start another fight or another argument . . . and . . . then they could like say something really mean about me . . . I don't know. It could, it would just start another argument and I wouldn't want to get into it because I wouldn't want to waste my time and I also wouldn't want to get my feelings hurt . . . Just to be in a fight anyways, is bad, because you know, you get mad and obviously you don't want to get into fights, and so I kind of wish I could, just to show him that he doesn't rule the world . . . I just wanted to show him that I wouldn't let him just say anything . . . I wanted him to know that that was really unfair, and that I think he was really irrational, just like really unfair and stupid, like silly . . . But I know he would have just gotten . . . so mad, and I just stayed out of it . . . I didn't want to take any chances.

Feeling her anger and knowing what she thinks of her teacher's unfairness, Noura thinks that she cannot risk the consequences of speaking and having her teacher know how she feels. Unlike herself at ten, when she held in her feelings, consciously covering them with the phrase "I don't know," or herself at eleven, when she created a way for herself and her friends to show each other how they really felt and what they really knew, Noura at thirteen sees no way to speak openly with her teacher. In the face of this relational impasse, Noura wavers between wanting and not wanting, knowing and not knowing, quickly becoming unsure of what she really thinks and feels about what her teacher has done and what she wants to happen:

> He could have just tried to ignore [my laughter], because we have to ignore a lot of things that a lot of our teachers do . . . like when they are really mean . . . not necessarily mean, but like we think of it as unfair, but I guess it really is fair in a way . . . It's

his class and he can, or any teacher can just assign whatever they want, but I mean it seems unfair to us . . . I hate it . . . It makes me mad when they make you do like, I mean I guess it's good in the long run, but I don't know.

Speaking her feelings and retracting them ("they are really mean . . . not necessarily mean"; "we think of it as unfair . . . it really is fair"), first sure of her feelings ("I hate it . . . It makes me mad") and then uncertain ("I guess it's good in the long run, but I don't know"), Noura, like a person moving from bright sunlight into a dark room, gingerly feels her way through her interview.

But there is no doubt Noura is angry this year. She talks about fighting with her brother; it infuriates her that he listens "physically" but not "mentally" when she gives so much to the relationship. She explains how annoyed she gets when her friends, including Mia and China, tease her, though now she does not express the depth of her feelings, despite her vow at eleven to do so: "I say one little thing . . . and then I drop it . . . I just want to . . . you know, be careful . . . I'll just forget about it." Noura, it seems, has forgotten the "simple" truth she learned after so much difficulty and pain two years before—that if things go unsaid they become enormous and that "the next time, I'm just going to say it."

"Just saying it" is now so difficult for Noura that she no longer seems to know what she feels and, as a result, finds it hard to say what is happening. When her friends get angry at China because "one day she will be really nice, and then the next day . . . she won't be with you as much," Noura is confused about how to respond. "I don't know . . . I don't know what to say, I usually just say something like, 'I don't know, everyone does things like that,' you know." When she was ten, Noura knew how she felt, though she made choices about what to say and when to cover up. At thirteen, she now seems both to know and not to know how she feels and as a result doesn't trust herself to read China's actions accurately. "I really don't know if she is kidding or not," Noura explains, and though "sometimes I think [China's] a little mean to other people," the problem "is just really confusing." "I am sort of split," Noura confesses finally. "I don't know what to think . . . I can't make a definite answer."

Out of connection with herself, with what she knows, Noura finds her relational world treacherous and opaque, and she becomes frightened of what she might feel and think. While one minute she convinces herself that what China does is "natural" and "normal," the next minute she admits,

> Sometimes I think it's just too confusing to think about, and I shouldn't really . . . Sometimes I'm afraid to think one way. That's more what I am afraid of. Like that I will start hating someone and I know that's not true, that I hate someone, or strongly dislike them even . . . So I am kind of afraid of what I will think, I guess.

Disconnected from her thoughts and feelings, Noura is confused, afraid her feelings will become uncontrollable. Saying and then retracting her feelings, Noura fears that if she really thinks (and feels, we might add), she might decide "that they're right and just forget about the other side's point of view." As a result, Noura stays safely "in between," afraid to get too close to what she is feeling and thinking, unsure whether she wants to move further into relationships, which she knows can be difficult and duplicitous, or to move away from everyone. Standing in between, out of relationship with herself and also with others, Noura struggles to remember and name the "it" of her feelings.

> I try to keep myself from thinking that I dislike it. Just so it doesn't get too like dominant or something . . . I sort of am afraid of it happening, but like it's just more, I guess it's just something that I do, like subconsciously . . . without really knowing it and um, I was going to say something. Shoot, I just forgot what I was going to say . . .

"Afraid of *it* happening"—perhaps that she will think and feel deeply, and thus have to know—Noura stops herself "at the time things make sense . . . before I confuse myself again." Like with a "math problem," where "I think okay, I understand why this works and stop thinking just so I don't bring up another point that makes more sense," Noura puts a halt to her feelings, to even "thinking" about her feelings. "Always taking precautions" against feeling too strongly or thinking too much, against making too much noise or taking too much time, the deep-feeling, outspoken world of relationships eleven-year-old Noura and her friends embraced is thus covered over or walled off through the amnesia of dissociation by thirteen-year-old Noura. We are struck by the clarity and specificity of Noura's description of this process, and the questions it poses for us: How will we respond to Noura? What will we say and do in the presence of this disconnection?

Judy: Losing Her Mind

Nine-year-old Judy listens intently as her interviewer talks about the study she is now a part of and the questions she will be asked in the next hour and a half.[1] "There are no right or wrong answers," the woman tells her, "We are really interested in how you think and feel." Nonetheless, Judy begins her first interview with a disclaimer: "I'm not a very good drawer," she says, as she describes her complicated family picture: "Okay, this is me . . . I have a hamster and he's Fred. And this is my mom and this is my little brother, he's seven, and my sister, who's four. My parents are divorced and I live with my mom. And my dad, and this is my stepmother, and this is my half-sister."

"Can you tell me a story about the people in that picture?" her interviewer asks. Judy, who has learned about relationships—about connections and disconnections, love and anger, closeness and withdrawal—here in her divided family, pauses a moment and then begins, in full voice, to tell a story about her brother and herself:

Okay, well. There is a boy named [Johnny] and he was walking along and then he saw his sister with her hamster. He wanted to see her hamster and she wouldn't let him, and he got really mad and started screaming at her, and so the hamster got killed.

"Oh, no!" her interviewer exclaims, "Why did the hamster have that ending?" "I don't know," Judy answers. "Because lots of my hamsters do."

Judy does not draw out the connection implicit in the story she tells. In one sense, the death of a hamster is a sad but rather inevitable event, a natural part of the landscape of facts and feelings she experiences in her life. Also part of her life are the pain, anger, and jealousy of her brother, which she returns to throughout her interview narratives. Here in this supposedly make-believe family story, Judy links the voluble anger of her brother with the death of her hamster, a member of her family. And this link can be read in at least two ways—as an astute commentary on a relational reality where male violence is explosive, and as a more personal commentary on the danger she feels, and her fears about what will happen to her or other members of her family if she expresses her strong feelings—specifically if she says no to her brother's requests.

Relational conflicts, Judy may have learned from her parents' irreconcilable differences, are explosive—fracturing relationships and making it necessary for others to resolve the disputes "in court . . . the court's decision would be best." Living with relational conflict, in Judy's experience, makes people "get grumpy after a while and they don't feel good. They get mad." The anger and intransigence Judy has witnessed and felt in her family, it seems, causes her to associate relational conflicts with unresolvable bad feelings or death.

For Judy and some of the other girls in this study, conflict in relationship has a gender-bias: brothers and sisters, mothers and fathers, boys and girls. That boys and girls differ and disagree seems factual to Judy. Judy says she knows this "by just experiencing it with my brother," who is different from her, who, she says, is "real mad and hyper," who tells her what to do, who covers his actions by lying to their mother.

But also Judy struggles to explain the conflict and constant "switching" that happens among her girlfriends. How can people agree, Judy wonders—talking now about friends, but also echoing the struggle in her family—"when they're both strongly feeling what they feel?" Like the shadow of a cloud that passes over the landscape, the question of how to have strong feelings and yet stay in relationship moves in and out of Judy's responses.

124

Judy, like other nine-year-olds, knows her world through the evidence of her senses; her knowledge of the relational world comes from what she experiences, sees, hears, and feels. Feelings and thoughts come through her experience of being in a body that feels and knows feelings, that lives in time and space. Thus it strikes Judy as particularly insensitive when someone just walks away from her best friend, leaving her all alone "just talking into space." Judy says she can tell that her friend is going to feel bad because "I just feel it in my mind." When her interviewer asks her to explain this, Judy has some trouble articulating what she means: "You can just kind of see them walking away or getting sad or something, but you can't tell right then and there she's going to get hurt or anything, but you just feel it. It's hard to explain." What Judy seems to be saying is that while she doesn't consciously think "my friend is going to get hurt," she senses and feels her friend's sadness, and thus knows it. Her mind knows what she feels in her body—and her body resonates by feeling with others.[2]

Judy's knowledge of the relational world thus springs from her body: her senses, her feelings, and her experience of living in relationships. She is grounded in that experience and takes the world at face value: hamsters die, brothers get furious, parents separate, friends get hurt and feel sad, and even best friends, she says, are sometimes boring. The differences she can readily pick up in people lead them to different perspectives, opinions, and, sometimes, to conflict. Judy understands feelings both as a means of knowing and connecting with others and as an obstacle to communicating—people sometimes feel their feelings so strongly they can't speak but just scream and then, as in her story, something or someone may die. What happens when anger turns into stubbornness or violence? Judy seems to be asking. Her world, it seems, is both colored and shadowed by feeling.

By age ten we hear subtle differences in Judy's voice and in her relationship with her self and her world. This year Judy hurries her answers and her voice frequently breaks into a giggle that subtly negates the seriousness or importance of what she has to say. In her nine-year-old interview, Judy, who thoughtfully paused before each answer and said "I don't know" four times—once after implying a connection between her brother's anger and her hamster's death—now says "I don't know" twenty-four times in an interview of comparable length. Judy has changed in a year, and while the changes are subtle, it seems that the ground of knowledge is shifting beneath her feet.

The disagreement and conflict that seemed at once so natural and so upsetting to Judy at nine is now, at ten, obscured for her, as for many of the other girls, by injunctions to be nice. "I hardly ever get into fights with my friends," Judy now says with pride, "because we both usually like the exact same things and we do the exact same things." Between nine and ten, differences and disagreements have evaporated into "the exact same things."

Indeed, liking and doing the exact same things seems to protect Judy from the danger of feeling strong feelings that she knows have the potential to disrupt and destroy relationships. The sense of reaching a crisis point with her friends or her family and the fear that someone might leave or "move out" lead Judy to struggle between holding onto her embodied feelings and the evidence of her senses and letting go for the sake of "relationships." Her feelings make her vulnerable or open to the pleasure and pain of relationships, something Judy seems to both crave and fear.

This sense of a hovering but ambiguous danger surfaces as Judy struggles to know what she feels, particularly when she tells her interviewer about an experience she can't quite fully recall, although, she remembers, "it was something dangerous":

[My friend and I] were deciding whether or not to do something and I don't know, it might have been, I guess it was kind of dangerous, because both of us were not sure whether to do it or not.
You can't remember what it was?
No, I have a short memory. It was recently, too. And so we finally decided not to do it, because we thought we really didn't need to do this thing, which was dangerous, so we just better not. We were just doing it to see if it was fun or something and decided against it.

As her memory gradually returns and the provocative "it" begins to take shape, Judy explains that she and her friend

found this thing that usually wouldn't be in the woods . . . It was metal or something, like a machine or something, but I can't remember what. But it was really tall and really big. And there was like an engine in it, and it was really tall. It wasn't a tractor or anything . . . it looked like there were sharp edges or something. It was more than that, but what else I can't remember.

While Judy cannot remember exactly what the thing was—"it's vague," she says—she and her friend, she recalls, were both afraid of "hav[ing] ourselves hurt" and also attracted to it, wanted to play on it and try to start it up, because "it sounded like really fun." "Excited at first," they also had an embodied, visceral response to the danger inherent in the situation and so they decided to "back off."

In response to eight different questions about this experience, Judy speaks of not wanting to get hurt by playing on "the thing"— she might, for instance, "break a leg." She is puzzled by her choice to speak of this situation in response to her interviewer's question about a time when she experienced conflict. "I kind of already knew that [I wasn't supposed to do something that could hurt me]," she says, "so it was kind of obvious." But what Judy seems to struggle with is the attraction she feels to powerful, pleasurable experiences—like this thing that was big and tall, that she could "start up," that promised to be fun to play on—even while she knows that such things are said to be dangerous for girls, that she should "back off" and go home where she will be safe.

As Judy speaks of vague dangers, dangers to her body that are both exciting and frightening, and begins to concentrate on the consequences of acting on impulse, she seems to back off from her strong feelings and rely more on her developing cognitive powers, powers that allow her to "pay . . . attention" and learn differently than she has in the past. And her interviewer backs off as well. This incipient split between cognition and emotion, thought and feeling, seem to help Judy understand and make sense of the world around her, but, as she herself says, this split distances her from her fear (and her attraction) and makes it impossible for her to remember what, in some sense, she knows. As Judy responds to the dangers of feeling her strong feelings by disconnecting from her bodily knowing, and as she associates knowing only with her intellect, with what goes on in her head, she loses the ground of felt experience and begins to talk *about*, rather than to speak, her feelings. As her interview comes to a close, we hear the profound consequences of this loss when Judy confesses to her interviewer, "I don't know what's wrong here, I keep stuttering here, it was tough . . . I knew what the question was, but as soon as you asked me my mind went blank." Judy's dissociation, along with her ability to think in new ways, is evident as Judy knows and then experiences her mind go blank.

While the phrase "I don't know" suggested the ground of Judy's knowledge was shifting at ten, eleven-year-old Judy punctuates her interview with the phrase "I mean." As Elizabeth Debold notes, "to mean," according to the *Oxford English Dictionary*, comes from the Old High German, to have in mind, to intend, to signify, to make known. The repeated tap of "I mean" in the patter of Judy's speech seems to indicate her desire to convey her thoughts, her intellect, her feelings, to her interviewer.

And indeed, this year Judy's voice sounds remarkably mature, almost self-consciously rehearsed, except on those occasions when her feelings enter the dialogue with her interviewer. In these moments Judy's voice shifts to reveal a different, less polished, uncertain Judy grappling for words to explain her experience. As her relationship with what she knows in her body changes, Judy seems to struggle to hold her thoughts and feelings together.

Although Judy at eleven does not talk about physical changes in her body, early in her interview she hints at the relationship between such changes in her body and change in her world. Asked what stands out for her in the past year, Judy says, "Well, this was the first year that I started meeting boys, just recently, because someone had a boy/girl party, and I started meeting boys." The category "boys" represents a new kind of person in Judy's world: a category set apart from all of the boys she has known, including her brother. Yet boys are not the center of Judy's life. Judy continues to struggle with the divisions she experiences in her family relationships.

"Lots of decisions are really simple things," Judy begins when her interviewer asks her about a time when she had to make a decision but didn't know what she should do. But the decision Judy chooses to talk about is anything but simple. "My parents are divorced and like next year I have a choice of which one to live with," she explains, "and I have just been thinking over that a lot recently. I haven't really decided. I have kind of made up my mind to stay here [with my mom]."

Judy's struggle to hold thoughts and feelings together resurfaces as she describes her conflict. Faced with a dilemma of feelings because "I would love to go be with [my dad] all the time, but I also love to be with my mom all the time," Judy tries to reason her way to a decision: "I think I'm getting a really good education and education means a lot to me now. And I like where I live, where my mom lives, and I like the neighborhood . . . and I like the way I am living right now." Judy tries to step back from what she loves and likes to evaluate these feelings against the standard of "the general, typical life of a child," which means "just growing up with a regular family and like I think I would get a regular family at my dad's, because there are two parents, they are a two-parent family with already two kids."

This concept of a "regular family" in which one lives the "general, typical life of a child" negates Judy's experience of loving and liking where she is living—with her mom—and blankets the complex feelings she has for all of the people to whom she is related—Fred, mother, father, brother, stepmother, and now two half-sisters. Alongside the ideal of a typical family are her feelings that "I like it better here just because it's regular and I'm used to it and also there I am lonely for the things I do, and, like, here I can do almost anything, I have almost any kind of freedom." Here Judy turns the word "regular" in another direction, indicating her own experiences of day-to-day living rather than cultural norms of "family."

Perhaps picking up that regular can mean both what Judy feels and knows and what others say ought to be, her interviewer asks her: "How did *you* feel about this issue?" "I don't know," Judy begins with uncertainty, "I feel like either my mom or my dad will feel bad, whichever decision I make." What Judy "feels" is her anticipation of her *parents'* feelings, and as she continues, she seems to move further and further away from her own feelings until she ends with a statement which sounds almost banal:

My dad . . . would feel bad, because he would feel like I really didn't want to live with him, but it wouldn't be that big a thing if I left my mom instead of staying with my mom, just the feelings, I think, would be different towards the parent, my parents, and it's a hard decision to make. It's like whatever I do, it depends a lot on my future.

Judy does not mention either her feelings or her mother's feelings, but "the feelings." In fact, her readiness to distance herself from or cover over her feelings is evident when she says "it wouldn't be that big a thing if I left my mom." Judy does not speak about her own sadness or love or fear or pain, or even her desire to leave. Instead she gives priority to her father's feelings and overrides her feelings with thoughts—"just the feelings, I think, would be different." And yet, on one level, Judy seems to know what she is doing and feeling. Judy thinks about and talks from her feelings—her loving and liking being with her mom—but she buries more difficult feelings under a lifeless "it": "It wouldn't be that big a thing . . . it's a hard decision to make . . . it depends a lot on my future." By filtering her feelings and desires through her thoughts and by objectifying herself and her knowledge of relationships, Judy moves away from what she feels and knows and instead moves to justify this separation.

And yet, we notice that Judy is, in fact, doing what she wants, though she finds this hard to explain: "I am thinking I am pretty much going to stay here . . . I think I'd be just as happy there, but it's hard to explain. I just think like this is what I want to do, so I think just me wanting to do this makes it right, because there is no really wrong answer unless I make it wrong." Judy struggles not to make what feels right, wrong—staying with her mom, staying with her regular life, though not having a regular family. In the face of this impasse between what she feels and what others say, Judy resists, and the intensity of her resistance consumes her at all hours:

> So here I am learning to think things through more and think about what I'm doing, and I think at night, and I always think about things and before I'd just go to sleep. And now I think about things to do and I think about the day and my future and my past and like a circle of those kinds of things.
>
> *Does it keep you up?*
>
> It keeps me up, like sometimes I'll do that when I can't fall asleep but sometimes I will keep thinking and keep thinking and I will look at the clock and it will be like 11 o'clock and like I'm "Oh, boy," because I like getting in bed by 9 or 9:30. So I need a lot of sleep.

The need to lie awake in bed late at night to think things through for herself becomes clearer when eleven-year-old Judy begins to speak about herself and her feelings in what sound like her parents' voices: she and her brother and sister are "troublemakers," "childish" for fighting. When Judy and her mother disagree and Judy "gets really mad," her mother tells her she has "a bad attitude" and grounds her. Sent to her room, Judy is left to sort out her feelings alone, and in her remorse thinks, "If I had just kept my mouth shut and didn't say anything . . . that would have been the end of it." Though Judy says "in my mind I was still angry," she realizes it's better not to "say anything" since when her mother "makes up her mind, there is no use arguing against it." Taking in what her mother is saying—that she is a "troublemaker," "childish," someone with "a bad attitude"—Judy struggles to hold onto and name what she feels, that "in my mind I was still angry." Judy learns to stop speaking in an attempt to hold onto her anger and also to avoid accusations and prevent further trouble. Instead, she lies awake at night thinking "about the day and my future and my past and like a circle of those kinds of things."

In school, as well as at home, Judy struggles to stay with the feelings "in my mind" in the face of what she is taking in—the voices of others and the awareness of what happens when she speaks. We notice how closely she follows these voices, how carefully she reads what others do. Judy notices, for example, how other girls in her class respond when "some high school student will come to talk to us [in assembly]." They "won't like the subject so they will look down," she explains. "And it's like sometimes like a couple of people use sign language." While Judy may agree with these girls that "something is wrong" with the speakers, she argues at least for the appearance of interest: "I think that you should at least show the people consideration . . . I mean, how would you feel if you were standing up there and you wrote something that was really good . . . and no one else is listening? I mean, I would feel like really awful." Judy considers her classmates "rude" and "selfish" for not "think[ing] about anyone else but themselves." But she also knows these girls, like her, "don't really want to hear it," and that they are responding indirectly to feelings and opinions she knows from experience cannot easily be said.

As a result, Judy finds herself in an uncomfortable situation when her friends confront her on her feigned interest. They will often ask, "'You actually liked that?' or something, or . . . everyone will say like, 'That was boring, did you listen to it?' and you'd be like, 'Oh, I didn't listen to it' and sometimes it makes you feel better if you really don't listen to it, instead of just saying that." Judy, struggling not to be rude and selfish but also to be honest, now finds herself caught between conventions of nice behavior and her real feelings, a place where truth, again, becomes slippery: "I mean . . . if someone asks me like, 'Wasn't that boring?' I mean I won't really answer because I don't want to say, I don't want to have people go, 'Ugh! You liked that?' But I mean I just won't say 'No.' I mean some people can call that lying, but if you don't answer, I don't think it is really lying." In order not to lie or to be made fun of, Judy finds herself sheltering her feelings and her opinion from her friends and, in turn, echoing her mother, explaining away her friends' actions as just their "bad attitude": "I mean they start out . . . with a bad attitude about it, so all during the thing they have a bad attitude about it . . . If they start out saying, 'Oh, this is something that really might be good,' then the whole thing will be really good."

Thus Judy continues to struggle with the interface between what is true and what is false, what is right and what is wrong in relationships; she is caught, it seems, by the difference between relationships in which people are "being really interested" and those in which "even if they don't enjoy it, I mean they should at least look interested." As relational reality for Judy often seems a matter of "attitude" rather than experience, the ground of Judy's knowledge—her thoughts and feelings in relationship—is in danger of giving way.

Two years later, Judy's interviewer notes how "sad" Judy looks. Judy's voice at thirteen is deep and resonant and often carries her sadness. Judy's speech is now riddled with the phrases "I don't know"—the bellwether of dissociation—and "I mean"—a sign of her struggle to connect herself with knowing, her mind with relationship. Taking the greater length of this eighth grade interview into account, Judy says "I don't know" nearly six times more often and prefaces her thoughts and feelings with "I mean" nearly twice as often as she did two years earlier.

Judy's psychological acuity remains apparent, however, as she recalls the list of events that led to everything blowing up at her father's the past summer:

> It was really tense like the whole summer because everyone was trying to be extra special nice to people, like the whole time, my stepmother, I was trying to be really nice to her, because we all feel awkward. And by the end, we were so tired of being nice, that everything blew up and we got in like huge fights.

Her stepmother, Judy explains, "is sort of scared about what [me and my brother] are able to do, because she has never had older children before," so Judy and her brother had "to get used to different house rules . . . we had to adjust" to less freedom. Judy also "felt weird" about bringing friends to the house "because I didn't feel like it was my house." Her father then "had a total spaz" when she "asked him for $5.50 to go to a movie with my friend." Judy and her brother were expected to watch her little half-sisters without notice and "a three-year-old and five-year-old can really get on your nerves after a while." Their stepmother, moreover, never seemed to say "thank you" or appreciate the attempts Judy and her brother made to help out. All this came to a head when, one night at dinner, her eight-year-old sister refused to eat her vegetables. But, Judy says knowingly, "the whole thing was not about the carrots, it was just about everything else, and so they got into a huge argument . . . and after that nothing seemed to be going right . . . I don't know."

Judy knows what led to her stepmother "crying in her bedroom and I was crying in my bedroom and my sister was crying in her bedroom and my dad was going around trying to fix everything . . . and he has no idea what's going on. He's totally lost." She is aware of feelings that run counter to voices that tell her to be "extra special nice": her anger at her stepmother, her frustration with her half-sisters, her dismay at her father's being "so icky about things." The pressure she felt (and we presume the others also felt) to be nice led them to get "a little stressed out . . . we couldn't keep it in any longer." Judy knows what Noura knows: if you keep feelings in, they become overwhelming and explode.

When her interviewer asks Judy, "Is there any way you could find to speak about the things so that they didn't, you know, get all bent out of shape and then blow up at the end?" Judy's throat tightens and her voice becomes thick with emotion. "I would feel so uncomfortable doing that. Like even saying anything that bothered me. I'd feel really bad," she explains, tears welling in her eyes, "I know what you're asking, but I don't know, I am trying to think." Struggling to think what she is feeling and to respond to the connection she feels with the question and with the woman who asks the question, Judy tries to explain: "You can't make someone change for you . . . I wouldn't want to ask [my stepmother] to be someone else or anything." And with this, Judy falters, knowing what her interviewer is asking and feeling the gap between what she wants and what seems possible for her. "I don't think, I mean, this sounds—I mean, if I was an outsider looking in, I would probably think they should just talk about it, that would be the best thing. But that's not even on my list." "Why?" her interviewer persists:

> I don't know, because I don't—I don't know. I mean, I do know. I just like—I can't explain it. I don't know what, how to put it into words.
> *What does it feel like? or what does it look like?*
> I don't know, it's just like if—I don't know, it's like, I don't know, I can't even begin to explain it, because I don't even know if I know what it is. So I can't really explain it. Because I don't know. I don't even know like in my brain or in my heart, what I am really feeling. I mean I don't know if it's pain or upsetness or sad—I don't know.

Judy is so close to knowing what she is feeling, even as she struggles to locate her feelings "in my brain or in my heart." As Judy, in response to the woman sitting with her, moves into relationship with herself, with what she knows and how she feels, Judy also knows what happens when she expresses feelings of "pain or upsetness or sad[ness]" to her stepmother or her father. Expressing what she feels disrupts the family scene others seem invested in maintaining. The interviewer's invitation to Judy to connect with her feelings reveals the disconnections Judy feels and her experience of relational impasse:

> I'm trying to think. Just because of the fact of we don't really, I'm not sure, I don't know. It's just—I mean, I don't really know why. It's just like a feeling I have, that I don't really want to talk about this. I can't really explain why though. Just because of the fact that we don't really know her. Especially, it's not really just [my stepmother], it's my dad, too. I mean, we want to make our vacation as good as it can be, and to do something like that might just bring it down. I don't know, it would just sort of ruin the whole point of a vacation with my father. So, I sort of avoid that and put it aside and don't worry about that, because this is our only time together.

Though she says, "this is our only time together," Judy and her family are not really together. Covering over her feelings for the sake of a good vacation, Judy cannot come to know her stepmother or her father, and they, in turn, are shielded from her. Their only genuine connections seem to be in those moments where their feelings, out of relationship, become overwhelming and out of control, and therefore destructive. And as a result, one week before they are to go back to their father's for Thanksgiving, Judy anticipates a painful struggle and her sister is "sort of scared to go."

Judy speaks of her choice to "avoid . . . and put . . . aside" her bad feelings as she attempts "not to be depressed for the rest of my life" like her brother seems to be.[3] And yet we feel the opposite is happening—by not speaking her sadness, Judy is in danger of being depressed. Trying not to be "bothered" or "never really think" about the steady stream of antagonism between her parents, Judy attempts to hold the bad feelings away from herself and not to feel her pain or her upsetness or her sadness but instead to silence herself. "Never mind," Judy says to her interviewer, in essence, articulating this disconnection and dismissing what she has just explained. "I just talk too much."

For Judy at thirteen, feeling and knowing have become "two different things":

The knowing sort of comes from the brain, like your intelligence part. Like your smartness, your brightness, your education part, and your feeling is something that it doesn't matter if you have an education or not, it's just like something that you can't put into words. That you can't really explain, but it's not, I don't know, it's just like a deeper sort of knowing than intelligence knowing. Because intelligence tells you "no," "bad," "yes," "good," and all that.

In referring to this "deeper sort of knowing," Judy says, "I am pointing to my stomach," which seems to be the bodily center of this knowing feeling. "Whenever I feel like something bad is going to happen or feel scared or something awful, I can feel it in my stomach . . . a gut feeling that you are not doing something right

136

or you are doing something that you don't really care about . . . whether it's right or wrong." This feeling, Judy continues, "is an internal sort of knowing, that it just has to do with like not your brain but more your mind":

A mind sort of has your real thoughts and a brain sort of has the intelligence . . . what you learn in school, like all that sort of thing, physics, and statistics and all that, but your mind is sort of associated with your heart and your soul and your internal feeling and your real feelings.

Yet, while "no one else can really affect . . . the feelings that you've had . . . because someone can't say you don't feel this, you do." People, Judy explains, "can control what they're teaching you and say 'This is right and this is wrong,' that's control like into your brain. But the feeling is just with you; [the feeling] can't be changed by someone else who wants it to be this way. It can't be changed by saying 'No, this is wrong, this is right, this is wrong.'" "Some people can . . . name lots of different things any different way, like you can name something 'innocence,' and you can name this 'wrong,' and that's the way someone put it into my head." Yet, she continues, "it still comes out inside of you the same way."

As Judy describes the very process of knowing what she knows through her feelings described by other names or covered over with what "people put . . . into my head," she finds herself "struggling for words that I don't even know exist, or my feelings that I can't even say, something like that, I don't know." But Judy does know that this has happened to her, that "when we grow up we sort of forget about our mind and we are behind . . . So that like right now, when I am trying to explain things I'm not familiar with [the mind], because I forgot about that part of me, so it is too hard to put into words." In an extraordinary moment, Judy begins to think and feel her way through her experiences and, in the process, comes to her own theory of development:

I think that maybe really young children have . . . [mind] more than anyone else because I don't know, they don't have much of a brain . . . and I think that's when you get all your mind stuff because that's the only thing you really have then because then you . . . transform some of the mind things to the brain, so then that starts to evolve and that's sort of like the way you are brought up. It goes into your brain. And I think that after a while, you just sort of forget your mind, because everything is being shoved at you into your brain.

"I mean," Judy continues, using the very language that signifies her own loss and forgetting, "it's sort of like something that happens gradually. And I mean, I don't know, it's sort of, I mean some people, I mean, everyone has it, a little of it, but they can't . . . really acknowledge what it is. I mean, they just know it's there." Working through the life-span, Judy retraces her own experience of how "you just sort of forget your mind":

> Like little babies, they can't understand . . . they have . . . really nothing, because they're just starting, but then . . . by like seven . . . they have the most mind, but they are starting to lose it actually.

With "what you learn in school" and all that's "shoved at you into your brain," Judy explains,

> people seem to just like sort of gradually forget about that and then just worry about the sums and totals of checks and stuff, and it is sort of stagnant . . . I mean, it's sort of just like they have other things on their mind and they don't want to worry about [the feeling] . . . or maybe perhaps that since they don't know what it is, they don't want to have to worry about it . . . they don't really acknowledge the fact that they don't really understand it. But they always sort of have it.

Shifting to speak of the "it" as she traces how people lose their minds, Judy reads into the future, to the end of life: "When you start to realize that you are going to be dying soon, I think that perhaps then some people start to get it back, because they are sort of sick and tired of all that brain stuff . . . maybe that's why grandparents get along so good with grandchildren, because they're really old and they're really young and they sort of connect."

In a poignant moment, Judy describes "my grandfather, I really

respect him . . . he has a lot of knowledge . . . in his stomach . . .
I mean, he has real feelings, he understands things easily." Yet, Judy
watches from the periphery as this man who "understand[s] . . .
people, the inside of them . . . the inside of their feelings," goes on
a "trip during the summer" with "all his male grandchildren . . .
when they're about ten." Judy adds, "I have never been on a trip
because he takes his grandsons with him." Although Judy says that
she can "understand what probably was going on," she doesn't voice
any feelings about being left behind.

Judy does not draw out the implications of her experience with
her grandfather—his preferential treatment of his grandsons and
the seeming failure of this man, whom she describes as having "real
feelings" and who "understands people . . . the inside of their
feelings," to understand her feelings. But she does have a theory
about "why the earth isn't the greatest place to live." All this
shoving of things into the brain "sort of loses the beauty of things,"
she says. "Someone looks at like a sunrise or something and says
how like 'The sun goes through this.' Why can't people just accept
the beauty of it?" That felt appreciation of the beauty, Judy says, is
"sort of like your stomach. That's the sort of thing that makes you
think, it's sort of a mysterious sort of thing." Maybe, she wonders
aloud to the woman sitting with her, "people are turning to crime
because they forgot about the beauty in life":

> Maybe . . . a lot of people have lost that sort of beauty, because
> they have been shoving brain things at them and no one can
> really realize that sort of a feeling and then when they try and
> think about it, it's just so overwhelming because they have never
> been able to think about that, that part to put into words. I don't
> know.

Trying to hold onto the feeling herself, Judy, standing and looking
at a setting sun, finds herself "want[ing] to shake them and say,
'Look! Look how beautiful that is!'" While her own path of development places her well on her way to worrying "about the sums and
totals of checks," Judy still struggles to "accept and let it be beautiful."

Judy, at thirteen, speaks of a felt reality that is beginning to elude her—a reality that holds mind and body, thoughts and feelings, reason and passion, together. Mind, for Judy, connects with the original meanings of the word: with deepest and earliest memory, integrating feelings, perceiving and thinking, which arises out of intention and desire to embody mental life. Losing her mind to the voices shoved into her brain, Judy also covers over bodily desires and sexual feelings with romantic ideals. Talking about a friend who "goes out with guys" and "goes farther than most people would," whose behavior is, for this reason, "disgusting," Judy places herself squarely within the conventions of the romance story:

> Because no one, except for her, everyone wants a really good relationship with someone. I mean, we are like thirteen, but still you want to be romantic . . . That just made me, if I had done something like that, I would feel like total dirt and totally worthless and she's so proud of it. I just can't know how she did that. No one else would ever do that, because they don't—that's not romantic, that's just plain disgusting.

Like other feelings such as anger and "upsetness," Judy "cannot know" how her friend could feel sexual desire, cannot imagine having such feelings herself. Instead, Judy looks to romance for "a really good relationship with someone."

Judy thus describes her education as a process by which information is "shoved into your brain" and defines so-called reality as the way she ought to know and see the world. Aware that she is "forgetting" the reality of her feelings, Judy is concerned that she is losing something of great value. Wanting the "regular" family, wanting romance without sexuality, wanting to be the "exact same" as her friends, Judy feels the pressure of norms and conventions inside her brain, particularly those of feminine goodness, which, taken in, are creating ideas of reality that are at odds with her experiences of living as a feeling mind/body. The "deeper knowing" that Judy mentions, the embodied knowing that led her as a nine-year-old to "feel in her mind," has been overridden by voices and romances that have entered her brain.

Victoria: Building a Shield

The image of the perfect girl looms large for ten-year-old Victoria, who, upon offering a picture she drew of her family, describes her picture as "really horrible" and compares it to that of her classmate, who "is good at everything," who's "perfect at everything." "How does that make you feel?" her interviewer asks her. "Bad," Victoria replies.

In fact, Victoria's family picture is not perfect, nor is it pretty; drawn in pencil, a line of small drab stick-figures hug the bottom of the page: "That's my mom, that's my dad, that's my brother, that's my sister, that's my cat, that's my other cat, that's my dog, that's my boss, and that's my horse barn." "And where are you?" her interviewer wonders. "I didn't put me in this," Victoria replies. But if she were to put herself in her picture, Victoria explains, she would draw herself "with a horse" on the opposite end of the paper, far away from the others.

Victoria, who has a part-time job working at a stable—her "home away from home," a place where she often sleeps on the weekends—is self-reliant and straightforward but also, it seems, lonely, sad, and disillusioned with the people in her life. Animals "are better than humans," she tells her interviewer, "They're nicer . . . because [if] you tell them something, they don't get mad at you, and they listen to you." At home, Victoria doesn't feel listened to, but feels, she says, "like a sandwich" between her younger sister and older brother, who are "spoiled"—one is "a baby," she says, and one is "a boss." Victoria is the girl who describes herself and her two friends as "leftovers" in the cafeteria of school social life. At school "you get picked on a lot," she tells her interviewer. People "get mad" and "can pass [their feelings] on to someone else, and it will keep on going around so everyone can pick corners."

Though school is socially difficult, Victoria's disillusionment and anger focus in large part on what happens at home. On the surface Victoria lives the life of the "typical" child Judy so dreams about—a member of a white, middle-class family living in the suburbs, a father who is a judge, a mother who is, for the most part, a homemaker. But inside the privacy of her home things are quite different than they appear from the outside.

According to Victoria, her "bossy" brother is both careless and cruel; he "doesn't listen" to anybody, she says, and "even talks back" to their mother. Victoria's anger is palpable when she recalls how her brother let her dog out of the house one evening and it was hit by a car—"He was only a puppy too," she explains. "It was so sad." "I'm mad at him," Victoria then tells her interviewer, "everything he's had, a bird and a hamster . . . he got them all killed, so my mom doesn't let him get a dog or a cat . . . [He] used to hang [my cat] by its tail, wrap a rope around its tail, and hang it and stuff. And that's why my mom doesn't want him to have anything more like that."

Now that Victoria has been promised a new dog, she knows she "should" share with her brother—some things "are nice but not fair," she explains. But to be nice, Victoria would have to ignore her brother's irresponsible and cruel behavior; she would have to disregard what she knows he is capable of doing; she would have to put her dog in jeopardy. Standing firmly against the idea, she says, "I'm not going to share it with him." Though she is willing to go so far as to say her brother may "not realize" what he is doing, Victoria is unwilling to cover over his cruelty or bury her own strong feelings of sadness and anger.

"In some things," like with her brother's treatment of her cat, Victoria can count on her mother to agree with her and support her. But more often she must deal with her father, who "doesn't really say anything" when she complains and who, according to Victoria, sticks up for her "unbearable" brother. "I don't think it's right," Victoria tells her interviewer, referring to her father's loyalty to her brother. "Do you ever say anything?" her interviewer wonders. "Yeah," Victoria replies. "My dad just gets mad at me."

Victoria knows from her own experience that "everyone's different." She, herself, is very different from her father and her brother most of the time. She knows, also from experience, that while one person can "be aggravated by one thing . . . the other may . . . just overlook it." Knowing that people see things "looking at an angle,"

Victoria nonetheless refuses to change the angle of her own vision. Instead, she stays with what she feels and thinks, even in the face of her father's and her brother's wrath. "It's not wrong to say what you think," she tells her interviewer, and even when it is too risky to speak, "I can think it always in my head." At such times, feelings move out of Victoria's body and into her head.

A year later Victoria, now eleven, describes her life: "I work at a stable, and I've worked there like every weekend for a long time now. And, I have a brother and a sister, and, I hate—my brother is a real jerk . . . He tries to boss you around, like my mom will tell him to empty the dishwasher and he'll go and tell *you* [to do] it. Or he will say, 'Victoria, I'm gonna beat you up,' and I'll say, 'Go ahead,' and he'll do it, and for no reason. He's just too wild, just kind of like a bully."

Her brother, who is thirteen, is now, Victoria says, "really tall"— "he's bigger than my dad." Daunted by her brother's rapid growth, afraid of what he is now capable of, Victoria does not feel protected from him:

> My mom told us to clean up the living room, including my dad. My brother took a towel he picked up from the floor snapping it at me, just kidding, so I sat down and my dad grabbed me by my wrist, he didn't hurt me or anything, he just grabbed me and pulled me up and said clean up this living room now. And he sat back down. And then I said, "Dad, why aren't you listening to me?" And he said, "Clean up this room now." And I started screaming, "Will you listen to what happened?" And he goes, "Clean up this living room now!" And so then he sent me to my room because I wouldn't do it and five minutes later he came up and said go clean up the living room and then come up here. But he would not listen to me and when I explained it to my mom she agreed . . . it's just like she is always on my side, it seems to me . . . she agreed that he should have listened because he had no right to grab me and pull me across the room when it was my brother's fault.

Victoria is not a passive player in such dramas—she screams to be heard, she refuses to do what she is ordered, she complains to the one person in the house who will listen. But though her mother "is always on my side" and aligns with her in private, Victoria notices that her mother often agrees with her father "when he's in the room." She senses why this is so as she ponders the differences in power between her father and mother. Her father, she explains, "knows exactly how much money [my mom] has, but [my mom] doesn't know how much money he has." Listening and watching her parents' stormy relationship, Victoria begins to worry that if they were to get a divorce, her mother would have no money. Since her mother "worked and made her own money" before her parents were married but now stays home, she would have no job "to fall back on."

Victoria's concern over the dissolution of her parents' marriage grows as she watches her mother and father play, in her words, "Mr. and Mrs. Shock," where they say things they don't mean just to upset each other, so that "now," Victoria says, "I don't know what to believe." Aligning herself with her mother, Victoria sees the effect these conversations have. "He mentally drains her," Victoria says, referring, as an example, to her father threatening one minute to sell the house because they have no money, and then the next assuring them that they have plenty of money—"We're not sure whether or not he was just saying it," Victoria explains, "or he really meant that we had to do something."

Victoria worries so much because she knows in vivid detail what is going on between her parents. "[My mom] doesn't keep [her thoughts and feelings] a secret from me," she says, but tells Victoria "what they were fighting about or how much money she's got and what would happen if they got a divorce or something." Allowed to see inside her parents' conflicts through her mother's eyes, Victoria is especially sensitive to the differences between what her mother and father do and say in public and what her mother feels and speaks about in private. Victoria aligns herself with her mother's view and notes with annoyance the polite games her father plays when, for example, he says to her mother every night: "Dinner was the best you've ever made." "He always says that no matter what," she says, "if it's awful or anything . . . and he makes it so exaggerated, it kind of like drives me crazy . . . I guess he wants to please her, but it drives her crazy, too."

Sensitive to the differences in power in her house associated with gender and money, Victoria begins to pick up these differences elsewhere in her life—she notices that the woman she works for part-time "likes boys better than girls," for example, and has been proving her preference by paying her less than the boys she works with. When Victoria, in anger, tells her mother, her mother "agreed that that was unfair but we couldn't really do anything about it." Again Victoria is confronted with the different angles of her parents' visions: "My dad says . . . she did it by accident, she didn't mean to and my mom agrees with me that she did it on purpose."

Victoria struggles to stay with what she knows from experience in the midst of these different constructions of psychological and social reality. The woman who interviews her seems really interested in what Victoria knows. And it may be her interest and responsiveness, her willingness to listen, that leads Victoria to speak out about the way power differences between women and men literally affect the renaming of her mother and, in Victoria's words, "drain her potential."

At the beginning of the interview you mentioned that referring to your mother and father as Mr. and Mrs. [Hanson] is unfair. Do you want to explain that to me?
Because it always says Mr. and Mrs. [Jim Hanson] and it's like, what about the woman, she's here too. And then it says, Mrs. and then not her name but my dad's name, Mrs. [Jim Hanson]. But it never says Mrs. Elaine or Ms. Elaine, something like that, her name, it just says Mrs. and then his name, and that's unfair because it makes it look like she's not even there.
Why does that bother you?
Well, because, like my mother, she's good and she's smart and she's understanding, but like everything about these names and stuff is kind of draining her, draining her potential and stuff.
Why because of the name?
Just because, because like everything always points to the man, like the man is most important and the woman is not even alive

. . . to put it that way, the men are the most important people. Just say it. Like God, this is not right!

Victoria, passionately invested in what she feels and thinks, sees and questions the consequences of a societal norm that suggests, because of "like everything about these names and stuff," her mother is less than who she could be, who, according to convention, "is not even alive." Yet Victoria seems caught between her personal knowledge of her mother—her own relational experiences of her mother as "good," "smart," and "understanding"—and a growing awareness that "if [her parents] got a divorce and [her mother] had to work, no one would know who she was." There is no public record of what Victoria and her mother know to be true privately; this knowledge, it appears, is not welcomed in the world and so it is not held up in the world—even by her mother. Perhaps, then, things aren't what they seem. What can it mean that the person with whom she has felt the strongest bond and with whom she has placed the greatest trust and value is made to "look like she's not even there"? What does it mean that her mother goes along with this construction of herself—says one thing in private and then says something different in public? What really can Victoria believe in, who can she trust on an emotional level?

Speaking up, Victoria observes, can be dangerous and disruptive. When she speaks directly and openly about what she sees and hears, her father warns her—and her mother, at least publicly, agrees— that "people are going to think you are dumb when you say that" or that "people don't appreciate you telling them that; it makes you look stupid." Struggling to remain visible and public when others seem to want her to go unnoticed and unheard, Victoria begins to feel pressure to not know what she knows, or at least not to say it. And so like Jessie in fifth grade, who carefully chooses when to stay with her feelings and speak and when to "pretend" to "agree to be nice," and like many other girls in this study, Victoria struggles to authorize her thoughts and give voice to what she knows in the face of pressure to be polite, presentable, good, and nice.

Victoria strains to understand all the layers of meaning and innuendo in what is being said by those around her, as she tries to anticipate how what she says will be heard and responded to and tries to decipher how people really feel beneath the nice things they say to each other. When her mother talks with her, confides in her, assures her, agrees with her in private, and then in public supports her father, Victoria feels betrayed and all alone. When her father so exaggerates his compliments that they have no meaning and when her parents, rather than say what they feel and want, play Mr. and Mrs. Shock, Victoria feels a little "crazy." In the face of these radical disconnections, eleven-year-old Victoria tries desperately to be "honest" and "trustworthy" with her family and also to stay in relationship with what she knows to be true from experience. But in this judge's family there are no rules of evidence, there is nothing she can count on, and no one who is reliable. And so when Victoria says in the beginning of her interview this year, "I don't know what to believe," we have a sense that her "confusion" is, in fact, a stunningly clear and astute commentary on her relational experiences.

A year later Victoria, now twelve and in the sixth grade, struggles to control and to contain her feelings. If the underworld and the surface appearance of relationships are so radically different, perhaps it makes sense to align with the world everyone else sees—at least she will not be alone, at least she will have witnesses. But in Victoria's life, by her account, she cannot expect loyalty—she will remain alone since the witness, most often her mother, will not speak publicly in her defense. Perhaps it is this realization that accounts for the change in Victoria this year, since her anger and sadness of the year before seem now transformed into a deep-seated bitterness and despair. "I think life stinks," she tells her interviewer, "My life stinks."

People who can't rely on other people, Victoria explains, "are people in trouble." And this year, it seems, Victoria is a person in trouble. Either the physical violence in her family has escalated or Victoria, in her attempt to hold on, has decided to speak about her experiences more openly. Victoria seems confused, however, about how to respond, how to feel and think about what is happening to her—at times protesting, at times denying the violence, at times hating, at times idealizing the perpetrators. Talking about a time when she accidentally broke something, for example, Victoria denies she has ever been "beaten" even while she introduces the word and imagines in detail the experience of being hit by her father: "I was kind of surprised and upset and afraid of being yelled at. Even though I hadn't been hit for a long time, I mean I was never beaten or anything, but I used to get spanked, so I kept thinking of his hand coming down on me."

And even though Victoria describes in detail how threatening her fourteen-year-old brother and his friends have become—"He has the worst kind of friends . . . One . . . has been in jail . . . for breaking a leg of a girl when he . . . threw her over a fence," and "[my brother] took one of my Reeboks and . . . started hitting me with it, on my leg and I was screaming"—her description of abuse turns suddenly to idealization as she tells her interviewer, "I always used to try to please my older brother, he is like my god." As Victoria insists over and over that no one is listening to her—"Whenever I am at home all my protests and all my screams and all my fits just go into deaf ears"—and as she follows scene after scene of intrusion and violence with denial and justification, we know something is terribly wrong.

If Victoria feels the physical pain of being in violent relationships, she continues to feel the emotional pain when her mother turns away. In disgust, she watches the relationship between her mother and her brother develop—as her mother attempts to set boundaries and rules for him, "he just talks my mom out of everything," including being with Victoria. The family story her mother hands down to Victoria further distances her from her mother and brother's relationship: "He's the first . . . he has always been really obnoxious . . . even when I was a baby, the only time she spent with me was when she was feeding me, even at night when I was sick, as long as he was awake he wouldn't let her near me, because he was really jealous all the time." Victoria feels her mother's absence even when she is most needy. Though she sees her brother as the cause of her mother's absence, she also sees her mother giving in to her brother's demands.

This year Victoria says that when her brother hits her, her mother says, "Well you deserved it," in essence treating Victoria as she, herself, is treated. "Life is not fair," Victoria concludes, echoing the words her mother so often says to her, "It is lucky." From Victoria's vantage point, where being "outspoken . . . has got me in trouble" and where "whenever I say something it goes in just deaf ears," it truly seems foolish to depend on people. As a result, Victoria says, "I don't care . . . The only person you can rely on is yourself." "There is a couple of people that I really trust that I will tell anything to in this world," she adds, "but most of them are dogs."

The bitter disillusionment and internal division we heard in Victoria at eleven remains acute for her at twelve. Her anger and mistrust of her brother has grown into intense hate as he continues to intrude on her life. "He has learned how to open up my diary," she tells her interviewer. "He has learned the combination." His intrusions begin to have sexual overtones when Victoria, now at the edge of young womanhood, complains that "he's learned how to open my door, so I'll be in the middle of doing something or I will be changing or something and he will just come in with one of his friends." Her brother's constant trespassing and voyeurism on Victoria's private life leads her to withdraw, physically and emotionally. "I only ask for peace and to be left alone," she tells her interviewer, "I just want to be private and to be left alone."

But Victoria, angry and hurt, longs for relationships that are authentic and trustworthy. Real friends, she says, "need to be able to trust each other and they need to be able to be loyal and stick up for them no matter what. [You need] to be able to tell them your feelings and not to have to worry about them going and telling someone else or showing them something." Though she has felt betrayed at home, she holds out hope for loyalty and cherishes her few "best friends" who "always listen to everything I say real carefully."

Still vulnerable, still open to feeling pleasure as well as anger and sadness, Victoria is nonetheless wary. Looking with clear, sharp eyes at the people around her, she concludes that none of them are perfect "obviously." In a sarcastic voice, she explains the changes in her life. "I was," she explains, "an idealistic child." "I have always tried to get good grades and do just what my mommy and daddy wanted me to do and if I got yelled at that means that I wasn't doing, I wasn't being perfect, which upset me . . . Now I do things to please me and not my parents . . . and if they yell at me I don't really care because they are not perfect either, obviously."

For Victoria, realizing she could please herself came as a revelation, something she learned quite unexpectedly from her music teacher, who said to her class after a concert: "You guys were wonderful . . . but I hope you did it to please yourself and not me." Now with three part-time jobs, proud and determined to buy her own clothes, unable to "stand . . . tak[ing] my dad's money," Victoria is claiming her "independence . . . my independence from everyone."

But "independence" in Victoria's mind is infused with many different meanings. It is a word passed down through generations of women—to her mother and, through her mother, to her:

> I am writing my autobiography now and my mom, I asked her if there was one family trait on her side of the family and she said there was, independence, because for the past five generations the women's husbands have been either like total alcoholics or they have not gotten along and the husband has walked out on them and she said that she thinks because of this the parents kind of teach them, their mothers kind of teach them to be independent towards men and I am just independent towards them.

But the underside of this story of independent women is another story—of duplicity and repetition—since why would each generation of women choose the same kind of man? Were these women not talking with their daughters? Warning them? Were they blind? Victoria's mother's experience with marriage explains this seemingly inevitable outcome, an outcome likely to happen to Victoria as well if she follows the same path of disconnection that, in her family, is called "independence." The complication of this story of independence is evident in Victoria's account of her mother's relationship with men: "I think [my mother] expected to marry the guy of her dreams and everything and have a happy life . . . My dad bought her chocolates and everything . . . [but] in a real person in life he is not like that at all. And so her life just hasn't turned out the way she has wanted it to . . . She has kind of shut out the world around her." As a result, Victoria says, "I don't blame her [for not listening to me, at times], her life is really terrible, I mean her life is worse than mine."

As Victoria sees it, her mother might have been able to listen to her and be happy if only she could have "married the man of her dreams." But when Victoria starts to write her mother's story—"what she regretted most in the past"—into her autobiography, her mother tells her to cover over the truth with a lie "in case my dad read it." Experiencing the duplicity, Victoria still wants what her mother once hoped for. Like in the romance novels she and her mother read, Victoria says, "I'm hoping some day I will fall in love with a man and we will be happy and live happily ever after." But, Victoria adds, hesitant not to make what she sees as her mother's mistake, "if it doesn't happen, I want one child, hopefully a girl, and I don't want to be married because I am not going to marry someone I don't love."

What Victoria longs for sounds only slightly different from the "idealistic" vision she had as a child, when she "used to believe in the fairy princess and happily ever afters." "I am related to the romance stuff," Victoria admits. And we hear this relationship when she describes the man she will love: "He is going to be at least six foot and have a beard and a mustache and he's going to be really nice and gentle and . . . the perfect prince. He is going to be rich, too. He's going to have money and it's all very strange." It is strange, it seems to us, to hear Victoria speak of her "independence" from everyone and yet hold firmly to her desire for a "perfect prince" who will, it seems, support her emotionally and economically.

Victoria's desires, though troublesome, are understandable—her hope for romantic love seems directly connected to the betrayals and losses she has felt; her expressed desire for independence seems connected to her disappointment and abuse in relationships, and to her fear of isolation and abandonment. Victoria's romantic ideal depends on her not knowing what she knows from her experience to be true—that "no one is perfect," that her "perfect prince" might well, "in a real person in life," turn out to be disgusting or an alcoholic like her father. But rather than take in the reality of her own anger and sadness at the frustration and violence that surrounds her and intrudes upon her and confuses her, Victoria, like her mother, who "shut out the world around her," longs to disconnect from this reality and take in the possibility of romance, crafted with the help of her mother and the novels they read. Claiming her "independence from everyone," Victoria thus tells a story of withdrawal from others to keep the pain of her relationships from hurting too much, and then covers her intense feelings of loss with a romantic ending. Perhaps to assure that what she knows and feels remains walled off from others' intrusion and violation Victoria says, "I try to build, it's kind of bad really to do it, but I try to build a little shield."

Two years later fourteen-year-old Victoria speaks with the same woman she has confided in for the past three years. Their relationship has grown. In fact, the year before Victoria had written to her interviewer for understanding and advice about her feelings. This year they greet each other in the small office that has become an interview room. Before turning on the tape recorder, they talk about how things are going for Victoria, how she has been feeling. However, when the interview begins—formally, publicly—Victoria becomes resistant and sarcastic:

Can you tell me something about your life during the past year?
Nothing's happened.
Nothing's happened? Anything? No? You are not going to talk about anything?
Nothing's happened.
You just told me a bunch of stuff?
Alright, my dad got married, that happened. I went out with a

bunch of scums, that happened. I went to work all summer long, that happened.

Trivializing their earlier conversation, Victoria begins to reveal in the here-and-now of the interview situation the vulnerability and mistrust she feels when what she has confided in private is now open to public scrutiny. The relationship between Victoria and her interviewer, tentative and honest in the preceding years, seems now choked by the interview questions, and Victoria, defensive and angry, dares the woman to stay with her in the presence of her self-proclaimed "craziness." If the interview is to go on, Victoria seems to have decided, she will play Mrs. Shock. The interview itself becomes a relational drama.

As Victoria throws out one provocative statement after another, we sense the depths of her sadness—her bitterness and despair. Relationships with guys—the "scums" she goes out with—are, she says,

like a little game you play. You know, you don't really care, and you sit there and say "I love you," and if they say they love you back, you know that means they want to go farther the next time they see you or whatever . . . Yah, it's a game. I mean it's like preparing you for the ultimate game which is like marriage, you know. The trick.

From what her mother told her, and then told her not to write in her autobiography, Victoria knows that her mother feels that she had been tricked into marrying her father. Marriage thus seems the ultimate trick in a long series of relational games. Although her parents now have divorced, Victoria, the incarnation of that marriage, also carries forward its radical separation between private feelings and public images; she feels disgust and disdain for the boys she goes out with and yet continues to "play for my image." Her emotional distance from the sexual relationships that she describes with boys, whom she deems worthy of her "dirty looks" but not her trust or true feelings, goes along with her fear that these boys have the power to make advances and then "dump" her, that they have the power to trick her.

Victoria is openly angry now at what she experiences as her mother's lies and betrayals—the "sweet" and nice public persona which conceals a private "bitchiness." Yet Victoria feels for the most part alone with what she has experienced in this relationship. Dismissing her father—speaking of him with disgust and disdain— she talks with corruscating bitterness and disappointment about her relationship with her mother:

> What annoys me about her is she's like really sweet [on the surface]. All my friends are like, "She's so sweet." The ones who spend a lot of time at my house [realize] she starts bitching at me, or she starts screaming at me for something or another. [The others] think she is really sweet, you know, "You have such a neat Mom."

Victoria's awareness of her mother's duplicity now seems joined with feelings of helplessness as she realizes how readily others are taken in by what she knows to be a surface. People who do not spend a lot of time at her house will not know the relational truth and thus will not understand or feel the grounds for her sadness and despair.

Victoria's aloneness also comes through this year as she speaks of her relationships with her friends. These friends tease and hit one another, they speak cruelly about one another, they categorize and judge one another according to the nature of their relationships with boys and their sexual behavior, they talk behind one another's backs and spread false rumors. Going down the list of her friends, Victoria says: "Donna likes someone, and Gina likes someone just to like someone, and Lucy is a major slut, she sleeps with anyone. Cloe is a slut, she sleeps with anyone, you know." As for herself, Victoria fears she will be called a lesbian—a girl who has "no emotion" for boys. Explaining herself, Victoria says, "I am in love with the idea of being in love. I want to be loved, you know, really, so much, that I'm in love with the idea of doing it."

Although Victoria imagines romantic love washing over her like a wave and carrying her into a place where she is loved, she does not expect this to happen to her. "I want to fall madly in love," she says, but "I don't think that will happen. I mean I'm not the lucky person, that will be the one in a million." In the face of her longing to be loved, she turns to self-help books: "I have read all about this," she explains to her interviewer, "the psychological impact of wanting to be loved, the little doctor books." And she recognizes herself and her family in what she reads. Because she is in love with the idea of being in love, she fears that she will "be stupid and go out and get pregnant when I'm seventeen because I think I'm madly in love." She connects the mistrust she feels for all but her best friends to the alcoholism she sees in her family and fears that because she too desires to "escape it all," she is "like the perfect person for alcoholism."

Victoria's hurt and anger and also her hope for genuine relationship repeatedly break the surface of her cynicism and despair, only to be overcome once again by her feelings of hopelessness—that what she most wants will never happen to her, that there is nothing that she can do to change things, that there is no one who can really help her, including the woman who is sitting with her and to whom she wrote. And yet she continues to wonder about the goodness in people: "How do you like view the good in people?" she asks:

> Like some people, when someone makes a mistake, they go, "Oh, it's a nice try." And other people, they go, "Gee, she was stupid for not getting that," you know . . . which is what I'm like. But some people are like, "Oh, nice try."

Victoria yearns for someone who will understand her, who will see that she is trying to be loved and liked despite her disclaimer that she does not care. Explaining herself, she says, "I had a distorted childhood . . . I don't care. I mean I know that a lot of people are a lot nicer than me. I'm just not a nice person . . . I'm spiteful and nasty." "Says who?" her interviewer asks. "Says me . . . I know what I'm like . . . I don't mean to, but I am . . . I hide it, but I am . . . I know a lot of people in my class don't like me . . . it's how you view me."

Victoria, a reader of self-help books, sees the connection between her "distorted childhood" and her not caring. When her interviewer asks about the connection between Victoria and her mother— "Aren't you doing the same thing that your mother did? Going out with or starting to have like dating relationships with people you don't like and respect?"—Victoria responds by differentiating herself from her mother, calling her mother "stupid" and "a slut" and then retracting these accusations as she begins to go underneath the labels into feelings that "are rather different," feelings that she cannot explain. Speaking of herself—of the fact that she is dating boys whom she describes as scums—Victoria says:

> Well, I know, but I'm not going to marry them. I mean I'm not stupid enough to marry them . . . My mother was a slut. No, actually she wasn't. She was stupid. No, not stupid. I just, I can't explain. My feelings for my mother are rather different.

Victoria in her effort to explain why her mother would have married a man she so disliked asks a series of emotionally difficult questions: was her mother a slut who would sleep with anyone, was she really tricked, or was she just stupid? And these questions are ultimately questions about herself as well. This year Victoria and her mother fight on a regular basis. Victoria's struggle is evident as she says, "You know, we fight a lot, but I still like her," and then backs away from this feeling: "We got in a fight one time too many . . . I learned my Mom was a bitch, that really changed a lot of things . . . because then I don't have to be nice to her anymore."

Giving full rein to her anger and disappointment in her relationships with women, Victoria calls her women teachers "phony" and "fake." Outwardly, they speak of fairness and strive to be "perfect" teachers. The reality that Victoria knows is that she feels treated unfairly, unloved, and left alone. "It's kind of my punishment in life," she says. When her interviewer asks, "Can you tell me about a time when something happened to you that was unfair?" Victoria answers: "Being born," and then adds sarcastically, "Does that count?"

Rejecting the possibility of relationship with this woman to whom she had written and who is now sitting with her, Victoria turns on her as well. The interview is "stupid," she says. The questions are stupid, and obvious: "like 'What's your name?' 'Victoria.' 'Why?' Like that. They're just, anyone with common sense would know." "I'm tired," Victoria says—suddenly vulnerable: "I didn't go to bed last night or the night before . . . When I close my eyes, I get the same nightmare back, you know." "What are you dreaming about?" her interviewer asks. "A lot of different things. Just having a lot of problems. I mean I go through stages. Usually, usually when I'm cold at night, I have nightmares. And it's been cold, so I start having nightmares again." Victoria is tired, she has been having nightmares, she has been having a lot of problems, it has been cold.

The coldness of Victoria's world is shocking. Throughout her interview, her experiences and stories read like a nightmare. Still playing Mrs. Shock, Victoria tells how her friend Lucy tried to run away. In doing so she refers matter-of-factly to rape, beatings, and suicide attempts. She tells of stolen credit cards, Lucy's mad dash to the airport, the last-minute discovery and capture. And she describes Lucy's suicide attempts and rapes in counterpoint to her own exhaustion and despair:

> If she wants to kill herself, she's going to do it herself. I was sleeping over at her house one night . . . and she wakes me up and she has like a razor blade at her wrist, and she's like, "I'm going to kill myself," and I'm like, "Don't kill yourself until morning, I'm really tired." And she was like, "No, I'm going to kill myself." "Lucy, promise you won't do anything tonight, I have to sleep, because I'm not awake." "I'm going to kill myself. I'm going to kill myself."

Speaking of Lucy, Victoria feels helpless, "not awake"; it seems that Lucy is trying to kill herself: "If she doesn't die from [suicide], she's going to die from AIDS . . . She is really strange. She is always getting raped, she has like a blade scratch like this because one of the guys she was making out with got mad at her or something, and so he, I don't know, he got mad at her, so he took a switchblade out in the car . . . She's also been pregnant already."

The interviewer struggles with how to respond to these stories of violence, violation, and despair. Victoria senses her uncertainty and discomfort; indeed, she plays to it, reminding her interviewer of her promise of confidentiality: "I was going to tell you [about Lucy running away]," she says. "You couldn't do anything anyway." In essence, she has put the woman sitting with her into the same position that she feels herself to be in: confronted with chilling realities, aware of the dangers women are in, and unable to take action to stop it.

Underneath the drama of relational violence, the depths of Victoria's pain and sadness seem clear. Through her stories about Lucy's suicide attempts and the "dash to freedom" on the part of this friend who is "psycho . . . just too strange . . . weird," Victoria points to what she herself seems most to fear and to long for: Lucy, she says, doesn't "trust anyone." She has been hurt and abused. She has learned "to duck when you're about to be slapped," to "say what you have to say" behind people's backs. Talking about Lucy allows Victoria to say, "I'm psycho too . . . I'm going crazy, I'm not kidding," without feeling herself to be too strange, too weird, too all alone.

Turning back to the question of the interview itself and the tape recorder, Victoria says that her friends "put me up to this . . . They told me I had to act really crazy to [convince you] that I'm going crazy." When the interviewer asks why she thinks that she is going crazy, Victoria says, "I don't know. I'm just not logical anymore. I think it is a logic thing . . . It is not appropriate to put on tape." Asked to explain ("Why, what do you mean?"), she goes on to voice the intensity of her anger: "I'm like, alright, [a guy] pisses me off, so . . . I tell them I'm going to castrate him. Or my brother gets me mad, and so I'm going to kill him. Not move away, I'm going to kill him. I mean violence . . . It's not normal . . . I am not acting myself."

The rage and violence that well up inside her do not feel normal to Victoria, do not feel like herself. The changes in herself are "not just development," she tells her interviewer, struggling to give words to what she is experiencing in herself:

> It's like different-minded. It's not like I am getting older and I understand things from a different point because I'm older. It's [that] I understand them because not only does the way I see things change, I don't know how to explain it . . . It's not crazy, like bad crazy, it's like good crazy, but it's not good crazy, it's just not me.

In her "craziness" Victoria "sees" a reality which should not be seen: that underneath sweetness, there is "bullshit," or "bitchiness"; that people who present themselves as fair and model perfection are unfair and imperfect and therefore "fake" and "just so phony." Victoria struggles to name what she experiences, to bring her feelings and her experiences into relationship with herself. And she wonders, is it "bad crazy" or "good crazy" to feel as angry as she now feels toward boys—toward her brother, her father, and the guys she goes out with? Is it like her or not like her to be so angry at her mother and to feel so betrayed and lied to by her?

Victoria knows with certainty that she has changed. She cannot not see the dark underside of the privileged world in which she is living, and yet she does not know if it is bad or good, crazy or not crazy, to comment "rudely" or to say what she hears and feels and thinks and sees. As though to underscore the bitterness she feels about her life, she pulls away the last remnants of pleasure when she tells her interviewer "I don't love . . . working at the horse barn anymore." "Now," she says, "I'm so sick of animals . . . they're so dirty and everything." "I'm just not myself," Victoria says again, "I'm messed up" but "I'm not confused."

Noura, Judy, and Victoria are involved in very different ways in a common struggle against losing something which feels essential: their voice, their mind, their self. Each girl describes fears and confusions which feel exhausting and potentially overwhelming, at the center of which is a relational problem: how to resist the pressures, internal and external, to let go of what they know through experience and take on images of women and stories about relationships which they know in some sense to be untrue and untrustworthy. And yet as girls reaching adolescence and experiencing changes in their bodies, in their feelings and thoughts, and in their relationships with others and with the world at large, they do not know whether or not they can still rely on what they feel and know—whether they can or whether others will take what they know from experience to be true.

As girls at the edge of adolescence gain the cognitive and emotional capacities to know the relational world in new ways—to bring to their understanding a new breadth of thought and depth of feeling as well as a capacity for abstraction and generalization— they begin to grasp the realities of relationships and of women's lives in new ways. In essence, they become capable of seeing the whole picture and also of learning how "people" speak of what is happening: the conventions, the explanations, and the justifications. What feels and seems unloving to girls is often called love; what feels and sounds mean or cruel in women is often covered by sweetness and called "sweet" or "nice." It becomes difficult for girls to listen and watch the relational world as they did in childhood and also to take on ways of seeing and speaking that are said to be true, or good, or at least not rude.

Seeing the framework for the first time—what is now commonly called "the social construction of reality"—and also feeling the power with which this framework or construction is enforced or held in place, girls pose genuine questions about love and power, truth and relationship. And their questions, if taken seriously, disturb the framework and disrupt the prevailing order of relationships. When their voices are muted or modulated, when their experience is denied, their reality questioned, their feelings explained away, girls describe a relational impasse—a sense of being unable to move forward in relation with others, a feeling of coming up against a wall.

The fears and confusion, the ambivalence and uncertainty, which many girls in our study give voice to seem to us not simply the natural consequences of the move from childhood into adolescence, as some might suggest, but also a sign of a truly disturbing and perplexing experience: a feeling of having to not know what one knows, of losing one's mind, of building a shield, an experience of losing voice and relationship.

We became aware of the wall girls face and their responses to the experience of relational impasse by listening to their voices and hearing their disillusionment and confusion, their sadness and their anger, but also their courage and their resistance to the pressures they feel from within and without not to feel what they feel or know what they know. One by one, these girls narrate their lives—what they see and hear, what they feel and think, and then over time their experience of anxiety and conflict when they find themselves in situations where it seems necessary either to disconnect from others or dissociate from themselves.

When Noura moves from knowing her distinctiveness from her brother—that her feelings are not his—to incorporating his opinion of her as paranoid, when she moves from speaking her feelings and thoughts in a loud voice with her friends to silently pondering her life late at night alone in the privacy of her room, we see—where others have seen a growth in subjectivity—a danger of losing voice and also a struggle against dissociation. When Judy moves from loving the regularity of her life with her mother to desiring to be in a regular or typical family, when she begins to sense the danger in the erotic and then narrates how she has come to split her feeling mind from her reasoning brain, we feel the power of the impasse and its effects on girls' psyches. And when Victoria buries her sadness and anger in response to the dangers of speaking, only to have them resurface as feelings of craziness, intense hatred, and idealization, we grasp what is at stake in girls' lives and also what is at stake for women.

As we listen to Noura, Judy, and Victoria narrate their journey to the wall, their struggle and finally their compromises with the

APPROACHING THE WALL

realities they face—their dissociation and feelings of disconnection—we wonder what choices these girls have, growing up in this time and this place, this society and this culture: what relational paths are open to them, what can they feel and know and say and still be in connection with others, what are the economic and political as well as the psychological and educational realities of their situation? Beginning with girls at early adolescence—at twelve and thirteen—may give us a clearer understanding of the gains and losses some girls experience and what becomes of girls' struggles and resistance.

5

Rivers into the Sea: Three Guides through Adolescence

We began with twelve-year-old Anna, to stand with her at the crossroads of adolescence. Returning now to Anna—tall, slender, with short brown hair and green eyes, quiet and wary—we place her amidst her twelve- and thirteen-year-old classmates. What we see are the signs of change all around. What we feel and sense is movement; like rivers flowing toward the open waters of the sea.

This is a time of visual change. Two thirds of the girls at this age will have begun menstruating.[1] There is no physical prototype: some girls appear childlike, tall and gangly; others look like young women, their bodies less angular, more rounded and full—bodies stirring, desiring, knowing, yet caught in the reality of the immediate, uncomfortable and shy in the gaze of others. Elizabeth Debold, a member of our research team, wishing to see a seventh-grade dance class, was told by the instructor that the girls were too embarrassed, too uncomfortable in their leotards to be seen by a stranger. This led Elizabeth to recall her junior high dances, herself and other girls standing in nervous, furtive groups, whispering among themselves in low voices. "Twelve-year-olds," she says, "cluster together like gangly trees in a dense patch of woods. Often when they speak, they put their hands over their mouths." She remembers the stance: "pinched posture, shoulders pushed awkwardly forward, head slightly bent. Between the lithe, jazz movement of the ten-year-old girls and the cultured grace of the seventeen-year-olds is the discomfort of twelve and thirteen."[2]

These changes in girls' bodies visually disconnect them from the world of childhood and identify them in the eyes of others with women, and thus with images of women and standards of beauty and goodness—physical and moral perfection. Girls become looked at, objects of beauty, talked about and judged against standards of perfection and ideals of relationship. And girls learn to look at their "looks" and to listen to what people say about them. Seeing themselves seen through of the gaze of others, hearing themselves talked about in ways that imply that they can be perfect, and that relationships can be free of conflict and bad feeling, they struggle between knowing what they know through experience and knowing what others want them to know and to feel and think.

At times they hold true to themselves. Kara worries out loud about "endanger[ing] the way I feel about myself or what I feel should be happening to me or the way I think," and her classmates echo these fears. Holding in their thoughts and feelings, holding fast to what they know through experience of themselves and their relationships, these girls attempt to stay with "how I feel, what my feelings are." The sense of threat is evident. Linda, reflecting with her interviewer on what makes her struggle so in her relationships, says, "You know, I have to pick the thing I will be happier in . . . there is a bad way of choosing, I could do something I don't like." Anna, explaining to her interviewer that it would be better for people, including herself, to "think more about what they really wanted to do, and not what other people wanted them to do," conveys this sense of foreboding: girls at this age feel in danger of losing themselves and losing touch with what they want. Voices which readily sound selfish or self-centered, when listened to more carefully, speak about losing relationship.

Girls' preoccupation with deciding what "would be better for you," "what I think about myself in the long run," or "what I feel should be happening to me" is a move into abstraction and differs from speaking their thoughts and feelings. Speaking up, as we heard from Victoria and other twelve-year-olds, can be dangerous and disruptive, and these girls, recognizing all too well the potential loss of relationship if they do say what they feel and think too forcefully or too directly, are up against a relational impasse which they describe: if they speak their strong feelings and thoughts—that is, if they bring themselves fully into relationships—they risk losing their relationships because no one will want to be with them; yet if they do not speak—if they take themselves out of relationship for the sake of "relationships"—they lose relationships that are genuine or authentic. Heard against this impending relational loss, girls' voices sound different and take on new meanings, because they are resisting losses which have been socially sanctioned and culturally inscribed—losses sustained by many women.

When these girls stay with the evidence of their senses in the face of this impasse, their relational capacities are striking. They clearly name the differences between what they know through experience and what others know or what is decreed as "reality." Neeti, whom we heard in Chapter 2, explains her decision to speak to the camp director on behalf of her cousin by saying at first that it is obvious why she did what she did, and then realizing that it may not be obvious to other people. However, she stays with what she knows in the face of others' rules and slogans:

It's obvious because—No, it isn't, but it is for me. It might not be obvious for you or for anybody else, but it's helping out my cousin. And that camp director, you know, it was a rule, but people are more important than rules, you know. So, he was just a little kid, you know, and they were trying out things, and the camp directors, they were saying, "We're just here to help our kids, to make them have fun," but my cousin wasn't having any fun, he was just contradicting the whole slogan, you know.

Neeti's repeated phrase "you know" suggests that she may have a question as to whether the woman sitting with her also knows what she knows: that it was helping her cousin, that people are more important than rules, that her cousin was not having fun at camp, or whether this woman will align herself with the camp directors and their rules.

Neeti explores the question of why what is obvious to her may not be obvious to anybody else in the situation. She knows that her cousin was "crying at night and stuff," "screaming," and having "nightmares," and knowing her cousin, she knows how he feels. Her viewpoint is not the same as the camp director's or that of her friends. Relationship is Neeti's access to knowing how her cousin feels, and she realizes that in the absence of that relationship, others cannot know what she knows. "It's like either you feel it all the way or you just recognize it, you know," she says. And given what she knows and feels, it seemed obvious although risky to act.

Yet we hear other girls struggle to fit what they know and feel into versions of reality which are inconsistent with what they have experienced, with the result that they—and also we in listening to them—readily become confused. Faith shifts from a first- to a second-person voice in trying to stay with her thoughts and her feelings in deciding what's "really right for you and you think it's right." In her struggle, we hear the power of the normative enter with the force of moral language, threatening to cover over what Faith feels and thinks by dictating to her how she should feel and think. For Faith to accept "what should be right to other people," she will have to disconnect from her sense of what is "really right" for her.

As these twelve- and thirteen-year-old girls stand at the threshold of early adolescence, they experience some of the implications of the prevailing social order of relationships as it complicates their efforts to stay in connection with themselves and with other people. As with Judy, Noura, and Victoria, culturally inscribed and socially institutionalized notions of womanhood which specify the normal, the typical, the desirable, the good, and the bad woman, enter girls' conversations and a struggle breaks out—a struggle to know what they know, to rely on their feelings, to hold onto their experiences and their relationships as a way of grounding themselves. Asked if she has ever been in a situation where what she knows to be true from experience is different from what others are saying and doing, Anna replies, "All the time . . . that's my life."

Standing at the edge of womanhood, girls begin to speak about themselves, about their thoughts and feelings, as something that might be "endangered" or "jeopardized." Twelve-year-old Becka, for example, struggles openly when she feels herself slipping away in relationships. Wondering whether to stay with a group of friends who make her life "miserable" or find "a new set of friends," Becka speaks with poignant clarity about what she lost in this miserable relationship: "I wasn't sure what to do, but then I realized that the good things weren't happening . . . I wasn't being happy, and I wasn't sure of myself . . . I wasn't being . . . with myself and I wasn't thinking about myself. I just wanted to have this group of friends," she continues. "I was losing confidence in myself, I was losing track of myself, really, and losing the kind of person I was."

Becka's choice not to give up relationship for the sake of having "this group of friends" is a sign of a healthy resistance—an active struggle against losing her voice and her sense of herself. Choosing to stay with herself and to take her unhappiness seriously, Becka will not call this false relationship real, but instead will look for new and, she hopes, better friends.

The generosity and openness that we saw in ten- and eleven-year-old girls when they created spaces for their own and others' voices tend to give way in these twelve- and thirteen-year-olds to self-protection. As girls feel pressure both from within and without to deny their feelings and thoughts for the sake of relationships, they can no longer afford to be so generous or open—or at least not in public. It is important to be "with myself," Becka says, as she faces an increasing number of alternative truths and interpretations, some with a legitimacy and authority that may feel overwhelming.

Like the younger girls, these twelve- and thirteen-year-olds are naturalists, bent on close and careful observation of the human world. But here at the borderland, where their "I" meets and for a short time self-consciously holds the "eye" of the culture[3]—where they see and hear clearly how they are being seen and spoken about—girls know to stand vigil over their thoughts and feelings. Visual metaphors characterize their conversation as they position themselves on this landscape. At once knowing themselves from their experiences in the relational world and seeing themselves as others see them, they find it increasingly difficult, as Judy says, to "feel with their minds" or even to believe in such a concept—to take what Judy experienced as "a deeper sort of knowing" as knowing or as trustworthy or as real, no matter how deep their feelings. And when such feelings threaten to place them outside of the realm of the acceptable or understandable—when they feel themselves too sad or too angry or too sexual or too loud, they may decide that it is better to bury their feelings and to go with what others say and know. In this brief time-out-of-time of liminal existence, this edge between childhood and full-blown adolescence, girls' minds may grasp the meaning others make of their changing bodies and they may feel themselves moving from flesh to image in an eroticized and frightening, tantalizing and ultimately terrifying fall.[4]

Trying to stay with their thoughts and feelings in the face of pressure to fit an image—for images, unlike bodies, do not know or speak[5]—these girls voice what they are doing and in doing so name the division they are feeling between what they know from experience and what has been socially constructed as "reality." Thoughts and feelings which expose that reality as unreal often seem too dangerous to speak out loud, and are retracted, taken inside, moved out of sight and hearing: hidden from all but the most trusted relationships or perhaps not spoken at all. Feelings are felt, thoughts are thought, but when no longer spoken, they are no longer heard— no longer endangered but also no longer exposed to the air and the light of relationship. As we heard Neeti say, when asked what was at stake for her in deciding to speak to the camp director, "Kind of like the ego, you know, and nothing physically and nothing that anybody else would see; it's just my feelings being hurt, and I hate being yelled at."

Even when girls choose not to risk their ego and bring their feelings and thoughts into relationships, they remain on the lookout for others by whom they can be safely seen and with whom they can safely speak. Moving themselves in and out of relationship, they listen for the ways in which others cover their voices and mask their true feelings. But in the absence of experience and in the presence of intense desires to be with people who are loving and genuine, they can rush too quickly into relationships and vulnerability. Becka, looking back at what now seems to her a rash decision to be friends with girls who made her miserable, says, "[I learned] not to rush into anything right away . . . I saw them, and it's like, 'Oh, wow!' you know. So, I rushed in right away without observing them, you know, and seeing what they were like."

The slipperiness of words and the treachery of relationships which ten- and eleven-year-old girls are acutely aware of have become solidified and normalized by twelve and thirteen. Knowing the threat of fraudulent relationships, Becka cannot act on the immediacy of her feelings; she must keep herself in check, remain on guard. Adolescent girls who do not learn this lesson well are in particular danger. For young women to be physically and emotionally safe, they must be aware of the treacherous undercurrents in relationships and also societal and cultural strictures. But this awareness, although protective, takes them outside of themselves; and, looking at themselves and listening to themselves, they begin to change their looks, modulate their voices, and monitor their behavior in relation to the looks and the voices of others in the world in which they are living. Thus at adolescence, girls can become more readily disconnected from what they are feeling, distanced from their own desires and pleasures, and therefore, ironically, more reliant on others who tell them what they want and feel and think and know. And their responses to these disconnections, their shock and their resistance, reveal the strengths of their connections in childhood.

These girls thus begin to look for the relational life which they know exists under the surface of what passes for relationships. They listen for and anticipate feelings and thoughts that are not spoken or shown but which they know will bubble up if not attended to. Erin, for example, plays out what would go on beneath the relational surface if she were to say something that hurt someone's feelings: "They wouldn't show it, but they would know," she says. "They would feel, like, kind of low, and they would not have as, they would not look at me as nice as they would have looked at me, they would just look at me as conceited and mean." Erin can "see if it would really bother them," not perhaps in the usual way, since "they wouldn't show it," but in the different way they would look at her and potentially speak about her to others. In the face of such delayed and indirect responses, girls begin to watch their footing and become more cautious in the relational world. Exquisitely attuned to the nuances of feelings and subtle shifts in relational configurations, they quickly learn the various ways in which people show what they feel and think; they pick up changes in voices, watch eyes and faces closely, scan bodies and clothes, and learn to read subtle cues, including cues about what can and cannot be spoken, what should and should not be known.

In this way, girls develop a sharp eye and ear for the disparity between what people say and what is really going on. But underneath there is a deeper and more confusing split: not between appearance and reality but between their experience and reality as it is generally constructed by other people. Then girls speak of feeling crazy or insane. Anna, who wonders if she is crazy, speaks into this confusion and asks how you can tell if what people are saying is true, "if what they are saying about you, if they really mean it . . . and it's hard to tell . . . with a lot of people, you can't tell how they are." Yet she feels that people can tell how she is, and this disparity conveys her sense of not quite knowing what she and others can and cannot tell. Anna, like many girls at her age, repeatedly says "I don't know." And this phrase enters our conversations with girls with rapidly increasing frequency at this juncture, marking girls' uncertainty about what they know and what they don't know, what can be known and what cannot be known.

Listening closely for what is not spoken, observing what is not shown or immediately known, many girls collude in covering over what happens in relationships in order to protect themselves and others from hurt or embarrassment. Melissa, for example, in a highly baroque passage, tells how she and her classmates would respond to someone who lied or cheated on a test:

> I mean, we don't like to say, "Oh, we hate you, you lied." We don't like to say that. So if we see somebody cheating on a test, which we haven't, we'd say, we'd pull the teacher out and say quietly, "Oh, so and so has two papers." And so that way we're not shouting it all over school, and that way they don't suffer any

blame. So it doesn't spread around because you don't say anything. It is just between the teacher and them to deal with it or something.

And why is that the best way, do you think, to handle it?

I think that's the best way because you're not hurting that person in any real way. You're doing some good for them because if they cheat on one test, then it's most likely going to lead to another one if they get away with it, and so you're just telling them that it's not right, and how are you going to get any place cheating on the test? And so that way you're not hurting them with their friends, and so it stays like confidential and nothing gets out. They're not losing anything; they're not being hurt.

For Melissa and her friends it is bad to say directly, "We hate you, you lied," but it is good to turn the girl in confidentially, behind her back, in what is said to be an effort to protect her from herself and save her from embarrassment with her friends. The disconnections in this move to act in a way that is said to be good and not hurtful are seemingly unobserved by Melissa, and yet her repeated insistence that "they don't suffer any blame . . . you're not hurting that person in any real way . . . you're not hurting them with their friends . . . they're not losing anything; they're not being hurt" suggests that at some level she is troubled and knows that what she and her friends are doing is in fact hurtful. Although Melissa says that it is better to speak *about* someone quietly than to speak *with* them in what undoubtedly would be a noisy conversation, she may suspect that under the guise of confidentiality and doing good for others, she and her friends are in fact protecting themselves against a cheater in the class and at the same time avoiding the possibility of being called tattletales for turning her in. What is most striking to us is that Melissa seems not even to consider the possibility of speaking directly with the girl, saying what she thinks, "It's not right," and asking *her* the question: "How are you going to get any place cheating on a test?"

Melissa's story marks the relational impasse many girls at this age feel: that it has become impossible for them to say directly what they are thinking and feeling, or at least to say it outside of the context of highly confidential or best-friend relationships. Knowledge of the power others have to look at them, to judge them, to spread rumors about them, to cause them harm, leads girls to protect themselves by removing their deepest feelings and thoughts from public scrutiny, and thus from public discussion, and taking them into an underground world. Girls thus become cautious or, in Anna's terms, "discreet." And yet Anna sees problems in discretion: "If you're afraid to stand up and say something," Anna explains, "I mean, if you just go along, if nobody else is discreet, you can't just go along with what everybody else says, because it happens all the time with young people, all being with one thing, and I really want to say something else."

Liza, also concerned about standing up, speaking out, and being silenced, tells how she would decide what's best if her friends disagreed: "I don't know, by doing probably what you wanted to do in a way that would be discreet enough so that you wouldn't . . . I don't know, make it too obvious." Liza brings her discretion to class where she takes herself out of public dialogue, choosing to keep her disagreements to herself. "Everyone I know takes the teacher's point of view," she says, "'cause it's—they're the ones holding the grade book and they're the ones that are going to be giving you the test on it, stuff like that. I mean, you can't just take whichever one you want." "Can you privately?" her interviewer wonders. "Yeah," she replies. "And how do you decide what to do privately?" "I don't know . . . you just examine what's there and stuff, and you try to decide which is more right to you and not like—without anyone else's opinion."

Liza's discretion, designed to bury her knowledge and protect her from exposure, is at least for the time being a conscious and calculated decision to take herself out of relationship. For Liza, discretion is another name for disconnection. For safety's sake she represents herself partially, uses her sophisticated understanding of authority and power to shield herself from the dangers of being seen: "You have to like keep your eyes open at all times," she says. "When you learn things about people," she continues, "you have to be more omniscient, you have to be able to see everything, not just like the physical appearance of a person or, you know, how well they can do something; you have to be able to see inside of them in a way."

Relationships for Liza, as for Becka, Melissa, and others, have become highly compromised as a way of knowing. No longer can they just ask people what they feel and think directly and listen to what they say; they have to see beyond "the physical appearance," they have to "see inside," they become experts at translation. Voice which has the capacity to reveal the inside world of thoughts and feelings seems increasingly untrustworthy to girls who no longer can imagine saying "go home" when they mean go home. Instead, they talk about seeing, seeing through, seeing into, as if one must step outside of relationships to know what is going on. And with this move, they align themselves with a long tradition that separates knowing from feeling, self from relationship, mind from body, voice from desire. By-passing relationship as a way of knowing, they attempt to become all-seeing, omniscient.

Knowing different perspectives, Liza confides, allows people to communicate, but only "if they're that way too." Otherwise, she adds, people are "like dictators," imposing their point of view on others and "punish[ing] people for what they haven't done." In the presence of dictators, an underground is essential. And Liza, clearly feeling such a presence, chooses to silence her astute and disruptive commentary. What she does in school is simply to voice "the teacher's point of view."

Disagreement makes Anna and Liza stand out, obvious, exposed to people's attention. Disagreement makes them vulnerable—open to the power of genuine relationship and also to the capriciousness of dictators. In the face of such vulnerability, Anna wonders whether it is better to be open or to be closed: "It's just better to stay out of things," she thinks, "'cause people can get mad if you say something." Aware of the realities of physical violence and also of psychological violation, girls have reason to fear arousing other people's anger. And their own anger, held in their bodies, unvoiced and out of relationship, loses its relational proportions and becomes in itself frightening and unclear. Girls who fear speaking their anger readily become confused about whether anger really exists, whether they are really feeling angry.

"You sort of have anger inside but not really," Jennifer explains. "You shouldn't let it out around everyone else. You should just like do it yourself." Jennifer's confusion about what is happening inside—"you sort of have anger inside but not really"—becomes understandable in the face of the relational threats that girls feel. Moral language comes into girls' voices to enforce cultural norms against women's anger ("You *shouldn't* let it out . . . you *should* . . . do it yourself"), and the dangers for women in expressing their anger may in fact override the psychological dangers of not saying or knowing how they feel. The power of moral language to cover strong feelings is apparent and also the ways in which morality can provide the rationalization for girls' and women's disconnection from their experiences and feelings—their taking themselves out of relationship.

The twelve- and thirteen-year-old girls in this study, desiring relationship, thus struggle with authority. On the one hand, they speak their strong feelings and thoughts and describe their relational conflicts in ways that suggest that they know what they want and what they will feel good about. On the other hand, they interrupt themselves constantly to say "I don't know"—sometimes because they genuinely do not know but often before going on to reveal remarkable knowing. Their stories about their lives—themselves, their relationships, their conflicts—are at once psychologically astute and filled with questions about the value and legitimacy of their experiences, their thoughts, and their feelings. How are they to stay with what they know empirically—knowledge of the human world which they have gained from close observation and through relationships with others—in the face of prevailing authorities who voice alternative truths that call such knowledge radically into question? In the face of this relational crisis, this seeming need to choose between staying with themselves and being with others, some girls stay with their thoughts and feelings—sometimes speaking what they know despite pressure to not know, sometimes choosing not to speak or speaking only to their friends, and in the process discovering where real relationships are and are not possible, sometimes at the expense of being deeply hurt. Other girls find the attraction to the normal and the typical irresistible. We heard Judy at twelve yearn for "the typical life of *the child*," and we hear Liza's preoccupation with being seen as the normal girl—"I don't want to sound really queer," she says, listening to the way she sounds as she tries to describe herself. "I fit in pretty well," she explains, "just an average, everyday person . . . just normal." And others, in the absence of experience, reiterate the promise of the romance story: that someday a prince will come and their life will be changed utterly. We heard Victoria's anger and sadness about her parents' relationship and her mother's betrayal turn to bitterness and denigration, and then to the idealization of relationships as she falls in love with the idea of love.

When these twelve- and thirteen-year-old girls engage in open resistance or disagree with those in power, relational conflicts— often a sign of healthy resistance to false relationships—take on political meaning, disrupting and interrupting the prevailing order of living. Poised at this edge in their own development, this place between girl and woman, girls yearn for authentic or resonant relationship at the same time as they begin to suspect that such relationships may be truly disturbing, may even be politically dangerous. And it is at this age that girls most commonly begin to be called "disturbed." Moving into a culture populated by images and models of young women, girls incorporate these images from reading magazines and books, from watching TV, and from listening in on the ways that other people, especially parents and teachers, look at and speak about them, their classmates, their acquaintances, their friends. And girls need to hold themselves away from the power of images and voices which encourage them to label their feelings and desires and needs as "selfish" and to see selflessness or self-silencing as the condition for being loved or approved of.

As girls become engaged in this struggle to hold onto the complexity of their relational experiences, they sound like the women whose voices resound in the literature on women's psychology. Their internal struggles with wanting authentic relationship and fearing that if they voice their feelings and thoughts they will jeopardize relationships and endanger themselves, and their external struggles against cultural images and voices that encourage them to make a series of divisions which undermine what they know through experience, announce their entrance into womanhood, or more specifically, a womanhood where staying with themselves feels selfish and actively being with others feels selfless—where it seems impossible or untenable for them to bring their voices into their relationships.[6]

Girls literally cannot bring their experience of living in relationship with others into this selfish–selfless construction. "It was me saving myself or saving him," Neeti says, in an effort to summarize a difficult and complicated relational conflict in one neat sentence when her interviewer asks her, "What was the conflict for you in that situation?" But the question itself leads her astray. The conflict for her was that she was in relationship with her cousin, that she felt miserable knowing that he was miserable, even though she knew that his feelings were not her feelings, and that she could not stay in relationship with her cousin and with herself without taking action. In doing so, she risked being yelled at and having her ego hurt.

The erosion of girls' capacity to stay in relationship with themselves and with others becomes clear as Michelle announces with pride, "Like this year I've changed a lot. I think of, more of what to do to be nice than . . . what I want to do." Doing what she wants to do is, in this construction, not nice. Marie, seeing her mother come home from work "tired . . . with circles under her eyes" and knowing that the dishes need to be done, also thinks about herself and the homework "I really should do." Her conflict, she says, is between "wanting to help my Mom because I know she's tired and wanting to help myself get my work done . . . It's deciding whether you're going to do something for yourself or for someone else." Marie calls this "a moral conflict," and once she has labeled it such, helping herself by doing her homework seems "selfish," at which point it seems clear what she *should* do. But her judgment is in fact more complex. "The person who needs the help," she explains, "is going to think you're being selfish if you don't." What Marie thinks remains unspoken.

Marie stays with what she sees—the circles under her mother's eyes, how tired she looks—and knows that she herself has work to do. But instead of representing the full complexity of this conflict, she superimposes a narrow moral framework in which her needs drop out—in which she voices only her mother's needs. In what seems at times an act of self-defense, these girls take on moral language like a protective shield, covering over the rich texture of their relational experiences and speaking as though there is an emotional or psychological scarcity of resources in the relational world.

Thus girls struggle with relational conflicts and exclusive choices—choices that destroy relationship whichever way they turn. The either-or framing (selfish or selfless, self or relationship) marks an inner psychological split or division. Taking on moral language, girls take in the dichotomies of a culture which splits good from bad women and divides the selfish from the selfless. People, in girls' descriptions, now sound less like people—the people in nine-year-old Margaret's life who have "a different mother and a different family, and a different skin, different color, different color eyes, color hair and intelligence"—and more like disembodied points of view, pre-formed and self-contained, juggled awkwardly to avoid making anyone hurt or upset. When differences were simply differences, relational conflicts were ordinary—to be expected. Now, as Marie says, "it's always a moral conflict."

While it is not unusual, in the midst of this juggling act, for these girls to exclude themselves to avoid being called "selfish," it would be simplistic to suggest that they gain nothing by such exclusive decisions. When girls act on behalf of others, seemingly at the expense of themselves, they gain in socially desirable ways. Jennifer talks about how she responded when an unpopular girl asked her if she was her friend in front of her best friend and an entire cabin of girls at summer camp:

> I wasn't sure that I should say that she was my friend because then I'd get my best friend upset and then I wasn't sure if I should say I wasn't her friend 'cause then I'd get her upset and then that would just get, like her against the whole cabin . . . I decided I'd say yes and explain [to my best friend] because that would be like the best thing to do. I'd make one person feel good and then I'd go back and make the other person feel good. So I figure that would be the perfect way to do it.

Attending to the needs of each person in turn, Jennifer avoids feelings of guilt and personal pain:

> I don't want to make someone upset 'cause that would get me into the depression age again and if I got them upset it would be a load on my mind and I'd hate myself and I'd try to get them to like me again . . . 'cause I like being liked even though I don't like somebody. And so I just figured, well, I'll make them both happy. Everything will be fine . . . so everything was great and then I went to sleep with no guilt on my mind.

Taking in the full burden of responsibility for this situation—hating herself if she made someone upset—Jennifer begins an exhaustive series of separate and private negotiations designed to cover over any appearance of conflict or disruption: "I'd make one person feel good and then I'd go back and make the other person feel good." Jennifer then describes what she gains in the process—other than a good night's sleep. She tells her interviewer of the sense of power she experienced—the power, or in her words "the domination," to make things "peaceful," to restore relationship (at least on the surface), the power to prevent one person from feeling bad or losing her self-confidence and to allow another to save face, to retain her pride:

> *How did you feel about it . . . about the whole situation?*
> Well, I wasn't too pleased with the fight or with someone asking

me if I liked them in front of everyone else who didn't, but I felt good that I said something 'cause that would have been, that was like, I was proud that I made the whole cabin suddenly get over a fight, and I was like, "Wow, do I have domination!" and I was proud.

What was it about making them get over the fight that made you proud?

Well, fights are really not the best things to have. Now there's a winner and a loser, nothing lands on the top, except when I stopped it. No. The fight ended, everything was peaceful . . . it's just like that. You don't have lots of like screaming or anything.

When you think over the conflict you described, do you think you learned anything from it?

Yeah. I think that I sort of learned how to get everybody happy at the same time. I learned how to get somebody happy by lying . . . I lied and got someone happy and then I told the truth to like all the rest of the people and got them happy, then I got myself happy because I'd made everyone else happy, and so everything was fine. So I figured I learned how to do that . . . I solved the problem that I figured was really important to solve.

The problem Jennifer takes on is real, but we are struck by the difference between her solution and Noura's—that in Jennifer's mind it is better to lie than to take the time and the space to say her feelings, to speak as Noura and her friends did, in loud voices. "I got myself happy," Jennifer says, "because I'd made everyone else happy." Although she lied to one person, it was more important to her that she prevent a fight and solve the problem peacefully, without "lots of screaming."

As the rivers of girls' lives flow into the sea of womanhood, it seems less possible to take the time and space to say what they feel and think to each other. The younger girls we listened to, who fight openly, are, predictably, less tired, less drained emotionally. While covering over her dislike with lies and quelling disruption and disagreement left Jennifer with a feeling of domination and control, these efforts were also duplicitous, time-consuming, and emotionally exhausting.

While creating the appearance of a surface calm over strong

feelings is labeled by Jennifer as lying, it provides a way for her to distance herself emotionally from the girl she doesn't like and, in this way, to exercise some control over the relational world. Jennifer has taken in displeasure with fighting, the desire for peaceful resolutions, the distaste for conflict, the wish to make everyone happy. Her bad feelings have gone underground. Like Melissa, who does not say directly "what you are doing is not right," Jennifer does not voice her anger toward the girl who put her in this uncomfortable situation. And like Melissa, who thinks only of speaking in private to the teacher, Jennifer speaks confidentially to her interviewer about feelings she cannot speak aloud in her relationships.

Holding themselves at bay, out of relationship, these twelve- and thirteen-year-old girls take in the vernacular of relationships all around them. Jennifer's words, especially her self statements—"*I made [them] get* over a fight; *I learned how to get* everyone happy; *I got myself* happy; *I made* everyone else happy"—mark a static, controlled relational language startlingly different from the fluidity of younger girls' relational dialogues and disagreements. This shift in her relational language, we suggest, marks Jennifer's movement into the sea of Western culture and a profound psychological loss.[7]

Removing themselves from relationship, these girls struggle daily with the seduction of the unattainable: to be all things to all people, to be perfect girls and model women. As their new-found capacities for abstract thought emerge, girls find it easier to disengage themselves from relational conflicts altogether. Faith, for example, has difficulty negotiating the problem of whose sleep-over invitation to accept. Finally, she says:

I stayed home. It's happened a few times, though, and I think I've sort of done each thing just to see how it would work out . . . I just start to think up these little solutions that I could have done. I'd just sit around and think about it, and think, well, what if this happened or what if this happened, you know, just try and rearrange the information . . . like if you do one thing, what's going to happen? If you do the other thing—maybe there might be one way you save both friendships, maybe one way you could save one, another way you could lose them all. So, it's really hard to tell what you should do if you want to keep your friends.

Approaching the problem at hand logically, Faith plays out various possible scenarios in her head. Since she has abstracted herself from the particulars of any one possibility—that is, taken herself out of relationship; quite literally, she has stayed home—she is free to "just try and rearrange the information." The viability of her solutions, then, depends on everything about the situation remaining the same—the invitation, her friends' reactions, their feelings, her own wishes, the relationships. Echoing Jennifer's language of "making" and "getting" relationships, Faith controls all the variables from afar—no muss, no fuss. Unsuccessful as she is in her plan to keep all her friends—she has done (or rather, thought) "each thing" and so far nothing has satisfied her—she is also seemingly unaffected. Her solutions depend on the rigid and unchanging nature of persons and situations; she keeps herself apart from the messiness and complexity of relational conflict. Choosing domination and separation over the heartbreak and difficulty of relationship, girls like Jennifer and Faith can use their ability to abstract knowledge to take themselves out of relational conflicts. Given their insights about difference, about dialogue, about the intimate relationship between thought and feeling and between feeling and action, as well as about the transforming power of relationships, girls are protecting themselves at the expense of what Judy calls "a deeper sort of knowing."

As girls learn to cover over their detailed knowledge of relationships, they learn to judge themselves differently and to reframe or revision the relational life they once lived. "My mom tells me that I'm rude sometimes," Erin explains, "and . . ." Her interviewer interrupts her. "Didn't she tell you that before?" she asks, wondering, perhaps suspecting, where Erin has been. "No . . . She just, I don't know," Erin responds. "Maybe she did, but I would, I would get really mad and I wouldn't listen to her. I still get really mad and I don't listen to her, but now maybe I'm listening to her more." Erin describes herself as someone who has "changed a lot," from someone who was once rude—meaning someone who would say what she felt and "get really mad"—to someone who now thinks "more of what to do to be nice than what I want to do." She explains:

> When I was in fifth grade I could do whatever I wanted and I could almost, and everyone would still like me. But now, I mean it was just rude, what I was doing. I can see now when I was little I was rude and it bugs me so much that I never wanted to be like that again, so I'm trying to make up for everything that I did when I was little and I was rude to people.

Erin's commitment to change has taken the form of a vow never to be rude—that is, "really mad"—again, to "make up for everything that I did when I was little and I was rude to people." This means Erin must forget what she knew as a ten-year-old—that relationships are complicated, that, as Allison said, people "process their thinking" differently, that people struggle to speak, and often do speak their feelings, in the face of pressure not to sound mean or bossy. There was a time when girls could say "I'm sad" or "I'm angry" and it did not seem rude and dangerously disruptive. Erin's memory both idealizes this time ("I could do whatever I wanted . . . and everyone would still like me") and rejects it ("I was rude . . . I never want to be like that again"). Her life becomes dedicated to undoing past indiscretions that, according to her ten- and eleven-year-old self, may not have happened in the first place. For Erin, a young woman entering this culture at this time, to retell or reconfigure her life in this way brings her into line with most prevailing accounts of psychological development, and also with accepted norms of female behavior.[8]

Once Erin takes in this foreign voice-over-her-voice—a voice she associates with her mother—and makes it a part of herself, she no longer needs her mother to "tell me I'm rude"; she can do so herself:

> Like kids, when they invite me to their parties or something, sometimes I won't want to go and I will use an excuse or something and that's a decision which, like, will hurt their feelings . . .

[When thinking about what to do I consider] hurting their feelings, being rude . . . it's like it's rude and it's mean and it's unkind.

Erin wonders how best to respond, how to include her wishes when doing so will hurt someone's feelings. Saying what she wants directly is now "rude," "mean," "unkind." She decides, finally, that it's "the way you say yes or no, it all depends on how you say it, on how you say no," she says. "If you just say, 'No, I'm not going,' if you say, 'No, I'm just really not in the mood' or . . . you take a bit of your time to explain to that person what you're going to do." To take the time to explain, Erin adds, is "to be nice. I don't know. Just not to be rude or something." What was once pretty simple and straightforward now takes all of Erin's attention and effort because it has become so elaborate and complex. What was once so ordinary—speaking about feelings like sadness, anger, pleasure— now seems transgressive.[9]

These twelve- and thirteen-year-old girls, coming of age in a particular place in culture and in time, show a healthy resistance to losing their voices and losing relationship. Their capacity for resistance is evident in their insistence on knowing what they know and their willingness to be outspoken. But at this juncture in development, girls' "ordinary courage" becomes extraordinary, an act of relational heroism. Girls' healthy resistance to psychological illness then takes on the dimensions of a political struggle—becomes a political resistance or a challenge to the existing order of relationship, to the prevailing lines of power and authority. But this is a political struggle which is anchored relationally rather than ideologically, psychologically rooted in girls' desire to be in genuine connection with others.

Because the relational problem is real, most girls we listened to show signs of this struggle, and its legacy reaches far into women's lives. For some girls, a healthy resistance finds a creative voice or expression; for some the resistance remains open and turns political; for some it moves underground—into a political underground where feelings and thoughts are secretly shared, or into a psychological underground where feelings become "nothing that anyone can see" and thoughts become private and protected. But once girls remove themselves from relationships, they begin to have difficulty articulating their feelings. Finding themselves in relationships that are not psychologically real, that are not psychological or emotional connections, they can no longer say what they know. Then girls begin not to know what they once knew, to forget the feelings and thoughts they once spoke but then withdrew to protect. We hear their confusion: "I don't know," they say over and over, as they struggle against dissociating themselves from their thoughts and feelings in order to connect to the world around them. We then hear girls position themselves with visual metaphors—determined to be "omniscient," to see all, aware that they are being seen and commented on by all—as they take in images of women's bodies and women's psyches that do not have room for their experience. Feeling the power, what Jennifer calls the "domination" of this image, girls who take it in expect to feel safe and secure, protected in part by being disconnected from themselves and other people.

Here at this watershed in girls' development, we again join with Anna and Neeti, and also Liza. Each will struggle with a central relational quandary: how to stay with herself and be with others, how to keep her voice in connection with her inner psychic world of thoughts and feelings and also to bring her voice into her relationships with other people. And each will exemplify different ways of going—different streams of development, different pathways of growth. Anna becomes outspoken—a political resister; after flirting with containment, she "bursts out." European-American and working-class, she finds her way through the relational impasse that many girls experience. Instead of learning what not to know, what not to say, Anna becomes invested in learning as much as she can and in saying what she knows. Staying close to her own experience, Anna's eyes and ears open wide as she watches and listens and names the way the world works.

Neeti is Indian and upper-middle-class. Outspoken at twelve, Neeti feels the pressure to cover over her strong feelings and go underground to protect her image and avoid hurting others. But she describes this move in vivid detail and is aware of leading a double life—knowing and yet pretending not to know what she really feels and what is really happening in her relationships. Neeti is the underground woman.

Liza is European-American and upper-middle-class and physically can fit the model or image of perfection. Underground at twelve, Liza gradually transforms herself into the image she desires—blonde, beautiful, and thin—leaving a wake of questions and confusion. Becoming blonder and blonder, thinner and thinner, Liza becomes anorexic. And her anorexia marks her move from the conscious underground where, like Neeti, she is connected to her feelings but strategically protects them from view, into a psychological resistance where she struggles to remain in touch with herself and her feelings.

These three girls, three rivers into the sea, demonstrate how girls' struggle to hold onto their voices and visions in the face of pressures to not know and not speak can lead some girls to risk the open trouble and disruption of political resistance and others to move their strong feelings and thoughts underground. Once there, in the absence of safe-houses where girls can say what they feel and think, girls' healthy resistance may turn into a psychological resistance as girls become reluctant to know what they know and fear that their experience if spoken will endanger their relationships and threaten survival.

Anna: A Political Resister

When Anna, at twelve, raises the question: How can you tell if what people are saying is true, "if what they are saying about you, if they really mean it, or if they are just doing it to be mean," she is trying to understand the difference between the surface banter of teasing, making fun, and putting people down that went on at the public school she once went to, and being "really mean" or cruel. Now, at her private girls' school, Anna notices that everyone is "nice" and she wants to be nice too—to not be mean or do something to hurt somebody. But sometimes, she says, "you just can't help it." "If you're feeling sad," Anna says, "you just can't make yourself happy." Thus she insistently rejects the otherwise tempting image of happiness or perfection, knowing perhaps that because of her working-class background she would never fit the conventional image of the perfect girl and her family.

But as a scholarship student, Anna is concerned about fitting in. "I don't think a lot of people like to be someplace where they're really different," she says. "You go somewhere and it's all a certain kind of people . . . So . . . you walk to the wrong door or something, and there's all these rich people inside, and you're just coming in off the street, and even if you look the same . . . you wouldn't *be* the same." And so Anna studies her surroundings. She is preoccupied with how people see her and how to interpret what others say and do, how to tell if relationships are true or false. Knowing that what people say and do can be different from what they feel and think, she searches for signs of authenticity in relationship, signs that friends are "really your friends."

Indeed, at twelve Anna wonders about the possibility of ever fully knowing another person. She thinks about how a person would feel if she could not make herself known to others. It "might be really hard on that person," she says, if you can't express "how you feel inside." And so Anna, who wishes to have "somebody to talk to or confide in . . . somebody [who] was there whom you could talk to," also knows the gaps in relationships that difference and disagreement can create—the places where people cannot express their feelings completely and the hurt they feel when they are misunderstood. Although Anna is clear about who she is inside—her "true self," she says, "is kind of however I feel; if I act that way, then I guess I'm being myself"—she wonders whether she can bring herself and her strong feelings into her relationships.

At home, Anna says it is unfair that her parents expect her to always remain in control of her feelings, to "ignore" her brothers' shouting and fighting, while they run rough-shod all over the house. When her "extremely violent" younger brother "attack[s] me" and "I try to defend myself sometimes . . . somebody gets mad at *me*," she complains. Anna concludes from this family drama that "you can't get mad . . . People think it's all your fault because you get mad at them." "I don't even try anymore," Anna tells her interviewer. "It is not worth anything because there is nothing you can really do about it."

Like other twelve-year-olds we listened to, Anna has a sharp eye for the disparity between what people say and what is really going on, evident as she describes her experience in going shopping for clothes with her mother:

> She will pull something out and she'll say, "Well, what do you think of it?" And then if I say I don't like it, then she'll get really mad, and she'll put it back . . . And then she'll forget about what happens when I really give her my opinion, and then she'll say, "Tell me what you really think about it." And then she gets mad when I tell her . . . And I'll say: "Well, you don't really want it because you already screamed at me when I gave it."

Though Anna says "sometimes I'm mad at the world," she concludes "it's better to stay out of things, because people can get mad if you say something." And yet, although Anna "tries to be better"—to contain her impatience and her anger—sometimes, she says, "I'll get really mad and I can outburst." Her ambivalence about these moments is patent as she explains, "I have to learn how to work with people, because sometimes I just get really mad at people who can't understand what I'm saying, and I get so exasperated. It's like 'Why can't you just . . . ? What's wrong with you? Why can't you see this my way?' And I have to really go for what I want, though. I can't let this stuff take over me . . . I have to, you kind of have to fight to get what you want."

Anna is passionate about knowing; learning is intensely personal and experiential to her: "I think one of the most powerful things," she tells her interviewer, "is experiencing something." School provides a space for Anna's passion and gives her a sense of personal power or efficacy. In school there is a place for Anna's opinion, and thus for Anna, since as she says, "You can be yourself when you think of your opinion."

But Anna is forever aware of the difference between herself and most of her classmates. "I can't take anything for granted," she tells her interviewer—not friendships, not answers in school, not what parents or teachers say. Particularly aware of the power adults have "to just . . . do what they want to do . . . [to not] pay any attention . . . [to] just ignore the whole thing," to dismiss her off-hand with comments like, "Well it wasn't your conversation," or "Nobody asked you," Anna carefully sizes up situations and, like Victoria, decides when to respond: "Sometimes I [say something] and sometimes I stop and think before I say anything, and then I realize that they are not going to listen anyway, so . . . I know it really wouldn't make a difference and might have just [made] things worse."

In essence, twelve-year-old Anna states the problem of resistance which enters girls' lives at the time of adolescence. On the one hand, she attempts to suppress her feelings, "not to be like that . . . not to get really mad" or, even worse, "outburst," and on the other hand, she realizes that "I can't let this stuff take over me." One resistance is psychological and will lead Anna to become "nice" or, as she views it, "successful" as she leaves the working-class environment of her family and boards the Noah's Ark of her private girls' school. The other resistance is political, and it will, as she realizes, make trouble in the world of her school and create conflicts in her relationships with others.

Anna struggles between these two forms of resistance a year later at the age of thirteen—when, it seems, she has gone underground. The phrase "I don't know" runs through the transcript of her eighth grade interview more than three times as often as the year before, pointing to her struggle to stay in relationship with herself and her knowledge. This year Anna speaks of keeping things to herself, of bringing herself out "just a little bit," of "playing a part," and of fitting into her new school, where she loves learning and where she is one of the top students in her class.

Well aware of "the way people make judgments," Anna no longer has to be told not to speak, no longer has to hear "Nobody asked you" or "It was not your conversation"; she has become adept at reading the signs. "They don't say it but you just get the feeling," she tells her interviewer. People make decisions without listening, Anna says. "You try and say something and people just don't listen

... They don't need to, like they don't have to listen, because they already know what they're going to do, so it doesn't matter."

Struggling to bring herself and her knowledge into relationship with others, revealing herself "bit by bit," Anna "torments" herself about speaking and not speaking—about not speaking out in class when she knows the answer, and about "messing up" in school. "Oh, don't do that again!" she says to herself when she has not spoken, or "Now, why did I do that? That was a really dumb thing to say," when she finally speaks, but in a way that "messes things up." Anna listens closely to herself as well as to others and monitors the changing rhythms and patterns, the sudden shifts in tempo or tonality that mark the human worlds she lives in, the disparate worlds of school and family which she traverses every day.

Anna at thirteen remains acutely aware of differences—of being different from the girls around her who live mostly in affluent families, whereas, she says, the centerpiece on her family's table is a pile of unpaid bills. "You don't know," she says, revealing her constant sense of double vision or seeing double, "how you should interpret [what people say] . . . whether you should interpret what they're saying the way that they're saying it and the way that they're meaning it, or get something different out of what they're saying."

Given her different angle of vision, Anna is seeing or hearing in the voices of the people around her something different from what they are—as they see it—saying and meaning. And she knows—as is evident when she speaks about herself as a knower—that you can interpret things differently, that thoughts and feelings cascade differently from different beginnings, so that depending on where you start—what questions you ask or where you begin, for example, in reading a poem—you arrive at different endpoints.

Yet, conformity also has its hold on Anna at thirteen, and she tries to arrive at the same endpoint as her classmates, watching to see which way they go so that she can follow: "I usually wait for like ten other people and sense where they are going," she says. "If fifteen people are going there, they have got to have some idea of where they are going." This year, she says, she does not "massively disagree on anything." With friends, if she disagreed, she would be "kind of mad at myself, have kind of a messed up feeling"; with adults the risks are different: "They would overpower me most of the time." "It could mean," she adds, "totally not getting along with the teacher for the rest of the year."

At fourteen, in the ninth grade, Anna becomes outspoken. When asked whether she sees herself as having changed, she draws her interviewer's attention to the change she hears in her own voice: "I used to be really quiet and shy and everything, and now I am really loud." Anna's choice to speak in a loud voice is evident as she—encouraged to speak in her school and seeing herself as "having a lot of choices"—says something her teacher does not wish to hear, something that makes her teacher angry. "I had to write an English paper," she explains:

And the English teacher didn't want me to write the English paper because we had to write a legend. And I see things from a lot of points of view, like I am creative. But it was a legend and we had to do a hero thing, and I didn't want to write about a hero: "There was a ladeedah good hero, and went and saved all of humankind and everything." So I like . . . if you see the hero from a different viewpoint, from a different standpoint, everyone could be a hero. So I wanted to write it from a Nazi standpoint, like Hitler as a hero. And [my English teacher] really didn't go for that idea at all . . . And I started writing, and she like, I mean, she got really mad . . . it was just really weird . . . I ended up writing two papers, a ladeedah legend and the one I wanted to write.

The interviewer asks, "Did you give the one you wanted to write to her?" "Yeah," Anna says:

I turned them both in . . . and she gave me an A on the normal one. I just gave her the other one to read because I *had* to write it, it sort of made me mad . . . I just had to write it and get it out . . . and I ended up writing it. I wrote it from the point of view of a little boy who was just joining one of the youth groups they had and he was going around like, he was so proud to have a uniform, and it just, it didn't come out about Hitler as much but it came out all about the things like the jobs and everything. And I turned in the paper and I turned in a letter like saying just, I had to write the paper . . . you know.

To Anna, the teacher was "narrowminded," meaning that she could not, in Anna's opinion, encompass this shift in perspective on heros and realize that Hitler was not, as the teacher would have it, an "anti-hero" in German eyes. "It wasn't," Anna insists, "if you wrote about it like someone remembering it and how great it was, it wouldn't be an anti-hero, it would be a hero . . . I don't know if she didn't understand that or because someone else was really against it." The teacher warned Anna she would sound like a little Nazi, but Anna, whose father was unemployed, whose household was the scene of violent outbursts on the part of her father and brothers, knows that the appearance of strength can cover a reality of weakness and vulnerability and that the need to appear strong and heroic can lead people to violence. "It was an urge," Anna says, capturing the physical insistency of her need to speak about the way she saw things. "I had to write the paper because I was so mad and it was, I had to write it to explain it to her, you know. I just had to . . . I just had to make her understand." The hero legend, from Anna's standpoint, is a dangerous legend. And at fourteen, Anna labels her ability to shift standpoint "creative" rather than "crazy."

In her outspoken effort to call things by their right names, Anna, at fourteen, observes and names and questions the inconsistencies in her school's position on economic differences—where money is available, for what reasons and for whom, and where it isn't—and the limits of the meritocracy which is espoused. Yet since getting the money to go to college is going to be a "big problem" and since "a lot depends on the people who do the college references," Anna also knows, wisely, that there are some things she does not want "to act out," some things she does not want to say to some people.

Anna's resistance to images of perfection becomes explicit this year as she rejects the premise of an ideal woman. Asked "What is society's image of the ideal woman?" she begins by saying, "Someone who could be successful and happy with what they're doing," and then adds, "I don't know"—the phrase which frequently introduces girls' most astute observations, those they are tempted to take underground or keep undercover—"It depends on, you know," she says, wondering, believing, perhaps, that the interviewer knows and that she is, in essence, a member of the underground also—"it depends on, you know, what you think about society, because there's all kinds of people, they each can have different thoughts." Freeing thinking now from the constraints of what Hawthorne calls "the iron framework of reasoning" which upholds the established order, Anna concludes: "Everybody has a different idea . . . I think everybody would have their own, and so there wouldn't be one image that says, 'Oh, the perfect woman. That's her, right there.'"

In eleventh grade, at the age of sixteen, with "a whole bunch of friends" behind her, Anna begins to ask some pointed questions about what is taken for granted, assumed to be unquestionable, in the public world in which she lives: questions about God and about violence and about privilege. The provocative nature of Anna's questions is evident as she observes to her religious classmates that there must have been a lot of "animal stuff" on Noah's Ark after forty days and forty nights. More pointedly, she notices "how close-minded people can be . . . how fanatical people can be about something they can't prove." What Anna likes most about school this year are the debates and arguments she has in her classes, and she recalls in amazement and with annoyance how, one day in class, in the presence of intense controversy and strong feelings, "there were just a bunch of people who sat there like stones and listened."

This year Anna speaks frankly and openly to her interviewer about the different pressures she feels at home and at school, differences that sometimes make her feel, as she says, "schizophrenic." She takes great pleasure in a singing group she has been involved in over the years because, she explains, "I kind of think I need it because it's an in-between, because it's different from school and it's different from everything at home."

Anna admits she has changed a great deal over the years, from someone who was "really, really, really shy and quiet" and at times "terrified" of speaking up, to someone who screams and yells—sometimes in fun and sometimes in anger. Along with her outspokenness, Anna has become, admittedly, somewhat cynical, particularly of those classmates she calls "annoying" and "superficial." Where once she wondered "how you can tell if what people are saying is true," now Anna is concerned about clarifying her own truths, critical of anyone who stands for nothing. Whether she is commenting on another student or on her own learning, shallowness or "superficiality" bothers Anna a lot: "You just can't stop from saying anything," she says. "I don't see how anyone cannot have a viewpoint and not want to say anything about it. And if you think someone else is wrong, how can you go on and not say anything?"

Anna speaks what she thinks and expresses what she feels, knowing she is disruptive and disturbing. Saying what she thinks, interrupting the flow of nice conversations, has in fact kept Anna out of school social clubs and popular cliques and has often made her classmates furious with her. But Anna has come to a conclusion: "I think I've hit a point where I don't care what all the popular people think," she says. "[Before] I really cared about fitting in, but now I have my own bunch of friends and I don't care what anyone else thinks of me. So, you know, a while ago I wouldn't have said anything, because I'd be afraid that people would say, 'What a strange person,' but I don't care anymore."

Anna distances herself from those people who seem "unreal" to her, or "irrational," or "superficial"—those people who don't look around themselves at the world, don't express their thoughts and feelings, but align themselves with popular opinions or nice appearances. She questions this "Pollyanna" view of reality where people don't want to know about people who are different, people like her, who are poor, who have unemployed fathers or violent brothers. "I've had to go through it," Anna says, speaking about being poor in what she terms a rich girls' school. Having been through it, Anna finds those people who will not listen or don't want to know "scary."

And yet she continues to speak from her experience, risking their disparagement:

> I get called a cynic all the time by everybody. They are, "you are such a cynic, and you are such a pessimist," but I'm not. You have to be, I think anybody who is living with somebody, you have to be cynical, you can't just . . . I mean Pollyanna would have problems . . . really, you have to be realistic about it. And thinking that life is peaches and cream is not realistic either, it's not real . . . And if you are not cynical about anything and think that every day is wonderful . . . it really grates on you when you have somebody around you like that, that is like Pollyanna. It's just like, 'Get away,' that's really scary, you know. You can't deal with someone like that.

Anna speaks about how she suspects others think of her—as a cynic, as a pessimist, as crazy—and by facing into these judgments, knowing them, repeating them, she lives with them, turns them from becoming somehow prophetic or overpowering to a self-conscious commentary on the distinction between her reality, her experience, and a Pollyanna existence. In this way Anna reveals the irony of polite masquerades, of hypocrisy and fraudulent relationships designed on the surface to protect people's feelings but which are, from her viewpoint, "crazy-making" conventions that separate people from one another, from themselves, and from reality.

Anna at fourteen, determined to get underneath this patina of niceness and piety, is not so sure she wants to join the elite or "normal" world to which she has entry. Instead, echoing Virginia Woolf's suggestion in *Three Guineas* that women gain a university education, enter the professions, and then form a "Society of Outsiders," Anna says that she "will be one of those people who go through college and get a Ph.D. and I'll live at the bottom of a mountain in Montana, just one of those weird people. Have a chicken farm. I don't know. Then I'll just write books or something." For the present, Anna imagines herself giving the senior speech she wants to give—"the best Senior Speech in the world in terms of shocking people," the speech where she tells what she knows through experience about reality.

Neeti: The Perfect Girl

Neeti, Anna's classmate—friendly, intense, her long dark hair elegantly braided, of Indian descent—is an outspoken resister at age twelve. But in contrast with Anna, who becomes increasingly outspoken over the five years of the study, Neeti becomes increasingly quiet, popular with other girls, striving to raise her grade point average from the imperfection of 3.7 to a perfect 4.0, active in sports and other school activities, and involved in increasingly complicated and futile attempts to be always nice and kind, never mean or rude. To stay with herself—to attend to her complex thoughts and feelings—is to risk being called "bad" or "mad," in both senses of the word, or more simply "selfish." To stay with others, Neeti chooses in effect to bury herself.

Listening to Neeti at age twelve, we are drawn by her knowledge of human relationships and psychological processes into an awareness of how closely and carefully she observes the relational world. Neeti tells us that "watching" and "listening" are key to the way she learns about people and the world. "I watch people," she says, "I watch over and over again . . . It's like, listen and learn, you know. Like I like learning from people's mistakes . . . It's not nice having people make mistakes, but it helps me out." If you want to know people, Neeti advises the woman who is sitting with her, "stand back," wait and watch, because "if you want to have friends and you are going to plunge into things, you can do it all wrong and never have a chance at having them as friends." You have a chance only, she says, "if you take things gradually . . . look out and see how they act, and see . . . whether I can fit in."

It is difficult to know to what extent Neeti is also commenting here on the interview process itself, her concerns about fitting into this psychologist's categories or her cautions about this relationship. The careful distinctions Neeti draws between her feelings and the feelings of others allow her to hold the difference between what authorities, such as the camp director, are saying and what she knows to be true or real. But these distinctions become more difficult to hold in her relationships with her friends. With friends, as Neeti explains, she is more cautious and less likely to plunge in and risk doing things "all wrong," less likely to disrupt or interrupt. Instead, she uses her keen powers of observation—her watching and listening—to assure that she will do the right things in order to fit in. To this end, Neeti sharpens her observational skills and listens more closely. As she becomes more and more adept at reading others and sizing up the prevailing order of relationships, she finds herself, her feelings and her thoughts, slipping away.

Twelve-year-old Neeti thus struggles to stay connected with herself—with what she knows through experience, what she hears and sees—at the same time that she wants very much to be connected to her friends and to fit into the world of her school. Like Anna at twelve, Neeti struggles with whether to speak out, to say what she is feeling and thinking, as she carefully takes in the relational world. Like Anna, she feels that she has to be herself—that she cannot cover over her feelings and her thoughts. "I can't look at something and ignore it," she says; "I look at everything before I make my judgment . . . I have to figure it out." Looking at everything, however, Neeti also wants to respond to everything that she sees. Seeing that some people are alone, she tries "to be friends with most people." And Neeti feels good about her responsiveness to others. "I feel good when there is a person and she doesn't have anybody to be with that day, so I stay with her and I feel good." "It's really rude to be mean," she tells her interviewer, and so, "I just smile all the time."

Underneath her smile, Neeti feels irritated that people do not notice or appreciate her or see what she is doing. "It's like people do things and nobody appreciates it, and you feel like why should I be doing it?" Yet Neeti chastises herself for these feelings and thoughts. When she begins to question why she buries her feelings for ungrateful people, a small voice inside says that she is not being responsive to others enough. "When I see something happen," Neeti says, "I always think to myself, I could have stopped that . . . I always think about it . . . I could have done more."

Neeti tries to notice everything. Carefully she watches and listens in on the relational world. The temptation to be perfect, to be always there for others, to always smile, to always do the right thing, is irresistible. But inside Neeti knows that she is not perfect, that "nothing's ever really perfect," that she does not always feel like being nice, and these feelings eat away at her. Pushing these feelings underground, she moves out of relationship with herself and into relationship with an image of herself that other people respond to and seem to desire or value—one that she herself has come to see as nicer or safer.

We hear the doubling of Neeti's voice and vision as she tells her interviewer that the only time she can really say she is being herself is when she meets someone else's standards of perfection, but then moves to describe her struggle to speak what she feels and thinks in her relationships. Neeti wants to be recognized for who she is and not how popular she has become:

> That used to be my whole past life, you know, people being like picked out and selected . . . not just myself, but other people felt like me. But now I don't care anymore because I realize I'm still there, and people, like if I walk down the hall, people will still see me . . . It's like as long as, like any friends I'm part of now, if they are really friends . . . if they're not going to be your friend unless you're famous or something, it's not worth it.

But while Neeti struggles to be "still there," to stay visible as herself and to have friends who are "really friends," she also knows the power of being chosen, and she wants to be popular. She herself acts differently around boys, because "I don't know if they'd like me for me, but I don't know if I act like myself, I can't tell." Playing the popular perfect game, Neeti risks not knowing what is an act and what is really her. "People think this is the only way," she observes; they think, "I can't have any other friends if I don't do it this way, so they'll just do it this way." Reflecting on herself, she tries to sort out what she is doing:

> I think I often do it, but I can't tell; just like I said, other people can't tell. Like I'm sure, like now it's hard to know the real you, you know, there are so many different people around . . . that are different, and so I have learned the way to act from people's

experiences, and my own experiences, and I guess that's the way I always act; so either that's me or something that I totally don't know.

Learning the way to act both from other people's experiences and her own experiences, Neeti cannot tell if she is being herself, if she is being real, or if she is "doing it"—acting different to be popular, to fit in, to make other people choose her, to make others feel good. And since other people can't tell either, the real Neeti who feels something different from what she is saying and what others are seeing seems in jeopardy. Her experience is now indistinguishable, at least on the outside, from others' experience of her. Neeti says uncertainly, "Either that's me or something I totally don't know."

A year later, thirteen-year-old Neeti continues to struggle with this relational impasse. Her desire to say what she feels and knows conflicts with her desire to have relationships, not to disrupt relationships, not to hurt anyone. As Neeti moves further out of relationship with herself, she also sounds emotionally uninvolved with her life. Although she appears self-assured in school and describes how she and her classmates disagree with one another and "get thrills out of seeing a teacher be wrong," she does not speak with passion or interest about learning. She is a hard worker, is considered smart, and strives for good grades. She says to her interviewer, "I just think that school is something, the only reason I'm learning all this is to get into college, and that's the only reason I'm here."

In fact, this year the public arena of school and the private world of personal relationships are split apart for Neeti, and we have no sense that she stands firmly in either. Saying that her relationships are "always there," Neeti monitors herself closely. Still struggling with the impossible task of living up to images of female perfection and never saying something that would lead another person to feel hurt, Neeti finds herself walking through a relational minefield. Asked to talk about an experience of conflict, she tells of "one friend I have and she is supposedly my best friend, you know, and I don't talk to her, because like everybody hates her in class . . . I mean I don't ever like her." This unpopular "friend" follows Neeti around and as a result Neeti feels she has to explain this encumbrance to her other friends. She cannot talk to the girls because "she's so sensitive." And so, Neeti concludes, shifting momentarily to a second-person voice, "There's not much you can do" before returning to her first-person experience of paralysis or impasse: "And I can't say anything to her, because she'll be hurt, so I have no idea what to do." With this change of voice, Neeti recapitulates in the interview session her giving up of her first-person voice and then not being able to say anything and not knowing what to do.

Neeti, feeling trapped in a scene which is not of her making, which is not what she wants, then tells a story of relational treachery, explaining that she and a friend who was really her friend backed out of a plan they had made to go to camp with this unpopular "best friend":

> [This girl] didn't sound offended; she said, "Okay." But we knew that she was hurt, you know, and so like we knew, we felt bad, but we didn't want to go there . . . So one day, this is me, not really, but there is another friend . . . she called up [this unpopular girl] . . . She and I were on the phone . . . and she pretended that I wasn't on the line, so I heard what they were saying. And so she mentioned my name and everything . . . [She said], "Do you know what they did? . . . [They] called me up one day out of the blue and said they weren't going to camp with me" . . . And she was upset, but there was nothing I could do about it . . . And she never said anything about it . . . She's nice to me . . . So her Mom called my Mom . . . and she was upset, but she didn't make it sound upset, you know . . . So now [my friend] and I and a few other girls had decided to go to another camp, and she goes, "Well, can I come?" And I go, "If you want to. It's up to you." Because I don't want her to come, but I can't say no.

Neeti, speaking now from the underground—protected by the confidentiality of the interview and perhaps by her sense of her interviewer as someone who knows her and someone who will stay with her—speaks her conflict clearly. Her dilemma is "that I don't like this girl at all, that I absolutely hate her, but I don't know how to act because I have to be nice." Neeti then describes with remarkable acuity the fraudulence woven into this relational drama—a drama involving both girls and women. The unpopular girl, after being abandoned and hurt by Neeti and her friend, does not "sound offended" but says "Okay" and continues to "be nice" to Neeti. Neeti finds out how she feels not by asking her but by secretly listening in on a set-up phone conversation. The girl's mother calls, upset, "but didn't make it sound upset." Neeti is clear that she does not want to be near this girl who follows her around, yet she responds to her desire to go with her to a different camp by saying, "If you want to. It's up to you." Neeti expresses her "hate" for this girl to the interviewer but does not know how to act because, as she says, "I have to be nice."

Neeti clearly knows the real and false of these relationships. She is a careful and deliberate observer: "I watch people and how they interact with each other . . . I look to see how people act differently when they are with some people and differently with others. And I think I can tell a lot about people." Yet Neeti feels intense pressure to be nice, to keep up false pretenses, and also does not want to upset this girl she dislikes so strongly. And there are other people to think about: "Her sisters and my sisters are friends," Neeti says. "Her mom and my mom are good friends, our parents have each other over for dinner." This unpopular girl, it seems, is omnipresent in her life—she lives close by, they carpool together. And Neeti knows this girl is easily hurt and depends on her friendship: "She called me one day and tells me, 'My world was shattered when you wouldn't talk to me.' So what am I supposed to say?"

Neeti wants to say "I hate you. Please leave me alone," but she also does not want to upset anyone—the girl, their sisters, their mothers—with these feelings. She has evidence that if she says what she feels this girl will be "shattered." And so Neeti describes a false and a "suffocating" closeness that feels like "being married" to someone she does not love. To protect the girl from being hurt, Neeti has to remove herself from the relationship. Unable to speak their feelings to each other, these feelings become amplified—the girl "follows her around," "suffocates her," and Neeti's dislike becomes an intense "hate." At the center of the dilemma, then, is an irony: By hiding her true feelings and reactions in order not to hurt this girl, to be seen as nice, and to avoid conflict in their relationship, Neeti participates in a relationship that is cruel and false. Her unspoken actions both betray her own feelings and leave this girl whom she wishes to protect confused and really alone, possibly more hurt than if Neeti were to say what she really felt. And so, ironically, to save a relationship Neeti participates in creating a false relationship in which there is no possibility for dialogue but only continued misunderstanding and bad feeling.

We watch Neeti's relational world darken as she becomes caught and seemingly hopelessly tangled in a web of fraudulent and ultimately cruel behavior. What she wishes for is an end to conflict. Unspoken, unvoiced, and thus taken out of relationships, her feelings and thoughts have come to seem out of proportion and out of perspective and thus impossible to bring into relationships with others. And yet, Neeti remains an astute observer of the human scene. In a trenchant and wonderfully ironic description of the relational world of her classroom, she notes that: "Nobody's mean from where I stand, but there are people who have hurt feelings." In this world of perfectly nice girls which she aspires to fit into, everyone—as she knows, including herself—"is talking behind people's backs."

At fourteen Neeti no longer speaks publicly—or even privately to her interviewer—about bad feelings, anger, or hatred. "I like to do the best I can," she says, when asked to describe herself. "I will do it to the best of my potential . . . I am conscientious about things that are going on around me, like I notice little things. I observe little things and I care for people around me." Asked how she has changed over the years, Neeti dutifully says that unlike when she was twelve, now she realizes "how important school is and how important friends are." Neeti appears to be the perfect girl this year—a straight A student with no bad thoughts or feelings, the girl everyone wishes she could be.

But when her interviewer asks Neeti to describe an experience of relational conflict, Neeti tells yet another version of the same story of relational impasse she has struggled with for the past two years. "I have a friend," Neeti begins, who "is thinking about running for president." "She's asking me if she is going to win, and I know she is not going to win and I don't know whether to say, 'Yah, I know you are not going to win,' or just say, 'Try for it, you never know.'" Though Neeti knows the "competition is going to win," she chooses not to say this to her friend, "because it would hurt her if I was honest." "In [such] situations," Neeti explains, "I think it's better to be nice," since "she might have been a little angry with me if I was honest with her."

Neeti still holds the distinction between what she really feels and thinks inside and what she feels she can say to her friend. This year, however, she seems less confused and less ambivalent about how to act and what to say. In this situation where the conflict, she says, is "whether it's more important to tell what you think or whether to tell what that person wants you to think," her decision is now somehow clear and justifiable—she will do the "nice" thing, she will do "what [her friend] wanted" rather than hurt her or cause her to be a "little angry."

Although Neeti knows what she is doing—knows she is telling her friend what she thinks her friend wants to hear and not what she really thinks—she no longer agonizes about being dishonest, no longer struggles much with the gap between what she feels and what she says. Carefully scrutinizing her friends and relationships for any sign of conflict, Neeti holds herself at bay and becomes a reflection—a mirror or sounding board for what others "want [her] to think." Doubling her voice, Neeti feels good that she can know what she knows and yet protect her friend from her knowledge.

But though the relational surface looks smooth and calm and may even feel smooth and calm, Neeti is involved in relationships that are not psychological connections. In contrast with herself at twelve, when she brought her feelings into relationship—feelings of concern and anger and fear and sadness that led to open conflict and disruption and eventually to a greater understanding of herself and other people—Neeti has now taken her feelings out of relationship, and increasingly has difficulty voicing anything but the nice and kind self she shows the world.

For Neeti to buy into this world of perfection, to become the model student and the model friend, is not to speak about—and, we suggest, eventually not to know—her thoughts and feelings. Unlike Anna, whose disruption will continue to put her at political risk, Neeti's movement underground may eventually place her at risk psychologically.

Liza: Cover Girl

For Liza at twelve the struggle around what to know is audible in her voice, visible in her face.[10] "I don't know," she says over and over again when the interviewer asks her what stands out for her over the past year, "I don't know, probably grades."

> *Why are grades important?*
> I don't know, I don't know, it's for me and for my parents and so
> I try to do well so that, I don't know, for my future, for my parents,
> so that they're not disappointed, I don't know, for a lot of reasons.

At twelve Liza says she feels great loyalty and indebtedness to her parents—"I mean, they pay for me to go to this school," she says, "they pay for a good education, and it's not right to disappoint them." She has taken in her parents' voices, repeating their maxims for good living—"you can't, you just can't do whatever you want, you have to do what you should do . . . if you're perfectly capable and you have potential and stuff, there's no reason why you can't, you know, use that to get what you want out of life . . . you know, I just think that that's the way it should be, you should always try to do your best." Switching out of the personal "I" to a general "you," Liza's first person slips into a second person and she disappears. At twelve she rarely says what she thinks and feels in first-person voice, only the words that precede them: "I don't know, I've been brought up to do the right thing usually, if I know what it is . . . you just know . . . if you were brought up, you know, learning the proper way to do things and, you know."

To Liza, learning the "proper way" seems to mean finding a way out of conflict and disagreement, "taking an in-between side," she says, as she does when she and her parents disagree. In school, Liza says, she, like "everyone I know," takes the teacher's point of view, "because they're the ones holding the grade book." Privately she tries "to decide which is more right to you . . . without anyone else's opinion." Consciously taking what she knows safely underground, where she can examine what she is learning and decide for herself what she thinks and feels is right, twelve-year-old Liza leaves the world of her family and her classroom unaffected and unchanged by her voice, her feelings, ideas, and opinions.

Like Judy and Neeti, Liza at twelve comes up against a powerful wall of cultural norms and the conventions of female imagination, as she traverses the terrain between childhood and adolescence and travels from girl to woman. Liza wants desperately to be seen as "normal." Taking in the shoulds and shouldn'ts around her, she begins to find it difficult to describe herself in her own terms. "Everyone could just like say a lot of good things and bad things about themselves," she begins, "but I don't really know what to say, because I don't want to sound really queer or something . . . I don't know, I think I work pretty hard in school and I fit in pretty well." The threat of falling outside the boundaries of what is considered appropriate and acceptable threatens to silence her as she judges herself by others' standards, knows who she is because she fits in, and knows she fits in because her relational life appears typical, normal. "I'm just an average, everyday person who goes to school," she continues, "who has a best friend, I don't know . . . likes guys, goes places on the weekends, stays home all Sunday to do homework, I don't know . . . just normal."

Liza molds herself into her image of the average girl, the good girl, the proper girl as defined by the upper-middle-class white world she has grown up in: she does well in school (though not so well that she stands out), "gets along with" her family, has a lot of friends, "likes guys." So careful about how she looks and how well she fits in, Liza says little about how she feels and what she thinks. She does not want to say or do anything to disrupt her carefully constructed image—"You don't want to spread anything around," she says, "You don't want to cause anything to occur that doesn't have to."

But Liza is anything but average. Her looks and the degree of her involvement with boys have already placed her on the periphery of her seventh grade class, where she must be ever vigilant of how the other girls see her. Because she has left her girlfriends for "guys," Liza says, she has to keep her "eyes open all the time." As she is with adults in her life, Liza has to "be omniscient" around other girls. "You can't just ignore something," she explains to her interviewer, touching briefly on the problem of her reputation among the girls in her school, because if you did "it might cause you to, I don't know, regret something."

Her eyes open wide, Liza sounds a bit like Neeti as she makes inferences about what is "inside of" people by watching "the way they relate to each other and the way they relate to you." Paying close attention, Liza says, "I think you know what to say and what not to say"; you are "like sensitive about what you say so that you don't disturb or hurt [a friend] in any way." "But how would you deal with a disagreement between you and your friends?" her interviewer asks, wondering perhaps what she really thinks and feels about this tiptoeing around in her relationships. "I don't know," Liza adds, "by doing probably what you wanted to do in a way that would be discreet enough so that you wouldn't like—so that you wouldn't . . . I don't know, make it too obvious." Unlike younger children who, she says, "kick . . . or punch" people, Liza says she prefers "a pleasant fight, you know, where you kind of ignore the person or just try to step back."

Liza does not wish to be alienated, to feel alienated, from others. But living always in the gaze of others, waiting for the judgments of others, and yet never wanting to be "obvious," Liza feels pressure to act in ways that feel uncomfortably false. In a halting voice that alternates between first and second person she describes a time when she feels she's not being her true self: "I don't know . . . when you're probably just—I don't really know, I mean, when you're talking with someone who really, you know, is putting pressure on you . . . I don't know, you're constantly like smiling and laughing and talking about things that you don't know anything about." In touch with the pressure and discomfort she feels during such moments, Liza also has her finger on the pulse of what others need and want from her. At twelve, she seems balanced on a precipice, one minute hoping for genuine relationships—friends who are "really friends," she says, "will always stick by you"—the next minute stumbling on the dangers of fraudulence, feeling pressure to talk "about things that you don't know anything about."

Liza wants to be a "role model" of what she defines as the ideal woman—"someone who is not afraid to speak up . . . who's not really stupid"—yet her ambivalence is palpable. "[You want to be] a person who can speak out?" her interviewer asks, wondering how this view fits in with the Liza who is private and discreet and normal. "Yeah," Liza replies, "but who's not too . . . I don't really know . . ." Who's not too what, we wonder, as we listen to Liza's voice trail off. Too outspoken perhaps, too indiscreet, too improper, too disruptive? Liza, who says "I have a guilty conscience," polices herself against such extremes; she keeps her eyes and ears open "at all times" for signs of her own indiscretion.

Yet, this twelve-year-old girl, whose main problem, she says off-handedly, is "that I don't have blonde hair," clearly wishes to be more than a reflection of others' expectations, more than a receptacle for others' opinions, ideas, and values. Though she appears on the surface to take in her teacher's point of view uncritically, underneath she wants a teacher who speaks with "feeling, . . . with an interesting tone in [her] voice . . . [who] brings some examples" from life experience. Liza wants to connect with what she is learning—to be, herself, a person who speaks out with feeling.

And so, twelve-year-old Liza struggles to stay with her feelings and thoughts as she tries to hold together the disparate voices she has taken in. Speaking sometimes in a voice laced with shoulds that promotes radical independence and autonomy, Liza tells of her desire to be mature, by which she means completely self-sufficient: Parents "are not always going to be there for the rest of your life," she explains to her interviewer. And you have to realize that "you either . . . take care of [things] by yourself or someone has to take care of [them] for you." Thus she abjures her relational desires and knowledge.

Mingled with this voice of emerging independence and separation is a voice of feminine silence and acceptance—a soft voice that knows when to be sensitive and when not to "disrupt," how to be "discreet" and compromising. Struggling with these competing voices, Liza sees the hint of an opening—"when people can see both ways, it's kind of like being bilingual, you know." The possibility of communicating with people in their own language is seductive to Liza because it removes the "reason for a lot of conflict." But as she dances back and forth between her "I don't know" and the all-knowing, all-seeing "you," which becomes the "eye" of the culture,[11] the already internalized self-scrutiny that she carries from home to school and school to home again, we wonder how she will, without conflict, negotiate these disparate voices.

"I am basically the same person," thirteen-year-old Liza tells her interviewer a year later. "I think like my ideas have changed and everything like that," but "there's been no like radical change. I haven't changed that much. I think that I have grown psychologically, but . . . I haven't changed. I have kept like the same consistency." Yet, Liza soon implies that she stands in the midst of a cool wind of change that whips and swirls around her, moving her, almost imperceptibly, "to a different level of life . . . a different psychological level." Thirteen is a "pressured time," Liza explains, "because like, you know, your friends change and everything becomes really different and then suddenly you are not like a little kid anymore . . . You are a lot more complicated now. You have more things to worry about; more things to deal with, social pressures, everything."

Indeed, Liza and Liza's life sound more complicated. Her struggle to "fit in" and remain a safely discreet member of her class has given way to open tension with the other girls as she leaves them not only for the world of dating but for a different kind of friendship.

"I've had lots of boy friends," she tells her interviewer. "Girls are not always the best friends to have. I'd rather have a guy friend more than a girl friend." "Why is that?" her interviewer wonders. "Because," Liza explains, "girl friends are really picky, you know, and like the slightest thing you do wrong, they're like, 'Oh,' and I don't know, guys are more accepting as friends I think . . . [girls] are more critical of you, you know, and they're always more, you have to be careful about what you do and say and all sorts of things like that . . . I think it is sort of generally true."

Liza connects her withdrawal from or disparagement of the world of her friends with their anger and criticism of her. Extricating herself from what she feels are the constraints of girls' jealousies, disconnecting from the girls who are in her mind so "picky" and critical, Liza maneuvers carefully in their presence, faking it for the sake of relationships which she sees as essential.

> You're either more careful about what you say or you are sort of faking it, you know. You are faking . . . I don't know. Like if you are, I don't know, if you're sort of like thrown together with someone you try to like adapt to like them, so I don't know. You just sort of have to, I don't know, sometimes, if you know you are not going to get along by being yourself.

Even as Liza pulls further away from the girls in her class, she feels bad and "a little down" about the changes in her relationships. She expects there will be times like this in her life when friends "sort of go against you" and "you are doubting yourself" and "you are just bummed out," yet she sounds defensive and bitter about the "little fights and squabbles" she has with these girls. "If you don't care," about a person, she says, "if you don't get along with them anyway, then it doesn't matter." "If you don't care, it must be useless." After all, she decides, her classmates lack a kind of psychological maturity. Speaking in the general "you," Liza seems to underscore her alignment with adult views of maturity against the childishness of these girls: "If you act mature . . . [adults] will probably accept you as that . . . If you are given the opportunity to act older and to get, you know, more privileges and to be more sophisticated . . . I think generally you will take it." Although she is "one of the youngest people in my whole class," she says, distancing herself further from her classmates, "I'm more mature than a lot of people that are older than I am." Moreover, it is "depressing," Liza says, that so many girls in her class act immature or "stupid." "That annoys me when someone is really stupid." "I don't have a lot of patience with stupidity, I really don't . . . I don't know, you can tell when they are faking it, you know, you can tell when they're acting dumb . . . I mean I don't understand why you would want to act dumb. That is not, I don't know, I would never try to do that."

To Liza, acting "stupid" or "dumb" means acting out, being silly or loud and speaking out. Perhaps for both reasons Liza distances herself emotionally and psychologically from the girls around her. She does not question how or why the girls in her class "that used to be the best class"—"We had teachers like you wouldn't believe saying how good we were"—now "frequently run laps in the gym" for breaking school rules and acting out. She does not question why a girl in her class who is "really bright" gradually, over the last few years, feels "worse and worse about herself, you know, getting really bad grades and everything." "She should have just worked," Liza says, rather than asking why such a smart girl would purposefully "write in the blanks [of a science test] like the Sesame Street people or something." "It just totally blows me over," Liza says in disbelief. "I don't understand." Yet Liza talks about these girls.

Distancing herself from her classmates and what they are doing and saying, Liza also describes moments of genuine relationship with herself and with these girls. "There is sort of like an instinct in every person," Liza tells her interviewer, "there is something in you that makes you want to do something . . . impulsive . . . spontaneous," like the time she and her girlfriends cut class: "Eight of us, you know, in a little line walking down the halls," Liza says, her eyes twinkling with the memory. "I mean, it was so natural, it was so successful . . . it felt good, I really did. It felt like we were heroes for a while . . . Sometimes it feels really nice to rebel, because I don't do it often." Speaking now in the first person, Liza places a moment of authenticity—a moment of genuine pleasure—in the context of a rare act of resistance with girls in her class. But neither she nor her interviewer comment on this scene that stands in such odd relationship to what she has said moments before about girls and girlfriends.

As Liza overrides this "I" with the "eye" of the culture, and her girlfriends for the "true friend relationships of boys," she exchanges those rare experiences of spontaneity, times when she feels "impulsive," "so natural" and like her "true self," for a maturity which sounds forced, artificial, and fake. The definition of maturity Liza espouses is at odds with her experience of the girls in her class. And yet she cannot resolve which is faked and which is real.

Against the story of cutting class, Liza describes her "mature" relationship with her boyfriend, four years her senior. This is a relationship of "limits" and control for Liza, since she has always been aware that her boyfriend "could want more than you could give, you know, in the sense that, the physical sense." Reflecting on her feelings about her boyfriend's desire, Liza says:

> I mean, I will refuse to a certain point . . . I think that every person has to establish a limit and then you should stick with it, you know, because as I said before, it's like you can't change your priorities in the middle of things, because if you do, then you are really weak, you know, you know that you are like a weak person. And it's really important to think things like that through. You know, just sort of, as if, you know, you had to get in the car with a drunk driver, it's sort of, you know, a decision like that, I think.

Equating her relationship with her boyfriend to getting in a car with a drunk driver, Liza conveys what she cannot say directly—her fear that she is in a life-threatening situation. Knowing about the dangers of getting "pulled under, so to speak," about being seduced into feeling "wonderful" without "thinking things through," she sets and patrols her boundaries.

Liza, who says she finds guys more accepting and easier to talk with, struggles to say what she feels and thinks to her boyfriend who, she says, "is sort of a possessive person." She cannot, she says, tell him she dislikes this in him and wants to see other people, for fear of making him "really mad . . . He acts sort of like, 'You are going out with me and that's it,'" she explains, "and I don't know." She decides to "let it"—meaning her feelings—"go" for a while, "put [my wishes] out of my mind," she says, "contradict" herself, by which she means override her voice, change her priorities, and, because "I wasn't sure of his reactions, so I didn't tell him . . . He could have gotten mad, he could have gotten upset. I mean, I didn't know what would come, you know, I didn't know what would come of it."

The social landscape has changed for Liza at thirteen but her struggle, so close to the linguistic surface,[12] has not. Now caught between relationships with her girlfriends, which are filled with ambivalence and conflict, and the world of "maturity" and romance, where under the shadow of a possessiveness which carries with it a threat of violence, she finds it difficult to know what she knows and speak her feelings, Liza does not know with whom she is safe, whom she can trust, "who's really worth it and who's not."

At fourteen and in the ninth grade, Liza has dyed her hair blonde, turning her wish for blonde hair at twelve into a reality. "I'm a busy person," Liza tells her interviewer this year, "Your social life seems to pick up when you get taller, get bigger, you know, older, and stuff." Observing herself from outside of herself, constantly aware of her "looks," Liza explains her changes in visual terms:

I think just getting older. I don't know, my appearance has changed a lot, like my physical appearance, like I am taller and thinner than I used to be. I don't know, I am all around better looking than I used to be, so I guess when you are being better looking than you used to be, you feel a little better than you used to feel . . . I don't know, like I used to be fat, be sort of fat . . . I just got sort of different looking than I used to be . . . I don't know, like if other people used to criticize me for the way I looked instead of look at me now, you know.

Seeing herself through the eyes of others, Liza proudly describes the extent of her physical changes:

> Like I walked into school this year and a teacher asked me who I was, and like I have been going here since first grade and I said, like, "No, you can't be that person." And I'm like, "Yeah. I just got sort of different looking than I used to be."

Liza's gaze has shifted to a point outside herself, the point in the social world where "everyone's always commenting," and as she aligns herself with this gaze, she is unrecognizable. "I still have my personality," she adds almost as an afterthought, as if to rescue herself from disappearing, as if she feels in danger of losing herself.

Liza's appearance (or disappearance) is striking. Becoming thinner and thinner has changed her "attitude" as well as her social life, especially her relationship with her boyfriend and her best friend. Through visual metaphors she positions her self and her relationships in space and in time: "I am all around better looking" she says, speaking again of how she has changed over the year. [Me and my boyfriend] "drive around in [a sports car] together," she says, explaining why her best friend calls their relationship "perfect." "You know, we look good together, have a good relationship."

Held in place by the gaze of others and now by her own self-observing ego, Liza nevertheless continues to feel an intense desire for relationships. "You can't survive like alone, you can't like sit on a mountain and be alone," she tells her interviewer. "You can't live alone, you need other people." Yet she feels "possessed" and "trapped" in her relationship with her boyfriend.

After returning from spring vacation with a girlfriend, feeling self-possessed and free, Liza finds it more and more difficult to talk with her boyfriend and to say what she feels: that she is angry with him and not sure she can stay with herself and remain in the relationship. When he overrides her attempts to speak with his arguments and protests, she finally breaks up with him:

> I mean he is very possessive of me . . . and he called one night and I just said, "You know, I am really tired of your possessiveness and I do have my own life, although you don't think I do" . . . I

said, "I really can't handle this anymore" . . . I was, "I told you
that I needed some space and I just need to breathe."

But her boyfriend is persistent and Liza, responding to his pursuit
of her and also perhaps to his recklessness and daring, decides that
she still likes him.

I said, "You are grounded and you just took the car and left." He
said, "Well, that was important to me. I wanted to get you." I
said, "Boy, he is going to get himself in trouble for me." I said,
"Alright!" It really showed me that he cared, I guess . . . That
action sort of taught me, he really cares, and I really still do like
him.

Although "he was just really possessive," and she initially thought
of "how I could be sort of free, how I could be unattached," Liza
stays in the relationship. "He cared about me enough to like pursue," she says. Thinking about the "really good time" they had
together and also the "security" of the relationship, Liza covers over
her feelings of anger and frustration by naming them "impulsive"
and "irrational": "It's good to be like your own person," she explains,
"but there is a point where you've got to say, you know, I really did
care about him and I was just being sort of irrational." After all, she
adds, "You can't criticize someone for caring too much."

Liza does not wish to hurt her boyfriend since "it is not good to
hurt someone," she tells her interviewer; "I didn't have anything to
lose." Yet what Liza loses is voice, saying that a relationship that
did not feel good to her is not good for her. Taken over by her
boyfriend's romantic sacrifice, swept away by his care and hurt
feelings, she justifies staying in a possessive and oppressive relationship by effectively retelling her story—renaming her anger and loss,
her desire for freedom, to "have my own life" "irrational."

Relationships pose unsolvable dilemmas to fourteen-year-old Liza.
Back and forth she slips on the thin ice of a paradox: To meet a
standard of maturity she calls "independent," she moves herself out
of relationship with others—with the girls in her class and with her
best friend: if you become too "dependent," she says, "you can
sometimes get mixed up as to who you are. You can sort of lose your

individual self." Out of relationship with others, however, she loses touch with herself and becomes really confused. Relationships then become truly dangerous and treacherous for Liza. With her boyfriend, for example, she no longer knows how she feels and what her point of view is and so she is persuaded in the name of love to remain in an emotionally abusive relationship.

Liza's insights about herself and her relationships seem to be gradually dissolving. Struggling to keep her thoughts and feelings above the pull of the currents swirling around her, she grabs first for the isolation or "maturity" of independence, then for the security of romance. She does not seem to remember the creative "private" strategies she used at twelve to stay with her voice, with the inner world of her thoughts and feelings when it was dangerous to speak aloud. Now fourteen and very blonde, Liza is also anorexic.

Girls at the edge of adolescence face a central relational crisis: to speak what they know through experience of themselves and of relationships creates political problems—disagreement with authorities, disrupting relationships—while not to speak leaves a residue of psychological problems: false relationships and confusion as to what they feel and think. Anna, Neeti, and Liza demonstrate three streams through this relational impasse, three responses to a crisis in women's development.

Anna, willing to be outspoken and disruptive, openly resisting becoming Pollyanna or taking on her view of the relational world, stays with what she feels and thinks and therefore knows. But she is not sure she wants to—or will ever be able to—bring herself fully into the world, to ever have a sense of place. Staying with her voice and also imagining herself living on a chicken farm in Montana writing books, Anna points to the dangers inherent in her resistance, the particular losses and the longings she feels.

Outspoken at twelve, Neeti moves her thoughts and feelings underground. She clearly names the discrepancy between what she feels and thinks and what she can say without hurting people or jeopardizing relationships. Neeti lives a double life. A perfect student, liked by everyone, she becomes, over time, emotionally disconnected from school and involved in relationships that are troubling to her. And Liza illustrates how the conscious underground can turn into a psychological resistance. A member of the underground at twelve, Liza disconnects from her childhood friends and aligns herself with standards of beauty and visions of maturity which for the most part have been defined by men. Out of relationship with others, Liza becomes more and more confused and out of touch with herself, until she no longer knows what she knows or can name what is happening in her relationships—her boyfriend's emotional abuse of her and her own abuse of her body.

For girls coming of age in this culture at this time, adolescence marks a potential point of departure from life experience. Because adolescence is a time when a variety of perspectives can be held and coordinated, a time when the hypothetical and the abstract can be entertained, girls risk losing touch with the specific—with their bodies, with their feelings, with their relationships, with their experience. And thus they are in danger of losing their ability to distinguish what is true from what is said to be true, what feels loving from what is said to be love, what feels real from what is said to be reality. Consequently, at a time of heightened physical and psychological risks in relationships, girls becoming young women are in danger of losing their ability to know the difference between true and false relationships.

6

Dancing at the Crossroads

At the crossroads of adolescence, the girls in our study describe a relational impasse that is familiar to many women: a paradoxical or dizzying sense of having to give up relationship for the sake of "relationships." As Jean Baker Miller has also suggested, this taking of oneself out of relationship in order to protect oneself and have relationships forces an inner division or chasm and creates a profound psychological shift. We heard this shift as a change in girls' voices as they reached adolescence. In essence, we were witnessing girls enacting and narrating dissociation.

Women's psychological development within patriarchal societies and male-voiced cultures is inherently traumatic. The pressure on boys to dissociate themselves from women early in childhood is analogous to the pressure girls feel to take themselves out of relationship with themselves and with women as they reach adolescence. For a girl to disconnect herself from women means to dissociate herself not only from her mother but also from herself—to move from being a girl to being a woman, which means "with men." For women, being with girls at this time means witnessing this process and listening to girls re-sound voices which many women have silenced or forgotten. Girls' development thus poses extremely difficult questions for women. How will we respond when girls who are doing very well by most standards of psychological as well as educational growth speak of losing their voices and losing relationship? In the course of this work, we began to appreciate the reality of the impasse—not only its psychological consequences but also its potential to defuse women's political power.

Our journey into women's childhood—our joining women with girls rather than comparing women with men—led us to hear, as if for the first time, the clarity and strength of girls' voices and the extent of girls' relational knowing. And we noticed how rarely girls actually appear or speak in writings about women's psychology. Women's disconnection from girls in the psychological literature mirrors the inner division we have been tracing—the tendency for girls as they become young women to dismiss their experience and modulate their voices. At adolescence, girls' ordinary courage—girls' seemingly effortless ability, as Annie Rogers says, to speak their minds by telling all their hearts—tends to turn into something heroic.[1] For girls at adolescence to say what they are feeling and thinking often means to risk, in the words of many girls, losing their relationships and finding themselves powerless and all alone.

Over the years of our study, even as they became more sophisticated cognitively and emotionally, young girls who had been outspoken and courageous in both an ordinary and a heroic sense became increasingly reluctant to say what they were feeling and thinking or to speak from their own experience about what they knew. Honesty in relationships began to seem "stupid"—it was called "selfish" or "rude" or "mean." Consequently, a healthy resistance to losing voice and losing relationship, which seemed ordinary in eight-year-old girls and heroic by age eleven, tended to give way to various forms of psychological resistance, as not speaking turned into not knowing and as the process of dissociation was itself forgotten. Girls reaching adolescence adopted survival strategies for spanning what often seemed like two incommensurate relational realities. And girls enacted this disconnection through various forms of dissociation: separating themselves or their psyches from their bodies so as not to know what they were feeling, dissociating their voice from their feelings and thoughts so that others would not know what they were experiencing, taking themselves out of relationship so that they could better approximate what others want and desire, or look more like some ideal image of what a woman or what a person should be. Open conflict and free speaking that were part of girls' daily living thus gave way to more covert forms of responding to hurt feelings or disagreements within relationships, so that some girls came to ignore or not know signs of emotional or physical abuse. And relationships correspondingly suffered. Girls, we thought, were undergoing a kind of psychological foot-binding, so that they were kept from feeling or using their relational strengths. Instead, these strengths, which explain girls' remarkable psychological resilience throughout the childhood years, were turning into a political liability. People, as many girls were told, did not want to hear what girls know. As girls' outspokenness or political resistance carried psychological risks, so girls' psychological resistance or not knowing had political as well as psychological consequences.

Witnessing these processes—seeing girls do well on tests of academic achievement, on standard measures of social and moral development, seeing them favored by their teachers and praised by their parents when they dissociated or dissembled—was deeply moving to us and to other women and men who were involved with us in this inquiry. As with the initial design of our study, we could not stay within the conventions of our profession and also listen seriously to what girls were saying. Girls' relational knowing made our own relational compromises transparent and also revealed the relational lies that are at the center of patriarchal cultures: subtle untruths and various forms of violation and violence that cover over or lead to women's disappearance in both the public world of history and culture and the private world of intimacy and love.

On a theoretical level, the evidence we gathered led us to consider early adolescence as a comparable time in women's development to early childhood in men's: a time when a relational impasse forced what psychoanalysts have called "a compromise formation"—some compromise between voice and relationships. Because this compromise removes or attenuates the tension between women's voices and the regeneration of patriarchal and male-voiced cultures, it tends to be seen as necessary and inevitable. In fact, it leaves a psychological wound or scar, a break manifest in the heightened susceptibility to psychological illness that boys suffer in early childhood and that girls suffer at adolescence. The timing of this loss of voice and this crisis of relationship can explain these asymmetries in women's and men's development.

In contrast with the murder at the crossroads that marks the Oedipus story and seals its relational deafness and blindness—Oedipus' need not to know what in another sense he knows (that his anger has become murderous and his love incestuous)—we offer a vision of women and girls dancing at the crossroads of adolescence, moving in relation to one another so that it becomes possible for girls and women to stay in relationship and to say what they know. In our interviews, we found that when women moved with girls, girls brought themselves into relationship with women and began to speak openly rather than trying to be good or bad girls. Women, coming into relationship with girls, became noticeably more radical—quicker to spot false voices and also to differentiate between real and idealized relationships. Thus a new kind of dance began between girls and women.

First steps in this dance came from the moves made by women who joined our project at Laurel School—psychologists and teachers who began to change their practice as we had, when they realized that they could do what they were doing only by not knowing what girls heard and saw. Patricia Flanders Hall, a psychologist and the former Dean of Students at Laurel School, writes about this process:

We could not avoid recognizing that [girls'] behavior reflected a similar kind of behavior among women at the school. We were not open with each other in public settings and, like the girls, had silenced ourselves beyond the walls of our classrooms or offices or in the presence of authority . . . We did not publicly disagree with policy, with each other, with men, with the Head of the School or the lunch menu. Above all, we began to fear that we were teaching girls to do exactly the same thing, and were perpetuating the same feelings of loss and inauthenticity that we recognized had colored our lives at the school. Clearly, how could we address questions of silencing without acknowledging and understanding our own silencing?

Women and Girls

Pat Flanders Hall was part of a group of sixteen women who, in the course of this project, began a series of three retreats to explore our relationship with our practices as psychologists, teachers, and administrators and also our relationships with the women and girls with whom we worked.[2] Judy Dorney joined the two of us as participants from the Harvard Project and took a leading role in charting the course of the retreats. Denise Andre, Claudia Boatright, Renee Bruckner, JoAnn Deak, Terri Garfinkel, Nancy Franklin, Louise (Skip) Grip, Marilyn Kent, Linda McDonald, Susie McGee, Sharon Miller, and Almuth Riggs joined Pat from Laurel. Reflecting on the outcome of the first retreat, Pat writes, "It took a very long time to exercise a modicum of courage to speak about this absence of authentic communication, and the resistance [to speaking] we mounted as a group of intelligent, educated women was remarkable." For the women as for the girls at the school, "being 'nice' to everyone was a familiar standard"—a seemingly safe way to navigate the relational waters of a middle-class, mainly white, largely female environment. As a member of the school's administration, Pat knew that in the presence of conflict her job was "to 'facilitate,' and that meant to prevent things from getting out of hand . . . [and] 'getting out of hand' meant any expression of feelings that could be construed as critical or disruptive to the smooth functioning of the school." And yet how can a girls' school function smoothly and without conflict if girls are becoming educated in the most basic sense—that is, learning to feel deeply, to think clearly, to draw out the implications of what they know through experience, to have the courage of outspokenness. A smoothly running girls' school within a patriarchal society and culture seemed an oxymoron.

After the first retreat, after moving into relationship and taking the first steps in speaking our feelings and thoughts, Pat writes about her own experience and that of others in returning to their work at the school. "We all sensed a frustrating 'lid' that we had put back on our conversations [after the retreat] and the bonds that had begun to form were only shared by eye contact in the hallways." Predictably, the conflict did not go away because the women did not talk about it or name it at the time. Instead, as the retreat process continued, women began listening to girls more seriously and took what they heard more deeply into themselves. The difficulty of this process becomes apparent in Pat's description:

It was first with a sense of shock and then a deep, knowing sadness that we listened to the voices of the girls tell us that it was the adult *women* in their lives that provided the models for silencing themselves and behaving like "good little girls." We wept. Then the adult women in our collective girlhoods came into the room. We could recall the controlling, silencing women with clarity and rage, but we could also gratefully recall the women who had allowed our disagreement and rambunctiousness in their presence and who had made us feel whole. And we recognized what it was we had to do as teachers and mothers and therapists and women in relationship. Unless we, as grown women, were willing to give up all the "good little girl" things we continued to do and give up our expectation that the girls in our charge would be as good as we were, we could not successfully empower young women to act on their own knowledge and feelings. Unless we stopped hiding in expectations of goodness and control, our behavior would silence any words to girls about speaking in their own voice. Finally, we dared to believe that one could be intelligently disruptive without destroying anything except the myths about the high level of female cooperativeness.

Asking then, "What did we do with what we learned?" she continues:

We first looked at disagreements among ourselves, and discovered that to take such a risk enhanced our relationships with each other. We looked beyond those relationships to the workplace and recognized that we had to bring this risk to our professional efforts

221

or continue to suffer a sense of frustration that was not worse because it had been named. We recognized that this is frightening work that cannot be done alone by a single woman but can only be successful in the supportive bonds of community. We also recognized that the sanctuary of a retreat setting allowed us to understand our knowledge and feelings with a clarity not possible in hierarchical work settings. And we agreed that the understandings we had reached sometimes conflicted with the vision of the school that we cared about and that we could not bring this knowledge back into our school effortlessly or without pain.

It was with girls that the women first began to experiment with change: "The easier time to begin to listen and speak in new ways was when we were working with the girls, and we all felt a sense of knowing wonder when they responded so quickly to us." Claudia Boatright, a most courteous and also scrupulously organized teacher, found herself permitting a loud personal argument in her classroom and was astonished to be thanked by the two girls for not interrupting them when it reached its natural conclusion. In another class, Claudia actively resisted her impulse to close off an emotionally tense conflict over a heated political question. She had come to see confronting conflict openly with strong feelings in public as essential to young women's education. Like Noura and her friends talking in loud voices on the phone and taking the time that they needed, the young women in her class spoke passionately about the Palestinian question, confronting rather than avoiding or defusing a political conflict that was confusing, frustrating, complex, and emotional. As Claudia resisted her impulse to defuse this emotionally volatile classroom conflict, so she also let the class run over and continue beyond the end of the hour.

Across a range of ages and contexts, women began listening to their own voices and also to the voices of girls. Strong voices and open disagreement still aroused discomfort, but we found ourselves hearing and encouraging girls' strengths. Linda McDonald, a preschool teacher, responded to a girl who came to her troubled by the behavior of the boys on the playground by encouraging her to speak directly to the boys and to use her "big girl voice." Nancy Franklin, an upper-school English teacher, stayed with her student when the student wrote about Andrew Marvell's poem "To His Coy Mistress" in a way that posed a radical challenge to conventional readings. Rather than interpret the poem from the point of view of the poet who "is trying to convince a reluctant young lady that they should make love while there is still time," her student, Anjli, "read it from the viewpoint of an innocent but perceptive and language-sensitive young girl" like herself. Anjli "called the poem morbid and found it terrifying and chilling." When Anjli received negative comments and low grades from Nancy Franklin's colleagues at other schools in a cross-grading exercise designed to ensure consistency of standards, Nancy chose to stay with her student and challenge the standards. Where her colleagues wrote "WRONG," Nancy said, "I don't think Anjli is wrong." Where her colleagues concluded that Anjli did not understand *carpe diem*, Nancy found in Anjli's response to the poem a new appreciation of the poem's power and a fresh reading.

Anjli's experience of hearing her feelings about the poem called wrong, and her identification with the young woman in the poem called "a misreading," are common enough experiences for girls and young women in schools and universities. Recent research shows what, as women, we remember—that in a myriad of ways girls and young women are given the message that their experiences and knowledge are not heard or welcomed in the classroom.[3] Perhaps we should not be so surprised when we hear Allisar, fifteen, tell the woman who interviews her that she has never experienced work that she loved. "See, that is what I want," she explains. "I want to do some work that I love doing, but I don't know if it is in my nature to love work." To Allisar, who radically splits work and love, education has little to do with personally trusting or believing: "I don't think you have to trust anything to get a good education. I don't think you have to trust any facts. You can know about them, but you don't have to believe in them to get a good education." Allisar has never had a teacher who, she says, "really makes you think and care about what you are learning," who asks the "type of questions that really makes you think so you feel exhausted" . . .

"that really revitalizes and massages your brain" . . . that would "relate everything down to the personal level . . . how is it going to affect you . . . That's how you get out the real emotion," she adds, "you know, feelings to understand or want to learn more about something." When girls are disconnected from what Audre Lorde calls "the erotic root and satisfactions" of their life work, girls' education can become, as Lorde might predict, "a travesty of necessities."[4]

Taking in the voices of girls like Anjli and Allisar, we began to move more authentically with one another and to become more willing to voice conflict and openly disagree. Listening to girls' voices, particularly in the time before adolescence, affected many women in ways that were unexpectedly powerful. Small voices began to give way to stronger voices, not knowing began to yield to memories of knowing, then of needing not to know or not to say what one felt and knew. And women began to speak in public and to act on the basis of what they knew through experience—to trust their own experience and the experiences of girls and other women.

At the center of this process, many women found themselves drawn by girls' voices into remembering their own adolescence and began to recall their own experiences of disconnection or dissociation at this time.[5] Such remembering seems essential if women are not going to justify or reimpose on girls losses which they have suffered. To reopen the question as to whether losses of voice and of relationship which many women have experienced are in fact necessary or inevitable, women have to experience the present as different from the past—to feel that now they are not without power or all alone. For this reason, the retreats, the opportunity to think and feel with other women, seem essential. Women's ability to ask new questions about voice and relationship and girls' development depends on experiencing ourselves as able to speak and also to stay in relationship with women—to feel sadness and anger without experiencing these feelings as overwhelming or as endangering relationships.

To answer Anna's question, then, what we have gotten out of this work with girls is an appreciation of the relational impasse girls experience at adolescence and a new understanding of women's psychological development, a relational theory that offers an explanation of developmental asymmetries between women and men, and a sense of an opening—a possibility for preventing psychological suffering and initiating societal and cultural change.

The girls in our study who keep their strong voices direct our attention to their mothers, but their mothers do not fit conventional images of good women. Anna's mother is strong in her relationship with Anna, but in describing this relationship Anna speaks of her mother's screaming at her and she feels her mother's feelings "gnawing at her." Eighteen-year-old Nawal, when asked how she has changed, describes the changes in her relationship with her mother which led to what she calls "my big realization":

> Okay, my Mom has black, curly wild hair, really dark skin. Dresses like, she wears a huge silver earring, does not fit the stereotypical Laurel mother image, does not. This is a woman who comes in from the senior luncheon and she says, "Nawal, am I dressed okay?" . . . and her hair was down and curly and she had enormous earrings, huge necklace, this black kind of fitted sundress thing, sandals, a lot of jewelry, and everyone was staring . . . And I love the way she dresses, and I love the fact that she is different . . . but when I was younger, it used to bother me, and I hated being Arabic. I hated being different, and I hated having an Arabic name. And I was really almost embarrassed by my Mom.

When Nawal's mother asked her directly, "Do you really want me to be like everyone else?" Nawal took the question seriously. "I thought about it for a while. At first I [thought] 'Yah,' and then I was like, 'Wait.' I thought about it and I tried to picture my mother like that. And I just couldn't . . . It makes me shudder, because that's not her." For Nawal, it was important to speak publicly about her realization. Devoting her senior speech to this subject, she voiced in the school's open assembly her resistance to American standards of beauty—the standards that led Nawal, a dark-skinned Arabic young woman, to wish for "long, long blond hair [and] blue eyes" and to judge herself and her mother as ugly or not beautiful. Nawal cried after her speech, her friends cried with her, and she felt "this weight was lifted and I finally said what I had to say to this school."

Nawal's comment echoed almost precisely the words of women teachers who spoke of feeling that they were working under a great weight in teaching what they were supposed to be teaching rather than what they felt it was important for girls to learn and know. For many reasons, it was harder for these women to finally say what they had to say to the school, and yet some of them did so by the end of the project. And the women's voices were in fact disruptive and associated with substantial changes in the lives of some of the women and also in the school.

As we witness so many of the perfect girls in our study become the perfect woman—the modern superwoman Catherine Steiner-Adair writes about or the "angel in the house" whom Virginia Woolf describes[6]—we feel ourselves tempted momentarily to forget or discount the resistant voices of younger girls, the girls who say what they are feeling and thinking, the girls who hold to what they are experiencing, the whistle-blowers in the relational world. In reentering girlhood and remembering images of perfection and various forms of psychological foot-binding that are imposed on girls at the time when they become young women, we found ourselves turning to the girls in our study who, because of color or class, live in the margins, who are so clearly at odds with the dominant models of female beauty and perfection as to reveal the cultural hand behind the standards.[7] These girls often spoke in loud voices, and among them we found many of our staunchest resisters. Like Anna and Nawal, they tend to have close confiding relationships with their mothers—relationships in which both mother and daughter speak, where they engage in open conflict and give voice to their feelings of anger and sadness, where both mother and daughter can feel the power they have to affect one another and thus the depths of their connection and love. It is for this reason that Nawal chooses her mother over the model: she cannot imagine a relationship with a model.

The daily reality of difference gives these girls sharp eyes for shallowness, for false commitments, "phony" relationships, and abuses of power, and gives their voices a strength and a clarity we found stunning. But for some there is also the painful reality of living in two worlds. The African-American girls, in particular, feel enormous responsibility to prove themselves in this microcosm of white society and, as Jenice says, "to wipe away some stereotypes that people have of blacks."[8] And yet because getting ahead is associated in this culture with being white, and since, as Jenice knows, "everyone's trying to get ahead," she resents that "as a black person I have been forced to assimilate." "Many of the people [here] really don't know that much about blacks," she explains, "and I think that blacks usually find out more about the ways that whites live than the other ways around." But "going to Laurel and going back to the black community" is also "really hard" for Jenice, because "blacks perceive me as someone who is trying to be white." Jenice feels the tensions and ambivalence and social pressure Signithia Fordham and John Ogbu describe of other black adolescents—their struggle between loyalty and identification with the black community and the "burden of acting white" if they act on their desire to excel in school.[9]

Jenice resolves this tension by finding strength in her relationship with her mother and listening to elders in her community who teach her to question what she is being taught, to wonder "what isn't written down" in her history books; who encourage her to transform her experience in school, "which wasn't a rewarding feeling," by insisting that school make "some kind of allowances for the way I think about something." As a result Jenice worked hard to "make sense" in her own mind and to "make order out of" her own experience. By the time she was eighteen and a senior, Jenice's goal was to continue on with school and rewrite history: "As far as education is concerned . . . I don't know that I felt as strong a commitment before . . . I mean, I know that a lot of young black students don't have the confidence in themselves that they should . . . and if they knew the things that blacks had done, it is something to be proud of, and I think it would help to advance the black race in general. And I feel some obligation."

Our dance with girls at adolescence began to move in new

directions as our project ended. At a national conference where we were presenting the results of our study, we suddenly missed the girls.[10] Their voices were so central to the findings we were presenting and were now powerfully affecting a large group of women and men. Carol decided to stay over in Cleveland for the weekend and to go to school on Monday morning to speak with the girls who were now thirteen and seventeen and who had been in the study for five years. We wanted them to know how strongly their voices were affecting other people and also to ask them how they wanted to be involved, now that we were writing about the work and presenting it in public.

The response of the thirteen-year-olds was clear: "We want you to tell them everything we said, and we want our names in the book."[11] With the seventeen-year-olds, it was far more complex: They sat silently in rows listening, and then answered by saying that they did not like us speaking about them behind their backs, that they wanted us to tell them everything we were saying about them, and then they would tell us whether or not they agreed and how they wanted to be involved. They wanted to go on retreat with us for a day. They wanted us to show them exactly how we did this work. We readily agreed.

Three of us—Lyn, Carol, and Pat—sat on the floor of a community center facing a room full of eleventh grade girls, some sitting cross-legged, some sprawled on their stomachs, a few sitting in fold-out chairs they found leaning against the walls. We had begun the retreat that morning by asking the girls to join with us by entering the process of our research. Our work rested on the belief that girls' voices were worth listening to, that it was possible for women to learn from girls and also necessary to listen to girls in order to understand women's psychological development. Since the girls' voices they would be listening to were their own voices or those of their classmates, these issues were issues of relationship in an immediate way. We asked girls to notice if they found themselves denigrating or trivializing or making fun of what girls were saying, and to ask themselves why they were doing this. We then explained our voice-centered method, the importance of listening to each girl's voice carefully by following the speaking self, the I who thinks and feels, through the interviews. Then we passed out excerpts from interviews with girls at different ages. We asked the girls to work in small groups, to listen for the voice of the girl speaking in each excerpt, and to describe what they were seeing and hearing and also how they would explain any changes or differences in the girls' voices. Now, after lunch, we sat together to talk about what they and we heard in these excerpts.

The girls clearly saw the empirical basis on which we had built our interpretation, and also experienced our way of working, but not all readily agreed with our interpretation of the changes in girls' voices. "We can relate to everything these people said," offered one girl, speaking for her group, "but not necessarily for the same reasons." "We were saying," said another girl,

> how we thought it was really strange that Victoria had this idea so powerfully in her mind and then we started . . . relating it to us and how we felt about Mr. and Mrs. things, and we were talking about how we wish there had been some background . . . about why she had come out and said this . . . You know, was she closer to her mom than she was to her dad. Or was she feeling her ideas . . . and she couldn't find her own self and she wanted to be an individual . . . And then we started relating to it . . . and how she was maybe trying to find herself and that she was saying how she didn't understand how her mom could find herself . . . when she didn't really have her own name.

Like seasoned researchers, these girls struggled to describe what they heard and what might account for the differences in the girls' voices: was it age, background, relational crises, personal experiences? "The one thing we noticed in this, as much as we really didn't want to admit it," said yet another girl, "was that we see how you can get the idea that we're confident when we're younger . . . [The older girl we read] didn't base her decision on what she wanted. She based her decision on what other people wanted . . . what other people felt. But the second grader . . . she just said, that's what I want."

And as they began listening to the voices of the younger girls, these young women were moved by what they were hearing—and surprised in ways that we found familiar. They too had forgotten these voices. They too called these honest voices "rude" and "mean." And hearing them again, they began to talk more freely about their own experiences and to remember what happened to themselves. Together we began to speak about the central questions of loss and prevention. "I mean," said one girl, "you have to have a distinction between [something superficial] and what you really, deeply, believe in. And that's what I don't understand. What stifles us from saying things like that."

As the conversation moved to the ways expectations of model looks and perfect girls affect girls' voices, Liza—herself outwardly perfect and cool—asked us what seemed, by the tone of her voice and the expression on her face, a most pressing question—a question about herself that she hoped psychology might answer for her:

> I would just like to know from you as psychologists or people with that kind of degree, is there such a thing as a person who is not necessarily perfect but who has everything together all the time? Not appears to but just does mentally, psychologically? Is there such a person? Is that possible?

A quiet settled over the room. The question was so real, so recognizable. Can there be a person, ever, who could be the girl everyone seems to want, not on the surface, but inside—who could really be her? The answer seemed obvious, perhaps—but the implication hung in the air—if the long journey did not end with perfection, what was all this expended energy about and for whose benefit?

For women to enter into relationship with girls means to break false images of perfection, to invite their most urgent questions into conversation, into relationship. One of the most difficult questions for the women teachers was whether it was legitimate for them to show girls their sadness and their anger and also whether they could reveal such feelings without losing control of themselves and of the girls. It seemed easier and also safer for women to try and model perfection for girls—perfect women, perfect relationships—and yet women's images of perfection were at odds with what girls know about women and experience in relationships. Thus women's success in being perfect role models for girls depended in part on girls' tacit agreement not to know what they know—their willingness to suspend their disbelief. Sensing women's fears about showing themselves in relationship, girls often were willing to withhold their feelings and thoughts in order to have "relationships" with their teachers. At the end of the day, when we were joined by some of the teachers who had been involved in the retreat process, this agreement unraveled. As the teachers expressed their wish for closer relationships with the girls, the girls pressed for authentic relationships with the women who teach them.

The teachers began by saying how deeply affected they had been as they began to listen more closely to what girls feel and know. Responding to this opening, one girl said that she preferred her men teachers because they "treat us like people" and "bring themselves into their teaching." The women were naturally taken aback by this observation. One offered a psychological explanation: mothers and daughters, she knew from experience, can have a hard time at adolescence. Perhaps these girls were projecting these conflicts with their mothers onto their relationships with their women teachers. The girls stayed with what they were saying, and one girl explained that, in fact, her own relationship with her mother was very close. Her problem with her women teachers was that they were not bringing themselves into their teaching and they were not treating girls "like people."

For women to bring themselves into their teaching and be in genuine relationship with girls, however, is far more disruptive and radical than for men. It means changing their practice as teachers and thus changing education. The wish on the part of both girls and women for more authentic relationships with one another and an appreciation of and also the difficulty in working out such relationships appropriately ended the day.

But we continued our conversations with girls. Anna and Neeti, whose voices had exemplified contrasting pathways of girls' development in our conference presentation, took copies of our paper home with them. We asked them to read the paper, especially the sections pertaining to them, and tell us whether they felt they were sufficiently disguised and also where they found themselves in disagreement or having strong feelings about what we were saying. Lyn would then meet with them and discuss the paper and their responses. Both girls showed the papers to their mothers and talked about it with them. Neeti's mother then spoke with Lyn at a meeting for parents. The paper had led Neeti and her mother to speak more openly with one another, so that Neeti was less alone and less hidden. Anna's mother showed the paper to Anna's father as a way perhaps of revealing to him what Anna knew and how she felt and thought about his violent outbursts.

We continue our relationship with some of the girls who have now left Laurel for college, and we remain connected to many of the women teachers. For ourselves, we are left with difficult questions about our practice as psychologists and also with a sense of discovery, of finding an opening in women's psychological development—a place where girls' development and women's psychology powerfully join. Girls' strong voices and healthy resistance to false relationship speak directly to the relational conflicts and problems that many women suffer. Our work with girls has clear implications for preventing psychological suffering in women, and also opens relational avenues through which women can recover their strong voices and their courage.

We are acutely aware of the need to listen to girls and explore relationships between women and girls in different settings. But what we have learned about women's psychology and women's development from our work with these one hundred girls is the power of beginning with girls' voices. From listening to girls at the edge of adolescence and observing our own and other women's responses, we begin to see the outlines of new pathways in women's development and also to see new possibilities for women's involvement in the process of political change. When women and girls meet at the crossroads of adolescence, the intergenerational seam of a patriarchal culture opens. If women and girls together resist giving up relationship for the sake of "relationships," then this meeting holds the potential for societal and cultural change.

Notes

References

Index

Notes

1. A Journey of Discovery

1. The "we" in this book refers, for the most part, to the authors, although at times the "we" may expand to include other researchers who have worked intensely on this project with us, particularly Elizabeth Debold, Judy Dorney, Barbara Miller, Annie Rogers, Mark Tappan, and Steve Sherblom. We will try to make such shifts in voice as clear as possible throughout the book.

2. Gilligan, 1977, 1982.

3. See Brown, 1989, 1991a, 1991b; Brown and Gilligan, in press; Gilligan, 1991a, 1991b; Rogers, 1992; Rogers and Gilligan, 1988.

4. Breuer and Freud, 1895/1955; Freud, 1895/1955, 1905, 1933/1965; Maudsley, 1879; Skey, 1867.

5. See Block, 1990; Demitrack, Putnam, Brewerton, Brandt, and Gold, 1990; Elder and Caspi, 1990; Hetherington, 1981; Peterson, 1988; Peterson and Ebata, 1987; Rutter, 1986; Simmons and Blyth, 1987; Werner and Smith, 1982.

6. Seligman, 1991.

7. Deutsch, 1944; Horney, 1926; Thompson, 1964; Miller, 1984.

8. Herman, 1981.

9. Much of the work of the Harvard Project on Women's Psychology and Girls' Development has been collected in a series of edited volumes: Gilligan, Ward, and Taylor, 1988; Gilligan, Lyons, and Hanmer, 1990; Gilligan, Rogers, and Tolman, 1991. In addition, see Gilligan, Johnston, and Miller, 1988.

10. Gilligan, 1977, 1982; see also Gilligan, Ward, and Taylor, 1988.

11. See Jordan, Kaplan, Miller, Stiver, and Surrey, 1991; also Jordan, 1987; Miller, 1976, 1988. Mary Belenky, Blythe Clinchy, Nancy Goldberger, and Jill Tarule (1986) describe women's connected ways of knowing; Ruthellen Josselson (1987) reports that women who have weathered crises in relationships have a stronger sense of self; Gisela Konopka (1966) reports the intensity of adolescent girls' desire for genuine connection with others and indicates that the need for

235

connection, by which girls mean involvement with others who "are real friends" or with an adult who appears as "a person," is unusually intense among girls who come to be called delinquent. Hilde Bruch (1978) describes anorexic girls' desperate need to know "what their parents truly feel and think." By refusing food, Bruch suggests, girls who feel unable to express strong feelings, "particularly negative feelings," in the midst of an idealized "perfect life" of "quiet harmony" push their families to "open fighting, angry outbursts." Catherine Steiner-Adair (1986, 1991) suggests that what girls can't say consciously and directly, they say "with their bodies": they are starved for genuine relationships, they "are dying" to be heard. Teresa Bernardez (1988) describes the psychological effects of cultural prohibitions against the expression of anger by women; and Dana Jack (1991) voices the inner dialogue of depressed women as a conversation between an "I" who wants and feels and knows from experience and an "Over-Eye" which looks at the woman so that she will see what she must or should want and feel and think, if she wants to be loved and to have relationships with others. The activity involved in silencing the "I" contributes to depressed women's feelings of exhaustion and despair.

12. Rogers, 1992.

13. Stern, 1985. See also Trevarthen, 1979; Murray and Trevarthen, 1985.

14. Scores on standard measures of sociomoral reflection (Gibbs and Widaman, 1982; Gibbs, Widaman, and Colby, 1982) and ego development (Loevinger, 1976; Loevinger and Wessler, 1970) reveal that both the seventh and tenth grade groups of girls in this study score higher than similar groups studied by other investigators. Individual scores on educational tests and grades provide additional evidence of the intellectual and cognitive development of these adolescent girls.

15. See Brown, 1989, 1991a, 1991b.

16. Lyn Mikel Brown, Sue Christopherson, Carol Gilligan, D. Kay Johnston, Barbara Miller, Jeannette McInnis, Lori Stern, Jill Taylor, and Janie Ward were interviewers from the Harvard Project; Kathy Manos and Carey Straffon were researchers from the Cleveland area. Because the Laurel School administration was interested in exploring the possibility of bringing such interviews into the life of the school on a more permanent basis, JoAnn Deak, then the school psychologist, and Nancy Strauss, the Director of the Upper School at the inception of the study, also interviewed a small number of girls. Dianne Argyris, Elizabeth Debold, Judy Dorney, Vivian Jenkins-Nelson, Annie Rogers, Deborah Tolman, and Tina Verba joined as interviewers in the second year of the project. We attempted to match interviewers and girls over the course of the study, though this was not always possible given some attrition on the part of the school (and also the transient nature of graduate school, in which many of our interviewers were enrolled). Brief written follow-up questions provided the girls with an opportunity to switch interviewers if they felt uncomfortable, though very few chose to do so.

17. Lorde, 1984a, p. 112.

18. Beginning in 1986, a number of us met weekly to discuss these issues and to create such a method. Initially this group was composed of Dianne Argyris, Jane Attanucci, Betty Bardige, Lyn Mikel Brown, Carol Gilligan, D. Kay Johnston, Janie Ward, and Grant Wiggins. Over time we were joined by David Wilcox, Richard

Osborne, Barbara Miller, and Mark Tappan. Our voice-centered method, described in Chapter 2, is a direct outgrowth of these early discussions. See Brown et al., 1988.

19. Dianne Argyris and Judy Dorney did the initial analysis of the girls' thoughts and feelings about the honor code by interpreting responses to a hypothetical dilemma we created about an honor code violation in the school.

20. See Rich, 1979a, p. 187.

2. The Harmonics of Relationship

1. Tina Verba, Gwill York, and Susan Libby also sat in on project meetings and volunteered a good deal of time and attention to the study. As an alumna of Laurel, Gwill was particularly helpful in familiarizing us with the school's unspoken expectations of the girls and the girls' responses to these expectations. We would also like to thank Laura Radin and Lisa Kulpinski for their contributions to this effort.

2. We are indebted to Mary Belenky and Blythe Clinchy for helping us to construct the initial "ways of knowing" questions, and also for their ongoing encouragement and advice as we revised questions to attend more closely to the changes in girls' voices.

3. Gilligan, 1977, 1982.

4. Lyons, 1982, 1983. See also Attanucci, 1988; Langdale, 1983.

5. Brown et al., 1988; Brown, Tappan, Gilligan, Argyris, and Miller, 1989; Brown, Debold, Tappan, and Gilligan, 1991; see also Brown and Gilligan, 1991; Gilligan, Brown, and Rogers, 1990.

6. Our understanding of voice draws centrally on the work of Kristin Linklater (1976), and our exploration of resonances in relationship has been deepened and clarified by the work of Normi Noel.

7. Rogers and Gilligan (1988), confronting both the assumptions of traditional developmental psychology and the language of psychological assessment, make "two translations of girls' voices": a musical language of voice, theme, counterpoint, and fugue and a stage language of positions, transitions, and levels, the traditional language of developmental psychology. Each translation carries its own language of development, but shifting to a musical language when interpreting girls' responses to sentence stems (Loevinger, 1976) allows Rogers and Gilligan to record evidence of both gains and losses over time and to notice that "two lines of development" appeared and disappeared "like a good magic trick" depending on how one defined psychological health and development. Listening in these two ways, Rogers and Gilligan find both clear evidence of emotional and cognitive growth in girls between the ages of twelve and sixteen and also clear evidence that girls lose self-confidence, that they capitulate more to constrictive norms of feminine behavior, and that they become less clear about their thoughts and feelings in relationships. See also Gilligan, Brown, and Rogers (1990) for a discussion of this shift in the language used to describe change and development.

8. In earlier discussions of this method and in previous papers about girls'

development that have drawn from this study, Neeti has been referred to as "Tanya." We have changed the pseudonym to better reflect Neeti's Indian heritage. Since there are few Indian girls in the study, we originally chose the name "Tanya" to obscure Neeti's ethnicity and thus assure her anonymity. However, now that we have established strong ties with Neeti, and since a person's race and ethnicity are so intricate a part of any interpretation of voice, we feel it is important to make this change.

9. We use colored pencils literally to trace different voices and to reveal their orchestration through the interview text. After attending to each voice, we move to worksheets where we record both the speaker's words (in one column) and our interpretation of these words (in another), so that we leave a comprehensive trail of evidence for our interpretations. These interpretations open up new conversations among our working group—conversations about the nature of evidence, about the complexities of interpretation, about the force of cultural messages and stereotypes that mute or drown out voice, as well as about the psyche's response to such messages.

10. Bakhtin, 1981, p. 276.

11. See Burke, 1969.

12. Rich, 1979b, p. 35; quoted in Schweickart, 1986, p. 52.

13. Schweickart, 1986, p. 50.

14. Fetterley, 1978, p. xxii.

15. Dana Jack's (1991) use of the term "Over-Eye" to represent moral "shoulds" has been extremely helpful and clarifying to us. The "Over-Eye" represents the internalization of outer imperatives and the perceived expectations to which one conforms in order to receive approval or to be seen as good. "The Over-Eye," Jack says, "carries a decidedly patriarchal flavor, both in its collective viewpoint about what is 'good' and 'right' for a woman and in its willingness to condemn her feelings when they depart from expected 'shoulds'" (p. 94).

16. See Gilligan, 1977, 1982; Gilligan, Ward, and Taylor, 1988.

17. Millett, 1970, p. 58.

18. Fetterley, 1978, p. xx.

19. Rich, 1979b, p. 35; see also Schweickart, 1986.

20. See Belenky, Clinchy, Goldberger, and Tarule, 1986; Fine, 1988; Fine and Zane, 1989; Herman, 1981; Jack, 1991; Jordan, Kaplan, Miller, Stiver, and Surrey, 1991; Josselson, 1987; Langdale, 1983; Lyons, 1983, 1990; Steiner-Adair, 1986, 1991.

21. Rich, 1979c, p. 35; see also Benhabib and Cornell, 1987; Flynn and Schweickart, 1986; Jacobus, 1986; Miller, 1988; Showalter, 1985b.

22. Woolf, 1938, p. 143.

23. See Brown, 1989, 1991a, 1991b.

3. Whistle-Blowers in the Relational World

1. Recent research reveals that girls and boys as young as four years old solve relational conflicts differently. Leaper (1991), analyzing the conversations of 138

middle- to upper-middle-class 4–9-year-olds, concludes that girls use more "collaborative" speech acts, while boys use more "controlling" speech acts. Miller, Danaher, and Forbes (1986), after studying over one thousand quarrels by 24 racially and economically diverse 5–7-year-olds, conclude that "boys are more concerned with and more forceful in pursuing their own agenda, and girls are more concerned with maintaining interpersonal harmony." In addition, Miller et al. found that girls changed their speech style depending on whether they were talking to other girls or to boys. Sheldon (1992) critiques the value-laden language these researchers use to interpret these gender differences. According to Sheldon, "to say that boys are more forceful persuaders hides the important work that mitigation does to further self-assertion in the conflict process and reinforces objectional stereotypes that portray girls and women as yielding, submissive, ineffective, and weak. It equates effectiveness in conflicts with aggression. It measures self-assertion and independence too narrowly." Moreover, Sheldon adds, such a conclusion "inadvertently values, or at least emphasizes a masculine mode of brute force over a feminine mode of conflict mitigation." Sheldon explains girls' tendency to shift speech style by suggesting that girls are more likely to use a "double-voice discourse." Three- and four-year-old girls' conflict talk has "a dual orientation," she suggests, "in which the speaker negotiates [her] own agenda while simultaneously orienting toward the viewpoint of [her] partner." That is, "in double-voice discourse, self-assertion is enmeshed in addressee-oriented mitigation." This example of Tessa and her friends also raises the issue of sexual harassment, a problem that has remained largely unexplored in the elementary years.

2. See, for example, Piaget, 1932/1965, and Lever, 1976.

3. Betty Bardige (1988) refers to children's moral thinking at this age as "face-value thinking" and explores the sensibilities of children who think in this way—their "profound sense of morality," their capacity for indignation at unfairness, for outrage and their deep sadness at abuse, accompanied by a pressing need to stop others' suffering. Bardige recognizes "the finely human" capacities of face-value or concrete thinking, even as she appreciates its cognitive limits.

4. The descriptions of the girls throughout the book are taken from interviewer notes written after the interviews were completed, and also from our memories of particular girls we talked with over the years of the study. In our longitudinal case studies we have occasionally changed small details—physical attributes such as eye or hair color, or family details such as parents' occupation—to assure anonymity.

5. This technique of using Aesop's fables to understand how children and adolescents understand and solve relational and moral conflicts was developed by Johnston (1988). Though we initially included the fable to replicate Johnston's findings—that young children can readily solve the same relational problem in at least two different ways, and that the preference for one solution over the other is gender-related—we became intrigued by the girls' involvement with the story and their personal investment in the relationship between the animals. We have since found this fable to be particularly useful in interviews with younger girls because it presents a story of relational conflict that contains elements of some of the hardest problems girls and women face: it is a story about someone getting

hurt, but it is also a story about exclusion, which carries with it the threat of abandonment, of freezing and suffering; and potentially it is a story about selflessness, which carries with it the likelihood of continual pain and abuse. This story can be heard in any number of ways, depending on the girl: as a story of domestic violence, as a story about difference, as a story about abandonment, about love, about caring for oneself or giving over one's own safety and comfort for the sake of another's.

6. Since "perfect girls" after a certain grade level may well have dropped out of math and science classes, this particular sign of perfection seems age-related. A recent survey by the American Association of University Women (1991) reports that girls tend to drop out of math courses after eighth grade. Most boys and girls, it seems, define math as a "masculine" subject.

7. Although we do not know that Sonia's resistance to the book her teacher chose had anything to do with race, it is important to note the scarcity of books written about children of color. By far the majority of children's books promote a white middle-class cultural identity. A *Boston Globe* article (February 23, 1992) reports that while more than 5,000 children's books were published in the United States in 1990, only 51 were written by black authors.

8. Annie Rogers (1992) has conceptualized a link between play and courage in girls' and women's healthy psychological development. She writes about the importance of play between women and girls in sustaining girls' courage because she has found girls' "ordinary courage" often becomes "transgressive" at adolescence.

9. Mark Tappan (1991) uses this excerpt from Lauren's interview to illustrate how language mediates and shapes experience. Drawing on the work of Vygotsky and Bakhtin, Tappan suggests Lauren's book is a "semiotic tool" enabling her to respond to the various dilemmas she faces. On this view, Lauren's book represents an early version of the internalized voice of her mother.

10. Rogers (1992) traces the etymology of the word "courage," and also describes what a practice of courage with girls would mean for women. Perhaps it is not coincidental that Annie is Lauren's interviewer this year.

11. Morrison, 1970, p. 16.

4. Approaching the Wall

1. We wish to thank Elizabeth Debold for an earlier interpretation of this longitudinal case and for her generous permission to include much of her interpretation here, particularly around Judy's dissociation of mind from body as she comes of age.

2. This connection between feelings and body draws from Elizabeth Debold's (1990, 1991) longitudinal analyses of girls' ways of knowing. Debold explores an embodied, passionate knowing prevalent in nine- and ten-year-olds, a world known through the senses, and she listens to adolescent girls' struggle to hold mind and body together as the desires and passions of childhood are appropriated and

translated into the narrow confines of cultural notions of femininity. See also Debold and Brown, 1991.

3. Judy's family situation, as she describes it, exemplifies the pattern researchers such as Elder and Caspi (1990) have identified—that when families are under stress, those who are most psychologically at risk are boys in childhood and girls in adolescence.

5. Rivers into the Sea

1. Rierdan and Koff, 1980; see also Brooks-Gunn and Peterson, 1983.

2. Debold, 1990.

3. Again, we are drawn to Dana Jack's (1991) distinction between an authentic "I" and the "Over-Eye" of cultural norms and values. Jack states, "Because the judgments of the Over-Eye include a cultural consensus about feminine goodness, truth, and value, they have the power to override the authentic self's view-point" (p. 94).

4. Tolman and Debold (1991) describe this move from embodiment to image and discuss the psychological costs of girls' identification with conventional images and models of female beauty.

5. Ibid.

6. Gilligan, 1977, 1982; Miller, 1976.

7. Listening to couples in crisis, Zimlicki (1991) traces a distinction between two languages of relationship—a static language of "to have and to hold" and a more relational, fluid language of love.

8. See Heilbrun, 1988. See also, Brown, 1991b; Gilligan, 1991b.

9. Again, Rogers (1992) writes about the move from the "ordinary courage" of younger girls—their capacity to speak what they know directly and easily—to a "transgressive courage" at adolescence, when to speak out becomes a violation of feminine norms, an act of trespassing or going where girls should not go.

10. We would like to thank Annie Rogers, and also Elizabeth Debold, for their helpful comments and insights about this case.

11. See Jack, 1991.

12. One hundred fifty-four "I don't knows" at age 12.

13. Steiner-Adair (1986) suggests that girls dramatize their protest of cultural ideals of femininity through anorexia and bulimia. Girls enact through their much politicized bodies a culture that is starving for genuine, full relationships.

14. Steiner-Adair, 1991; see also Sidel, 1990.

6. Dancing at the Crossroads

1. Rogers, 1992.

2. As we began to generate findings from the project, a group of women teachers and psychologists began to meet together to discuss our working papers. The group

referred to themselves as the Laurel-Harvard research affiliates. During an early meeting at the school, where a number of issues arose having to do with what it means to be women teaching girls in this culture at this time, what girls observe in their women teachers, and what power differences exist in the school, Terri Garfinkel, an early childhood teacher, suggested that to talk about these issues openly and in depth we needed to leave the school and spend an extended amount of time together. The teachers crossed school divisions, so that women in the early childhood program, middle school, and upper school were involved. Doris Bartlett, who began the retreats with us, could unfortunately not attend after the first weekend. Judy Dorney wrote the curriculum and facilitated two of the three retreats, drawing heavily from Maria Harris' (1988) outline of a feminist pedagogy in her book, *Women and Teaching*. Judy documents our experiences of relationship and community over the course of these retreats in her doctoral thesis, "Courage to act in a small way: Clues toward community and change among women teaching girls." We continue to be grateful to Leah Rhys, then the Head of School at Laurel, who encouraged and supported these retreats by finding extra money when necessary and arranging substitutes for the teachers.

3. Recent research on girls' experiences in school commissioned by the American Association of University Women (1991) illustrates the connection between self-esteem and messages girls receive daily in school. Furthermore, a research report entitled "How Schools Shortchange Girls," commissioned by AAUW and written by Susan Bailey on behalf of the Wellesley College Center for Research on Women (1992), reviews the literature on girls' experiences in classrooms and the gender bias in curricula and standardized tests. Also see Spender's (1982) discussion of girls' experiences in school in her book, *Invisible Women*.

4. Lorde, 1984b, p. 55.

5. Emily Hancock (1989) suggests that this process of remembering and recovery is essential if women are to claim themselves fully. According to Hancock, "Women's full development depends on circling back to the girl within and carrying her into womanhood" (p. 260). On the basis of interviews with twenty adult women, Hancock suggests that "reclaiming the authentic identity she'd embodied as a girl" (p. 4) "appears to be key to women's identity" (p. 25). However, our studies with young girls reveal the underside of girls' relational experiences—the feelings of being silenced and the experiences of powerlessness—as well as the embodied, pleasurable experiences. And our longitudinal work with girls as they move into adolescence reveals that young women tend to either dissociate themselves from the painful experiences of their childhood or reinterpret and rename their actions and experiences in idealized terms. Listening to girls' voices, then, is critical to understanding the difficulty of women's recovery of what Hancock calls "the girl within."

6. See Steiner-Adair, 1986; Woolf, 1921/1944, pp. 58–59.

7. "To be in the margin," bell hooks (1990) says, "is to be part of the whole but outside the main body." For some of the girls in this study, marginality was truly a place of resistance, what hooks calls "the site of radical possibility." But

with the capacity to see and name, and also to resist pressure to meet cultural (white, middle-class) ideals, arises the pressures of exclusion and the pain of ostracism. The emotional residues of enduring such pain—cynicism, anger, and resentment—were more evident in these girls. Though we laud their capacity for resistance, we also want to make clear the emotional costs of living in the margins.

8. Listening to the African-American girls as a group in this study, Judy Dorney (1990) found these girls spoke with overwhelming clarity about issues of race. Judy focused on a theme she heard over and over in the interviews: the girls' struggle to become themselves in the black community, from which they received much of their strength, courage, and hope, while also to negotiate a place in the dominant white culture. In describing how they see themselves as black women, Dorney suggests these girls' voices resonate with a pattern Janie Ward (1990) has described in listening to other black female adolescents: that to move toward self-affirmation, these girls must first negate, oppose, or resist the definitions, stereotypes, or negative images imposed on them by the dominant culture. See also Robinson and Ward, 1991.

9. Fordham and Ogbu (1986) write about the power of fictive kinship as a symbol of collective social identity for black Americans, an identity created in opposition to white American social identity. Because working hard to get good grades in school and being a "brainiac" are often identified by black students as examples of "acting white," those black students who wish to pursue academic success find themselves torn between doing well academically and behaving in ways that validate their loyalty to the black community.

10. The Laurel-Harvard Conference on The Psychology of Women and the Development of Girls was held in April 1990 in Cleveland, with the generous support of the George Gund Foundation and the Cleveland Foundation.

11. Given the findings of our study, that girls feel differently about this question when they get older, and given our need to protect the confidentiality of all the girls in this study, we decided after much discussion and some mixed feelings that we could not, in fact, honor this request.

References

Adelson, Joseph, ed. 1980. *Handbook of adolescent psychology*. New York: John Wiley.

Adelson, Joseph, and Margery Doehrman. 1980. The psychodynamic approach to adolescence. In Joseph Adelson, ed., *Handbook of adolescent psychology*. New York: John Wiley.

American Association of University Women. 1991. *Shortchanging girls, shortchanging America*. Washington, DC: AAUW.

———1992. *How Schools Shortchange Girls*. Washington, DC: AAUW Educational Foundation and National Education Association.

Apter, Terri. 1990. *Altered loves: Mothers and daughters during adolescence*. New York: St. Martin's Press.

Attanucci, Jane. 1988. In whose terms: A new perspective on self, role, and relationship. In Carol Gilligan, Janie Ward, and Jill Taylor, eds., *Mapping the moral domain*. Cambridge, MA: Harvard University Press.

Bakhtin, Mikhail. 1981. *The dialogic imagination*. Austin: University of Texas Press.

Bardige, Betty. 1988. Things so finely human: Moral sensibilities at risk in adolescence. In Carol Gilligan, Janie Ward, and Jill Taylor, eds., *Mapping the moral domain*. Cambridge, MA: Harvard University Press.

Belenky, Mary. 1983. The role of dialogue in human development and in the reduction of family violence. Paper presented at Teachers College, Columbia University.

Belenky, Mary, Blythe Clinchy, Nancy Goldberger, and Jill Tarule. 1986. *Women's ways of knowing*. New York: Basic Books.

Benhabib, Seyla, and Drucilla Cornell. 1987. *Feminism as critique*. Minneapolis, MN: University of Minnesota Press.

Bernardez, Teresa. 1988. Women and anger: Cultural prohibitions and the feminine ideal. Wellesley, MA: Stone Center Works in Progress.

Block, Jack. 1990. Ego resilience through time: Antecedents and ramifications. In *Resilience and psychological health*. Boston: Symposium of the Boston Psychoanalytic Society.

Breuer, Josef, and Sigmund Freud. 1895/1955. Studies on hysteria. In *The standard edition of the complete psychological works of Sigmund Freud.* Vol. 2. James Strachey, ed. and trans. London: Hogarth Press.

Brooks-Gunn, Jeanne, and Ann Peterson. 1983. *Girls at puberty.* New York: Plenum Press.

Brown, Lyn Mikel. 1989. "Narratives of relationship: The development of a care voice in girls ages 7 to 16." Unpublished doctoral diss., Harvard University.

———1991a. A problem of vision: The development of voice and relational knowledge in girls ages seven to sixteen. *Women's Studies Quarterly,* 19, 1/2: 52–71.

———1991b. Telling a girl's life: Self-authorization as a form of resistance. *Women and Therapy,* 11, 3/4: 71–86.

Brown, Lyn Mikel, and Carol Gilligan. 1991. Listening for voice in narratives of relationship. In Mark Tappan and Martin Packer, eds., *Narrative and storytelling: Implications for understanding moral development.* New Directions for Child Development, 54: 43–62. San Francisco: Jossey-Bass.

———In press. The psychology of women and the development of girls. *Feminism and Psychology.*

Brown, Lyn Mikel, Dianne Argyris, Jane Attanucci, Betty Bardige, Carol Gilligan, D. Kay Johnston, Barbara Miller, Richard Osborne, Mark Tappan, Janie Ward, Grant Wiggins, and David Wilcox. 1988. *A guide to reading narratives of conflict and choice for self and relational voice* (Monograph no. 1). Cambridge, MA: Project on the Psychology of Women and the Development of Girls, Harvard Graduate School of Education.

Brown, Lyn Mikel, Elizabeth Debold, Mark Tappan, and Carol Gilligan. 1991. Reading narratives of conflict and choice for self and moral voice: A relational method. In William Kurtines and Jacob Gewirtz, eds., *Handbook of moral behavior and development: Theory, research, and application.* Hillsdale, NJ: Erlbaum.

Brown, Lyn Mikel, Mark Tappan, Carol Gilligan, Dianne Argyris, and Barbara Miller. 1989. Reading for self and moral voice: A method for interpreting narratives of real-life moral conflict and choice. In Martin Packer and Richard Addison, eds., *Entering the circle: Hermeneutic investigation in psychology.* Albany: SUNY Press.

Bruch, Hilde. 1978. *The golden cage: The enigma of anorexia nervosa.* Cambridge: Harvard University Press.

Burke, Kenneth. 1969. *A grammar of motives.* Berkeley: University of California Press.

Crockett, Lisa, and Ann Peterson. 1987. Pubertal status and psychological development: Findings from the early adolescence study. In Richard Lerner and Terryl Foch, eds., *Biological-psychosocial interactions in early adolescence.* Hillsdale, NJ: Erlbaum.

Debold, Elizabeth. 1990. Learning in the first person: A passion to know. Paper presented in April at the Laurel-Harvard Conference on the Psychology of Women and the Development of Girls, Cleveland, Ohio.

———1991. The body at play. In Carol Gilligan, Annie Rogers, and Deborah

REFERENCES

Tolman, eds., *Women, girls, and psychotherapy: Reframing resistance*. Binghamton, NY: Haworth Press.

Debold, Elizabeth, and Lyn Mikel Brown. 1991. Losing the body of knowledge. Paper presented in March at the annual meeting of the Association of Women in Psychology.

Demitrack, Mark, Frank Putnam, Timothy Brewerton, Harry Brandt, and Philip Gold. 1990. Relation of clinical variables to dissociative phenomena in eating disorders. *The American Journal of Psychiatry*, 1479: 1184–1188.

Deutsch, Helene. 1944. *Psychology of women*. New York: Grune and Stratten.

Dorney, Judy. 1990. Who am I now and where is my home?: Black adolescent females in a predominantly white school. Paper presented in April at the Laurel-Harvard Conference on the Psychology of Women and the Development of Girls, Cleveland, Ohio.

———1991. "'Courage to act in a small way': Clues toward community and change among women teaching girls." Unpublished doctoral diss., Harvard University.

Ebata, Aaron. 1987. "A longitudinal study of distress during adolescence." Unpublished doctoral diss., Pennsylvania State University.

Elder, Glen, and Avshalom Caspi. 1990. Studying lives in a changing society: Sociological and personological explorations. In A. I. Rabin, Robert Zucker, Robert Emmons, and Susan Frank, eds., *Studying persons and lives*. New York: Springer.

Eme, Robert. 1979. Sex differences in childhood psychopathy: A review. *Psychological Bulletin*, 86: 574–595.

Fetterley, Judith. 1978. *The resisting reader: A feminist approach to American fiction*. Bloomington, IN: Indiana University Press.

Fine, Michelle. 1988. Sexuality, schooling and adolescent females: The missing discourse of desire. *Harvard Educational Review*, 58: 29–53.

Fine, Michelle, and Nancie Zane. 1989. Bein' wrapped too tight: When low-income women drop out of high school. In Lois Weis, Eleanor Farrar, and Hugh Petrie, eds., *Dropouts from school*. New York: SUNY Press.

Flynn, Elizabeth, and Patrocinio Schweickart, eds. 1986. *Gender and reading*. Baltimore, MD: The Johns Hopkins University Press.

Fordham, Signithia, and John Ogbu. 1986. Black students' school success: Coping with the "burden of acting white." *Urban Review*, 18: 176–206.

Freud, Sigmund. 1895/1955. Fräulein Elisabeth von R. In *The standard edition of the complete psychological works of Sigmund Freud*. Vol. 2., James Strachey, ed. and trans. London: Hogarth Press

———1905. Three essays on the theory of sexuality. In *The standard edition of the complete psychological works of Sigmund Freud*. Vol. 7. James Strachey, ed. and trans. London: Hogarth Press.

———1933/1965. Femininity. In *New introductory lectures on psychoanalysis*. James Strachey, ed. and trans. New York: W. W. Norton.

Gibbs, James, and Keith Widaman. 1982. *Social intelligence: Measuring the development of sociomoral reflection*. Englewood Cliffs: Prentice-Hall.

Gibbs, James, Keith Widaman, and Ann Colby. 1982. Construction and validation of a simplified, group-administrable equivalent to the Moral Judgment Interview. *Child Development,* 53: 895–910.

Gilligan, Carol. 1977. In a different voice: Women's conceptions of self and of morality. *Harvard Educational Review,* 47: 481–517.

———1982. *In a different voice: Psychological theory and women's development.* Cambridge, MA: Harvard University Press.

———1986. Exit-voice dilemmas in adolescent development. In Alejandro Foxley, Michael McPherson, and Guillermo O'Donnell, eds., *Development, democracy, and the art of trespassing: Essays in honor of Albert O. Hirschman.* Notre Dame: University of Notre Dame Press.

———1990. Teaching Shakespeare's sister. In Carol Gilligan, Nona Lyons, and Trudy Hanmer, eds., *Making connections: The relational worlds of adolescent girls at Emma Willard School.* Cambridge, MA: Harvard University Press.

———1991a. Joining the resistance: Psychology, politics, girls and women. *Michigan Quarterly Review,* 29, 4: 501–536.

———1991b. Women's psychological development: Implications for psychotherapy. In Carol Gilligan, Annie Rogers, and Deborah Tolman, eds., *Women, girls, and psychotherapy: Reframing resistance.* Binghamton, NY: Haworth Press.

Gilligan, Carol, and Jane Attanucci. 1988. Two moral orientations: Gender differences and similarities. *Merrill-Palmer Quarterly.* 343: 223–237.

Gilligan, Carol, and Mary Belenky. 1980. A naturalistic study of abortion decisions. In Robert Selman and Regina Yando, eds., *Clinical-developmental psychology.* New Directions for Child Development, 7: 69–90. San Francisco: Jossey-Bass.

Gilligan, Carol, Lyn Mikel Brown, and Annie Rogers. 1990. Psyche embedded: A place for body, relationships, and culture in personality theory. In A. I. Rabin, Robert Zucker, Robert Emmons, and Susan Frank, eds., *Studying persons and lives.* New York: Springer.

Gilligan, Carol, D. Kay Johnston, and Barbara Miller. 1988. *Moral voice, adolescent development, and secondary education: A study at the Green River School* (Monograph no. 3). Cambridge, MA: Project on the Psychology of Women and the Development of Girls, Harvard Graduate School of Education.

Gilligan, Carol, Nona Lyons, and Trudy Hanmer, eds. 1990. *Making connections: The relational worlds of adolescent girls at Emma Willard School.* Cambridge, MA: Harvard University Press.

Gilligan, Carol, Annie Rogers, and Deborah Tolman, eds. 1991. *Women, girls, and psychotherapy: Reframing resistance.* Binghamton, NY: Haworth Press.

Gilligan, Carol, Janie Ward, and Jill Taylor, eds. 1988. *Mapping the moral domain.* Cambridge, MA: Harvard University Press.

Gilligan, Carol, and Grant Wiggins. 1987. The origins of morality in early childhood relationships. In Jerome Kagan and Sharon Lamb, eds., *The emergence of morality in early childhood.* Chicago: University of Chicago Press.

Gove, Walter, and Terry Herb. 1974. Stress and mental illness among the young: A comparison of the sexes. *Social Forces,* 53: 256–265.

Hancock, Emily. 1989. *The girl within.* New York: Ballantine.

Harris, Maria. 1988. *Women and teaching: Themes for a spirituality of pedagogy.* New York: Paulist Press.

REFERENCES

Heilbrun, Carolyn. 1988. *Writing a woman's life*. New York: Ballantine.

Herman, Judith. 1981. *Father-daughter incest*. Cambridge, MA: Harvard University Press.

Hetherington, E. Mavis. 1981. Children of divorce. In Ronald Henderson, ed., *Parent-child interaction*. New York: Academic Press.

hooks, bell. 1990. *Yearning: Race, gender, and cultural politics*. Boston: South End Press.

Horney, Karen. 1926. The flight from womanhood. *International Journal of Psycho-analysis*, 7: 324–339.

Jack, Dana. 1987. Silencing the self: The power of social imperatives in female depression. In Ruth Formanek and Anita Gurian, eds., *Women and depression: A lifespan perspective*. New York: Springer.

Jack, Dana. 1991. *Silencing the self: Depression and women*. Cambridge, MA: Harvard University Press.

Jacobus, Mary. 1986. *Reading woman*. New York: Columbia University Press.

Johnston, D. Kay. 1988. Adolescents' solutions to dilemmas in fables: Two moral orientations—two problem solving strategies. In Carol Gilligan, Janie Ward, and Jill Taylor, eds., *Mapping the moral domain*. Cambridge, MA: Harvard University Press.

Jordan, Judith. 1987. Clarity in connection: Empathic knowing, desire, and sexuality. Wellesley, MA: Stone Center Works in Progress.

Jordan, Judith. 1991. The meaning of mutuality. In Judith Jordan, Alexandra Kaplan, Jean Baker Miller, Irene Stiver, and Janet Surrey. *Women's growth in connection*. New York: Guilford Press.

Jordan, Judith, Alexandra Kaplan, Jean Baker Miller, Irene Stiver, and Janet Surrey. 1991. *Women's growth in connection*. New York: Guilford Press.

Josselson, Ruthellen. 1987. *Finding herself: Pathways to identity development in women*. San Francisco: Jossey-Bass.

Kaplan, Alexandra. 1991. The "self-in-relation": Implications for depression in women. In Judith Jordan, Alexandra Kaplan, Jean Baker Miller, Irene Stiver, and Janet Surrey. *Women's growth in connection*. New York: Guilford Press.

Konopka, Gisela. 1966. *The adolescent girl in conflict*. Englewood Cliffs, NJ: Prentice-Hall.

Langdale, Sharry. 1983. "Moral orientations and moral development: The analysis of care and justice reasoning across different dilemmas in females and males from childhood through adulthood." Unpublished doctoral diss., Harvard University.

Leaper, Campbell. 1991. Influence and involvement in children's discourse: Age, gender and partner effects. *Child Development*, 62: 797–811.

Lever, Janet. 1976. Sex differences in the games children play. *Social Problems*, 23: 478–487.

Linklater, Kristin. 1976. *Freeing the natural voice*. New York: Drama Book Publishers.

Loevinger, Jane. 1976. *Ego development: Conceptions and theories*. San Francisco: Jossey-Bass.

REFERENCES

Loevinger, Jane, and R. Wessler. 1970. *Measuring ego development*. Vols. 1 and 2. San Francisco: Jossey-Bass.

Lorde, Audre. 1984a. The master's tools will never dismantle the master's house. In Audre Lorde, *Sister outsider*. Freedom, CA: The Crossing Press.

———1984b. The uses of the erotic. In Audre Lorde, *Sister outsider*. Freedom, CA: The Crossing Press.

Lyons, Nona. 1982. "Conceptions of self and morality and modes of moral choice: Identifying justice and care judgments of actual moral dilemmas." Unpublished doctoral diss., Harvard University.

———1983. Two perspectives: On self, relationships and morality. *Harvard Educational Review*, 53: 125–145.

———1990. Listening to voices we have not heard. In Carol Gilligan, Nona Lyons, and Trudy Hanmer, eds., *Making connections: The relational worlds of adolescent girls at Emma Willard School*. Cambridge, MA: Harvard University Press.

Maudsley, Henry. 1879. *The pathology of mind*. London: Macmillan.

Miller, Jean Baker. 1976. *Toward a new psychology of women*. Boston: Beacon Press.

———1988. Connections, disconnections, and violations. Wellesley, MA: Stone Center Works in Progress.

———1991. The development of women's sense of self. In Judith Jordan, Alexandra Kaplan, Jean Baker Miller, Irene Stiver, and Janet Surrey. *Women's growth in connection*. New York: Guilford Press.

Miller, Nancy K. 1988. *Subject to change*. New York: Columbia University Press.

Miller, Patrice, Dorothy Danaher, and David Forbes. 1986. Sex-related strategies for coping with interpersonal conflict in children aged five and seven. *Developmental Psychology*, 22: 543–548.

Millett, Kate. 1970. *Sexual politics*. Garden City, NJ: Doubleday.

Morrison, Toni. 1970. *The bluest eye*. New York: Washington Square Press.

Murray, Lynne, and Colwyn Trevarthen. 1985. Emotional regulation of interactions between two-month-olds and their mothers. In Tiffany Field and Nathan Fox, eds., *Social perception in infants*. Norwood, NJ: Ablex.

Peterson, Ann. 1988. Adolescent development. *Annual Review of Psychology*, 39: 583–607.

Peterson, Ann, and Aaron Ebata. 1987. Developmental transitions and adolescent problem behavior: Implications for prevention and intervention. In Klaus Hurrelmann, ed., *Social prevention and intervention*. New York: Aldine De Gruyter.

Piaget, Jean. 1932/1965. *The moral judgment of the child*. New York: The Free Press.

Rich, Adrienne. 1979a. Women and honor: Some notes on lying. In Adrienne Rich, *On lies, secrets, and silence*. New York: W. W. Norton.

———1979b. Vesuvius at home: The power of Emily Dickinson. In Adrienne Rich, *On lies, secrets, and silence*. New York: W. W. Norton.

———1979c. When we dead awaken: Writing as re-vision. In Adrienne Rich, *On lies, secrets, and silence*. New York: W. W. Norton.

Rierdan, Jill, and Elissa Koff. 1980. Representation of the female body by early and late adolescent girls. *Journal of Youth and Adolescence*, 94: 49–58.

REFERENCES

Robinson, Tracy, and Janie Ward. 1991. "A belief in self far greater than anyone's disbelief": Cultivating resistance among African American adolescents. *Women and Therapy*, 11, 3/4: 87–103.

Rogers, Annie. 1988. *Developmental voices: A method for identifying a fugue of themes in sentence completions.* Unpublished manuscript, Harvard University.

————1992. The development of courage in girls and women. Unpublished paper, Harvard Project on the Psychology of Women and the Development of Girls, Harvard Graduate School of Education.

Rogers, Annie, and Carol Gilligan. 1988. *Translating the language of adolescent girls: Themes of moral voice and stages of ego development* (Monograph no. 6). Cambridge, MA: Project on the Psychology of Women and the Development of Girls, Harvard Graduate School of Education.

Rogers, Annie, Lyn Mikel Brown, and Mark Tappan. 1991. Interpreting loss in ego development in girls: Regression or resistance? Paper presented in August at the annual meeting of the American Psychological Association.

Ruddick, Sara. 1989. *Maternal thinking.* New York: Ballantine.

Rutter, Michael. 1986. The developmental psychopathology of depression: Issues and perspectives. In Michael Rutter, Carroll Izzard, and Peter Read, eds. *Depression in young people: Developmental and clinical perspectives.* New York: Guilford Press.

Schweickart, Patrocinio. 1986. Reading ourselves: Toward a feminist theory of reading. In Elizabeth Flynn and Patrocinio Schweickart, eds., *Gender and reading.* Baltimore, MD: The Johns Hopkins University Press.

Seligman, Martin. 1991. *Learned optimism.* New York: Random House.

Sheldon, Amy. 1992. Conflict talk: Sociolinguistic challenges to self-assertion and how young girls meet them. *Merrill-Palmer Quarterly*, 38: 95–117.

Showalter, Elaine. 1985a. *The female malady.* New York: Penguin Books.

————1985b. *The new feminist criticism.* New York: Pantheon.

Sidel, Ruth. 1990. *On her own.* New York: Viking Penguin.

Simmons, Roberta, and Dale Blyth. 1987. *Moving into adolescence: The impact of pubertal change and school context.* New York: Aldine De Gruyter.

Skey, F. C. 1867. *Hysteria.* London: Longmans, Green, Reader and Dyer.

Spender, Dale. 1982. *Invisible women.* New York: W. W. Norton.

Steiner-Adair, Catherine. 1986. The body politic: Normal female adolescent development and the development of eating disorders. *Journal of the American Academy of Psychoanalysis*, 14: 95–114.

————. 1991. When the body speaks: Girls, eating disorders, and psychotherapy. In Carol Gilligan, Annie Rogers, and Deborah Tolman, eds., *Women, girls, and psychotherapy: Reframing resistance.* Binghamton, NY: Haworth Press.

Stern, Daniel. 1985. *The interpersonal world of the infant.* New York: Basic Books.

Stern, Lori. 1990. Disavowing the self in female adolescence. *Women and Therapy*, 11, 3/4: 105–117.

Stiver, Irene. 1991. The meanings of "dependency" in female-male relationships. In Judith Jordan, Alexandra Kaplan, Jean Baker Miller, Irene Stiver, and Janet Surrey, *Women's growth in connection.* New York: Guilford Press.

Surrey, Janet. 1991. The "self-in-relation": A theory of women's development. In

REFERENCES

Judith Jordan, Alexandra Kaplan, Jean Baker Miller, Irene Stiver, and Janet Surrey, *Women's growth in connection.* New York: Guilford Press.

Tanner, J. M. 1971. Sequence, tempo and individual variation in the growth and development of boys and girls aged twelve to sixteen. *Daedalus,* 1004: 907–930.

Tappan, Mark. 1991. Narrative, language and moral experience. *Journal of Moral Education,* 20, 3: 243–256.

Tappan, Mark, and Lyn Mikel Brown. 1989. Stories told and lessons learned: Toward a narrative approach to moral development and moral education. *Harvard Educational Review,* 59: 182–205.

Taylor, Jill. 1989. "Development of self, moral voice and the meaning of adolescent motherhood: The narratives of fourteen adolescent mothers." Unpublished doctoral diss., Harvard University.

Thompson, Clara. 1964. *Interpersonal psychoanalysis.* New York: Basic Books.

Tolman, Deborah. 1990. Just say no to what?: A preliminary analysis of sexual subjectivity in a multicultural group of adolescent females. Paper presented in April at the annual meeting of the American Orthopsychiatric Association, Miami.

Tolman, Deborah, and Elizabeth Debold. 1991. Made in whose image? Paper presented in August at the annual meeting of the American Psychological Association, San Francisco.

Trevarthen, Colwyn. 1979. Instincts for human understanding and for cultural cooperation: Their development in infancy. In Mario von Cranach, Klaus Foppa, Wolf Lepenies, and D. Floog, eds., *Human ethology: Claims and limits of a new discipline.* Maison des Sciences de l'Homme and Cambridge University Press.

Ward, Janie. 1988. Urban adolescents' conceptions of violence. In Carol Gilligan, Janie Ward, and Jill Taylor, eds., *Mapping the moral domain.* Cambridge, MA: Harvard University Press.

————1990. Racial identity formation and transformation. In Carol Gilligan, Nona Lyons, and Trudy Hanmer, eds., *Making connections: The relational worlds of adolescent girls at Emma Willard School.* Cambridge, MA: Harvard University Press.

Werner, Emmy, and Ruth Smith. 1982. *Vulnerable but invincible: A study of resilient children.* New York: McGraw-Hill.

Woolf, Virginia. 1921/1944. *Monday or Tuesday.* New York: Harcourt Brace and Company.

————1929. *A room of one's own.* New York: Harcourt Brace Jovanovich.

————1938. *Three guineas.* New York: Harcourt Brace Jovanovich.

————1942/1970. Professions for women. In Virginia Woolf, *The death of the moth and other essays.* New York: Harcourt Brace Janovich.

Zimlicki, Birute. 1991. Speaking of love: From a study of relationships in crisis. Unpublished manuscript, Harvard University.

Index

253

INDEX

Conflict, 198–199; avoiding, 3, 41, 80, 103–104, 105, 176–179, 201, 207; voicing, 4, 222, 224; response to, 6, 103–106, 116–117 *See also* Disagreement; Relational conflict

Connection, 2, 3, 5, 28, 32, 90, 97, 110, 112, 133; to self, 20, 70–71, 75, 196, 206; to family, 138–139; to childhood, 169. *See also* Disconnection

Cooperation, 45–46, 56, 57, 79, 88, 221. *See also* Collaboration

Courage, 3, 6, 73, 84–86, 105; ordinary, 4, 183, 217; in relational conflicts, 115–117, 161

"Craziness," 68, 107, 147, 153, 158–159, 161, 170, 191

Culture, 4, 7, 19–20, 21, 174, 180, 182, 183, 204, 215, 225; male-voiced, 29, 215, 216, 218–219, 220, 232; "I" vs. "eye" of, 167, 207, 210; images of women in, 175, 176. *See also* "Over-Eye"; Patriarchy

Cynicism, 155, 193, 194

Dana, 48, 51

Dating. *See* Boys: relationships with

Deak, JoAnn, 220

Debold, Elizabeth, 18, 19, 128, 163–164

Depression, 2, 100, 119, 120, 136. *See also* Sadness

Diana, 43, 44

Difference, 50–51, 55, 66–67, 69, 100–101, 109, 142–143, 186; gender, 145–146, 154, 189. *See also* Class difference; Racial difference

Disagreement, 4, 13–14, 50–51, 69, 82, 106, 126, 186; avoiding, 3, 62, 173, 218; voicing, 56–57, 109; with friends, 82–83, 102, 103–104, 111–112, 114–116, 121–122, 124, 190, 205. *See also* Conflict

Disconnection, 3, 4, 5, 6, 7, 10, 17, 32, 161, 162; response to, 16, 169; from self, 105–106, 110, 113, 122, 174, 217; in families, 135–136, 147, 150–151; from reality, 152; physical change and, 163–164; protection and, 170–171, 184; from friends, 208, 215; emotional, 214–215; girls from women, 216, 217. *See also* Connection

Discretion, 170–172, 205, 206, 207

Dissociation, 4, 6, 7, 17, 20, 107, 123, 128, 133, 161, 162, 193, 216–218

Divorce, 107, 123, 129, 144, 146, 153. *See also* Stepfamilies

Dorney, Judy, 18, 19, 220

Double standard, 107

Double vision, 72, 87, 91–93, 189, 197

Double voice, 72, 87, 197, 202

Ear training, 56

Edie, 96–97

Embodied knowing, 127, 140

Empathy, 31–37, 38, 176

Erin, 169–170, 181–183

Erotic, 161, 168, 224

Exclusion, 29, 54, 63, 64, 65, 70, 98, 116; fear of, 90–91, 112, 113; from family, 139

Experience/"reality" split, 29–30, 170, 193–194, 195

"Eye" of the culture, 167, 207, 210

Faith, 166, 180–181

Families, 107, 108, 115, 141; violence in, 123–124, 191; divisions in, 129, 135–136, 143, 144–145, 150–151; regular/traditional, 129–131, 140, 161; connections in, 138–139; rules in, 148. *See also* Divorce; Stepfamilies

Fathers, 129–130, 142, 143, 154

Fatigue, 117, 118, 131, 157, 176, 177

"Feeling what you feel," 67, 68, 90, 93, 95, 113; relational conflict and, 124, 125

Fetterly, Judith, 29, 30

Flanders Hall, Patricia, 219–221, 228

Fordham, Signithia, 227

Franklin, Nancy, 220, 222–223

Friends, 48, 50–51, 63, 65–66, 100; disagreement with, 82–83, 102, 103–104, 111–112, 114–116, 121–122, 124, 190, 205; fear of exclusion from, 112, 113; moving away from, 167, 207–209, 210

Gail, 91–93, 95–96, 97

Garfinkel, Terri, 220

Goldberger, Nancy, 3

"Good women," 2, 30, 61, 225; good woman/bad woman split, 177

INDEX

INDEX

About the Author

Lyn Mikel Brown is Assistant Professor and Co-chairperson of the Education and Human Development Department at Colby College. Carol Gilligan is Professor in the Human Development and Psychology Program at the Graduate School of Education, Harvard University. Gilligan is the author of *In A Different Voice*.